**Library of Philosophy**
EDITED BY J. H. MUIRHEAD, LL.D.

# KNOW THYSELF

# NOTE

THOUGH well acquainted with the English language, being half-English, I was glad in the preparation of this translation to have the assistance of Professor A. E. Taylor of the University of St. Andrews, who has carefully gone through the whole manuscript; and I wish to express my very special obligations to him for his kindness. He is, however, in no way responsible for the final form of the text, even in those places where I have followed literally his suggestions.

I have added an Index which has been restricted as far as possible to proper names and the most characteristic doctrines of the author, so that it should not be a mere repetition of the Table of Contents; and I hope it will be found useful by the English reader.

THE TRANSLATOR.

# KNOW THYSELF

BY

BERNARDINO VARISCO

PROFESSOR OF THEORETIC PHILOSOPHY IN THE UNIVERSITY OF ROME

TRANSLATED BY

GUGLIELMO SALVADORI, Ph.D.

LECTURER IN MORAL PHILOSOPHY IN THE UNIVERSITY OF ROME

LONDON
GEORGE ALLEN AND UNWIN, LIMITED
1915

[*All rights reserved*]

*First printed 1915*

# INTRODUCTION

## 1. A DOCTRINE OF THE PHENOMENAL UNIVERSE. WHAT IS A PHENOMENON?

"INTELLIGENDO se, intelligit omnia alia." These words,[1] applied to the individual subject, sum up the doctrine which I propose to set forth: a doctrine of the phenomenal universe. Of this doctrine I shall premise a brief summary which, though requiring for its right interpretation the developments afforded by the book, will, I think, make it more intelligible. To begin with, what is a phenomenon? I see a colour: there is the colour seen, and there is my seeing it. There is, correlated with my vision, a feeling, for instance, of pain.[2] There is my wish that such a feeling should cease. And there is the act by which I contrive to make it cease (for instance, the act of turning my head). Lastly, there is my cognition of all this. The colour, the feeling, the vision, etc., are commonly considered as so many phenomena. And that all these, as well as many other facts of the same kind, are separate phenomena, is quite obvious. But it is no less obvious that a phenomenon, though separate, has no exact lines: for instance, this colour merges insensibly into that other colour (the surrounding colour); this

---

[1] Of S. Thomas, who applies them to God. The reason of the change of reference cannot be given in a word: it will become manifest in the sequel. To avoid misunderstandings, I warn the reader at once that I have no intention of identifying God and the particular subject.

[2] Generally, the feeling correlated with an optic sensation is so weak that it passes unnoticed, but, whether disagreeable or agreeable, it is always present.

wish of mine merges into another wish, into a more complex state of consciousness, and so on. A phenomenon which could be called absolutely single and simple, never presents itself; and while on the whole it is undeniable that the given is an aggregate of phenomena, it is yet impossible to resolve the aggregate into its components, exactly defined. Further, the colour—I mean, the colour as seen—obviously does not exist without my seeing it; on the other hand, I cannot see without seeing a colour. Can I see without knowing that I see? I do not mean to inquire here whether or not the act of vision is enough to enable me to know that I see. No doubt, I distinguish between my mere seeing and my knowing that I see. And certainly vision, or any other phenomenon which should present itself outside my cognition, would be for me as if it had not presented itself.

### 2. REALITY AND COGNITION. THE SUBJECT

It is then to be concluded that what is usually called a phenomenon, is something, the existence of which is a being distinguished in the continuity of an experience or conscious life, a life or experience which is, at the same time and under the same aspect, reality and cognition. Each of these terms (reality and cognition) has a meaning, in so far as both express the indubitable and inevitable nature of the phenomenal complex. To deny either character to the complex is to destroy the possibility of ascribing any meaning whatever to the terms reality and cognition. As a distinct element in the complex of an experience, a phenomenon is always the phenomenon of a subject. Vice versa the subject is nothing but the unity of its phenomena. The existence of the subject may be resolved into the unity, whereby each of its phenomena is apprehended, that is to say, whereby each of its phenomena exists : if all its phenomena were to vanish, the subject also would vanish.

Consequently, the subject of which we speak is phenomenal, although it cannot certainly be resolved into any of the phenomena, of which it is the unity : the subject is phenomenal in so far as it is the form of phenomena. Obviously, in the phenomenal subject cognition coincides with reality, that is to say the subject knows itself. It does not however follow from this that reality and cognition coincide absolutely. That cognition which the subject has of itself at a given moment, is a reality coinciding with this cognition. But an actual cognition always implies some other. So it is possible that a subject should recognise as implied by its actual cognition a preceding reality, which, as preceding, is not the actual reality, although it exists in the actual cognition, and although in its preceding reality it did not coincide with a preceding cognition. For instance, I know that last night I slept without knowing that I was sleeping ; this knowledge of mine is not the same thing as my sleeping or my having slept.

By distinguishing phenomena from one another, and by inferring one cognition from another, the subject is able to arrange its own experience, that is to say to organise itself. It distinguishes extended phenomena from unextended.[1] The unity of unextended phenomena is a portion of the unity in which all phenomena are included ; and this is what the subject, after having reached a certain degree of development, calls its self ; we shall

[1] These two orders are connected with each other by phenomena, which, though extended with respect to some characters, are unextended with respect to others, and which make it possible to recognise one's own body amid other bodies ; of this intermediate kind of phenomena we shall say no more.

call it the subject in the strict sense. Relatively to the more closely connected unity of unextended phenomena, the extended are called external; and the subject, even after reaching the degree of development which we have mentioned (the common man, for instance), does not recognise them as its own. But that they are its own as much as the other phenomena (the unextended), is obvious: the colour which I see, is something seen by *me;* it is an element of that fact, indubitably mine, which is the act of seeing it. Again distinguishing among the phenomena which more properly constitute the self (in the strict sense), the subject distinguishes between its own doing (always associated with a feeling, of which we propose to take no account) and its own knowing. These are, as usual, moments constituting conscious life—inseparable, although distinguishable. Let us note their distinctive characters: knowing is nothing else but the existence of known experience, its reality; while doing is always followed by some modification of experience. Obviously, the distinctions mentioned imply the unity of experience, or the subject, which consequently cannot have had a beginning. On the contrary the subject in the strict sense is a product of organised experience, and has a beginning. That there has been a beginning, is a necessary inference from actual cognition.

### 3. EXISTENCE OF OTHER SUBJECTS

Along with the process above mentioned, by which the subject in the strict sense arises and develops out of the fundamental unitary experience, there evolves the process by which the same subject comes to the conviction that there are other analogous subjects distinguished from itself. My life, in so far as it is mine in the strict sense (unextended experience), is a doing-thinking; hence a doing as well as a thinking. Now, as thinking has necessarily two correlative poles—that of unextended thinking (activity as consciousness) and the extended object,[1] analogously doing (consciousness as active) implies also two correlative poles—strictly subjective activity and resistance. That the resistance is not absolutely outside the unitary experience, is clear. Resistance is the other pole of activity, without which there would be no activity. But in so far as it is the other pole of activity, resistance is distinguished from and becomes opposed to it : the consciousness of activity implies the consciousness of the distinction. In short, the subject distinguishes activity as a constituent of itself only in so far as it distinguishes activity from resistance : we have not here two distinctions, but the two correlated terms of the same distinction. To apprehend resistance, it will be objected, is not of itself, and is not always, the same thing as to apprehend another object as such. But neither is the apprehension of activity (which, as an element of the unitary experience, is always apprehended) of itself alone the apprehension or existence of the subject in the strict sense. The subject in the strict sense is a result of the organisation of the acts of apprehension of its constitutive activity. And, as these acts of apprehension become organised, so and at the same time do the correlated acts of apprehension of resistance. Further, resistance is necessarily apprehended as resembling activity : it is apprehended together with activity ; it can be conceived at first only as a duplicate of activity. What is presented is at once one and double. In the first distinction, rendered necessary because the unity is apprehended as double, it is inevitable that

---

[1] The immediate object is sometimes unextended, but an extended object, at least a mediate one, is never absent.

the two distinct parts should be apprehended as identical; for instance, if I pull a cord which is fixed at the other end, I do not become aware of my pulling without apprehending the resistance, and without apprehending it as a pull in an opposite sense but identical with my pulling. So, while the activities are becoming organised to constitute the subject, the resistances become organised to form the other subject; as appears also from the fact that a child and a barbarian are inclined to ascribe every resistance to another subject. Moreover, that the other subject is not apprehended as single, results from the various complications of resistances with activities and among themselves.

### 4. EXISTENCE OF EXTERNAL BODIES

The process through which we reach a belief in the existence of external bodies, independent of ourselves, is simultaneous with that above mentioned; indeed the two together constitute a single process. I see the looking-glass and my reflection in it. If I go away, I no longer see the looking-glass, nor the reflection. I know that, with my going away, the reflection has disappeared, the looking-glass has remained. The question is, how I know it, and what precisely is the meaning of this knowledge of mine. The reflection I can only see, while I see, touch, etc., the looking-glass. This is something, but it is not enough. I can only see the moon, and yet I consider it independent of me as much as the looking-glass, and more so. The reason of reasons for which I do not think that the looking-glass has vanished when I go away, consists in the testimony of another subject, who continues to see the looking-glass when I am absent, although he no longer sees my reflection in the looking-glass.[1] The

---

[1] My experience once systemised, I no longer need such attestations; but once I needed them in order to systemise my experience.

conviction that bodies cannot be resolved into phenomena exclusively belonging to each of us, is justified and significant, but is so inasmuch as it is the result of a systematisation, not merely of the experience of each single individual, but of the experience of each together with that of others. That this conviction is justified and significant in any other way, nobody has ever shown or will show; in fact, whatever proof be alleged of the existence of bodies, is reducible to phenomena or laws of phenomena, that is to say, is founded on an order of experience and is reducible to the assertion of such an order.

The existence of bodies " in themselves " (independent of any subject) is therefore to be excluded as an arbitrary and meaningless hypothesis. Be it observed that I do not say—a body is a phenomenon of myself in so far as I feel it, and therefore it is nothing but a phenomenon of myself; I say—my assertion that a body is more than a phenomenon of myself, is an assertion that extended experience, my own and that of others, is ordered in a certain way. The existence of a body is relative, not to me only, as is for instance the existence of a pain which I feel, but also to the other subject; it is clear then that, if we understand the phrase " in itself " as opposed to " in relation to me," we can and must speak of an " in itself " of bodies; but the meaning of this " in itself " is only to express " in relation to more than one subject." We do not declare the common conviction erroneous; we interpret it. The common assertion of the other subject has, on the contrary, no need of interpretation: the other subject is a reduplication of myself—a unity of extended and unextended experience like myself, although the content is different, at least in part. I cannot deny myself, because by the same act by which I deny, I assert myself. Consequently I cannot even deny the other subject,[1] because: (1) I recognise the action of the other subject as an element essential to my action, that is to say as a condition of my experience; (2) in denying the other subject I should deny the value of the process by which I have systematised my external experience, and of which I myself, considered as a subject in the strict sense, am a result. In recognising that bodies are independent of my sensing them or not, in recognising (explicitly asserting) myself, and in recognising other subjects, not subordinate to me, although I have gone beyond the matter of my experience, I have not yet gone beyond the field of experience: I have recognised in my experience, over and above its matter, a form; which form leads me to recognise, what it necessarily implies, another matter (phenomena of other subjects) and other analogous forms (other subjects).

What we have said so far about the phenomenal universe includes no arbitrary assumption; indeed we have simply given a clear account of what everyone knows, excluding any kind of arbitrary assumption. But what has been said, has further implications which we have still to make clear. Subjects are irreducibly distinct from each other, in the sense that an unextended phenomenon is never common to any two of them: my apprehending is not the apprehending of another. But the doing of a subject and the doing of another condition and modify each other mutually; they interfere, that is to say they are in some way reduced to unity, without ceasing to be two (so, for instance, the poles of a magnet are two, but neither exists without the other).

---

[1] The assertion of another determinate subject is not always infallible: the reflection of myself in the looking-glass may seem to me a man. Nevertheless, the assertion that other subjects exist, is as infallible as the assertion of myself.

## 5. MUTUAL INTERFERENCE OF SUBJECTS

The doing of a subject seems to interfere only with that of a few other subjects; but it is easy to convince oneself that, indirectly at least, the doing of any subject must interfere with that of every other subject. This mutual interference obviously implies that the existence of a subject has as its condition the existence of the others; that what exists is not a collection of subjects, but a system; or in short, that the multiplicity of subjects can be reduced to unity. Naturally this unity must be such as not to exclude multiplicity, such indeed as to be the condition of multiplicity and conditioned by it. A unity of such a kind may seem inconceivable. On the contrary, each of us has an instance of it in himself; every subject is the unity of many phenomena, the existence of which is the existence of a manifold which implies the unity of the subject, while vice versa the unity of the subject implies the multiplicity of its phenomena. Whence we conclude that the higher unity of subjects, for which we are seeking, is constituted precisely by each of the subjects themselves. The phenomenal universe is unified or has its centre in each of the subjects of which it is the result. It has a polycentric structure; and such a structure is essential to it; its existence consists in having it.

## 6. CONSCIOUSNESS AND SUBCONSCIOUSNESS

No doubt, to admit this conclusion, indeed to understand it, we must admit that the constitutive consciousness is not all equally clear in every subject; over and above the clear or actual consciousness, there is another, and much larger, sphere of subconsciousness. And that such a subconsciousness exists, is an undeniable implication of consciousness.[1] I remember; that, which I now remember, would not be that element of my consciousness which in fact it is, if it had not already been an element of my subconsciousness. Our being clearly conscious is in every case the result of a process which implies subconscious elements, and partly takes place in subconsciousness. Moreover, subconsciousness is not a *deus ex machina* introduced with the object of eliminating difficulties; this would be an illusive contrivance. Consciousness is nothing but subconsciousness organised. As we have already observed, the subject, in so far as it is a unity of clear consciousness, has a beginning; nothing is better known and more certain than this. But in so far as it is a subconscious unity, the subject cannot have had a beginning, because every process is conditioned by the unity of experience, the at least subconscious unity of the subject. The existence of the phenomenal universe resolves itself into the existence of certain unities which imply one another, and which act by interference with each other, each being the centre of all the others. In each unity there goes on a process due to this interference, on which it depends whether the unity develops or envelops itself, whether consciousness prevails over subconsciousness or the reverse.

### 7. UNITY AND MULTIPLICITY

The polycentric conception above mentioned eliminates two difficulties at once, difficulties which must be eliminated, if we would not forego the understanding of anything at all, and neither of which could be eliminated in

---

[1] Remember what we have observed above (second paragraph, p. vii): "actual cognition implies always some other." Whence it follows that besides the reality coinciding with actual cognition, it is necessary to assume another, which in fine is a subconscious reality.

any other way. The thought of each subject implies a necessity which has a universal value. This necessity implies first of all the unity of the particular thinking subject—is indeed no more than such a unity demands. But it holds good in relation to everything; we must therefore conclude, that the unity of the subject is the unity of everything—that the subject, whatever it may know, always knows itself (I do not mean self in the strict sense). But on the other hand the process of cognition, the thinking develops in time, is composed of facts which are connected as successive, and each of which is a temporal sequence, while necessity is absolutely outside time. As there is a principle of extra-temporal necessity—the unity of the subject and its being the unity of everything—there must be also a principle of temporality. The succession of phenomena [*l' accadere*][1] may not have had a beginning, but it requires a condition —a principle [2]—which makes it possible. This condition, or principle, cannot be unity pure and simple; that is to say, it cannot be reduced to that condition which by itself alone would resolve the universe into a system of extra-temporal relations, as is the case, for instance, in geometry. But neither can the condition of succession be a multiplicity apart from unity, for it is in succession that extra-temporal necessity asserts itself; therefore it must be a multiplicity implicit in unity. And it must be a multiplicity

---

[1] [The absence in the English language of a perfect equivalent has obliged the translator to render the word *accadere* (literally = "the happening," "what happens," or "the act of happening") in several different ways, as "succession," "variation," or "the course of events." To make the meaning clear, the Italian word has been inserted, when it was found necessary, in parentheses.]

[2] Aristotle (indeed, Plato before him) and S. Thomas after him recognised and showed, that the inevitableness of such a principle is not removed by assuming the eternity of the world, *i.e.* by assuming that succession has had no beginning. The two questions, whether succession has had a beginning, and how succession is possible, are distinct and mutually irreducible.

essential to unity, for extra-temporal necessity only asserts itself in succession, is nothing but a law of succession. Succession may be resolved into a sequence of new facts necessarily connected with each other. Hence succession implies a multiplicity of absolute beginnings, the existence of which must constitute a strict unity. We know that every subject is active, that is to say, gives rise to absolute beginnings. And the interference, according to necessary laws, of the beginnings to which a subject gives rise, with those to which other subjects give rise, is made possible by the mutual implications between the subjects. Extra-temporality, temporality, and their mutual implication, can be reduced to the polycentric structure of the phenomenal universe.

After having shown that each subject must imply all other subjects, we have to see in what way it implies them. The existence of a subject consists in its being as thinking.[1] Now, every thought implies the concept of Being, of which it is a determination; therefore a subject exists, in so far as it thinks Being. On the other hand, every phenomenon, and every subject, exists; in other words, is a determination of Being. We conclude, that the phenomenal universe exists in so far as it is implicit in each subject. When I say that something exists, in whatsoever way, I assert that the thing is a determination of Being—to be precise, of the Being thought by me, of that Being of which I too am a determination, since my existence is a thinking of it. Vice versa, Being is nothing else (as yet we do not know it to be anything else) than the element common to every subject and to every phenomenon. Hence, I think Being only in so

---

[1] We said just now that it consists in its being as active; but we had already observed that activity and thought are two only in abstraction: the subject thinks in so far as he acts, and acts in so far as he thinks.

far as my thought, in a most indeterminate form, includes everything, or in so far as my thought is the form of all matter. Being, according to what we have said of it, is not anything, not even anything thinkable, the existence of which consists in something else than in being thought: it exists in so far as every subject thinks it; and every subject thinks it in so far as his thinking requires simply such and such further determinations to coincide with some concrete thing. Being does not exist apart from its determinations; but it does not follow from this that Being is nothing, and that only its determinations have existence: the existence of the determinations is not the existence of independent things, separate or separable; their common character, in virtue of which they are determinations of an identical Being, is essential to their existence. Being, we said, is a concept, and exists only in so far as it is thought by some subject; it is thought in so far as it is the supreme form of the process of thought. And, as such, it must be thought by a multiplicity (by an infinity ?) of subjects; for none of those its determinations, which consist in its being thought by a determinate subject, can exhaust, or become identified with, the form of thinking.

8. DISTINCTION BETWEEN EXISTENCE AND KNOWLEDGE

The doctrine so recapitulated establishes the only nexus between reality and cognition which can be reconciled with the possibility of cognition. Cognition taken in its full sense, that doing-thinking which is the conscious life of a subject, coincides with a reality for which to exist and to be known are one and the same thing. And nevertheless it is necessary to distinguish between existence and knowing, because: (1) Abstract cognition, thinking as distinguished from doing, cannot be identified with reality, which coincides, not with the cognitive process taken in abstraction, but with the actual fulness of the vital process, which is at once knowledge and activity; (2) Actual cognition has necessarily implications, to recognise which is to know actually, *i.e.* to know actually, by a process following a preceding actual cognition, that the latter implied more than its explicit content: it is a knowing that the preceding cognition did not coincide, in its explicit form, with the whole reality implied by it. This is, in other words, to recognise subconsciousness as something beyond consciousness and essential to consciousness. The number of phenomena which each subject knows actually from time to time, is as nothing in comparison with those which happen. But the cognition of a reality and the reality known are the two constituents of one and the same vital act, so that the knowing is not, what is commonly imagined, an (impossible) going out of ourselves to arrive at something external. And there exists no reality, in the field of phenomena, which is essentially unknowable by a subject, because no reality exists (that is to say, we have no reason to suppose the existence of any) which is not implicit in each subject, and this its implicitness is an essential constituent as much of the reality as of the subject, whatever these may be.

Further, the existence of any reality, even if not explicitly known by how many soever subjects, always consists in vivid and full cognition on the part of some subject, because all that happens may be resolved into the doing-thinking of subjects. And finally, while to each of us the matter of reality is almost entirely unknown, its form on the other hand consists in our knowing or in our existence, for each of us is a centre of the

## Introduction

phenomenal universe (a centre which is essential, although not unique, indeed because not unique), and the form of forms, Being, coincides ultimately with a thought essential to each.

### 9. DISTINCTION BETWEEN TRUTH AND ERROR

The relation so established justifies the distinction between truth and error, *i.e.* accounts for error. My conscious living is constituted by a temporal process, which breaks up into distinct acts, is connected with subconsciousness, and at every moment detaches itself from it and falls back into it again. The process in so far as it becomes actual is always at the same time true and real. But it may or not conform to other analogous processes, which are implied in it subconsciously. In the first case, it constitutes a vital phase of my development; in the second, it is on the contrary an obstacle to my development, and the obstacle, if it goes beyond a certain limit, ends in the disorganisation of the narrowly subjective unity. In the first case we think what is true, *i.e.* we know; in the second, we fall into error. That error has its root in spontaneity, *i.e.* in that possibility of absolute beginnings which is a constituent of the subject, is quite obvious. The spontaneity of one subject is essentially connected with that of other subjects, but remains nevertheless spontaneity; from which it follows that a subject can, in manifesting its spontaneity outwardly, either adapt itself to a requirement of the whole by developing itself, or oppose that requirement by impeding its own development and working towards its own disorganisation. The possibility of phenomena, and the possibility of errors, coincide: this coincidence is not without importance as enforcing the doctrine here expounded.

## 10. BEING AS THE SUPREME FORM OF PHENOMENAL REALITY

Even in passing to Being we have not gone beyond the field of phenomenal reality. By this transition we have recognised a form of phenomenal reality—in fact, the supreme form, that by which phenomenal reality is connected within itself or unified, and to which is to be referred the necessity dominating in it. But the form is nothing but the form of matter, and, analogously, extra-temporal necessity applies only to temporal succession, and outside this it is nothing. Hence it follows that the contemplation of things *sub specie æternitatis* is in no sense superior to the contemplation of them *sub specie temporis*. Indeed the real or true view is the second, albeit it is not possible without regard to the unity of things—to forms which are valid for all time, and outside time. We can abstract from what is temporal something eternal, which therefore must be said to be immanent in the temporal, and which certainly is not ineffectual there, because the existence of the temporal would vanish with the vanishing of the eternal which is immanent in it. But to recognise that in the temporal there is, and cannot but be, immanent an eternal, is perhaps the same thing as to ascribe to the eternal an existence separate or separable from that of the temporal? Evidently not. Phenomenal reality cannot be resolved into the eternal which is immanent in it (an abstraction), nor into the merely temporal (also an abstraction): it is a temporal with a form the existence of which is outside time. The question, whether, beyond the eternal immanent in phenomena, there is an eternal independent of phenomena, remains unsolved. Has the Being, of which phenomena and those secondary unities called subjects are determinations, other determinations beyond these? I have called attention in this book to the several further consequences which follow from answering this question affirmatively or negatively. The answer can be drawn only from an exact and complete doctrine of the phenomenal universe, but it must be possible to draw it from such a doctrine.

## 11. CRITICISM OF AGNOSTICISM AND IDEALISM

The doctrine which I present, is no doubt incomplete, but I believe it to be exact: it is an outline which would require a further development, but as an outline it is definitive. This assertion will seem superlatively presumptuous to the agnostics, who are always the greater number; but it is high time to convince ourselves that agnosticism, though justified from the scientific point of view, is philosophically nonsense. The philosopher who is incapable of reaching anything final, ought to conclude that there is nothing final; and this would be a final conclusion. So I have also answered those idealists who, identifying reality and cognition, and so taking away from cognition a fixed term at which it ought to aim, consider final cognitions as excluded; cognition, they say, develops itself, *i.e.* changes continually, and this changing of it is the changing of reality. Although I do not believe that reality and cognition are identifiable in the sense in which those idealists identify them, I can accept the conception which is brought up against me. But I remark that this same conception, either has no value nor meaning at all, or is final. To say—cognition always goes on developing, without ever reaching a fixed result, and then to add—this is true to-day, but might not be true to-morrow, is to say and unsay the same thing. Certainly, reality and cognition are unceasingly changing, that is to say they consist in a succession, in a temporal process. But this temporal process implies a necessity, a form, an eternal which is immanent in it. It is impossible to recognise that such a process is a process of knowing, impossible to speak of reality in a serious way which transcends the fragmentariness of popular knowledge, if we are unable to abstract the immanent eternal from the temporal which realises it. And when we have been able to reach such an abstraction, the cognition so obtained, although it is only the cognition of a condition of actual knowledge, although therefore it does not exclude but indeed implies an unceasing change of cognition with respect to its content and its transitory forms, has reached a point which cannot be believed to be superable without denying at the same time the possibility of going beyond it. The doctrine so recapitulated is simply the formula which expresses the abstraction of which we were speaking.[1]

---

[1] As regards agnostic philosophers (about scientific agnosticism something is said further on in the book) see R. NAZZARI: *Massimi equivoci e minimi presupposti*, Roma, 1911, p. 146 : "Suppose there should be nothing *conclusive*," that is to say, definitive "either in knowledge or in life?" The author adds immediately : "Even this might be a conclusion." Might be? It *is;* or else it is a phrase without meaning. I cannot conceive how the author who gives undoubted proof of talent and culture has failed to see the irrationality of making the Kantian agnosticism an objection to me, me who, after so many others, have deduced from it the inevitable consequence : admitting that it is impossible for us to know beyond certain limits, why persist in asserting that there is anything beyond those limits? With regard to the idealistic objection see a review by me of the *Filosofia della Pratica* by B. CROCE in *Cultura Filosofica*, Firenze, 1910, N. IV. The doctrine expounded in the present book is substantially identical with that which I have already put forth in the *Great Problems*. The two books are independent of each other, but they are mutually complementary by reason of differences in their development and of many particular points. When I published the *Great Problems*, I promised that in a short time it would be followed by an historical commentary. In fact my doctrine is in the end the relatively clear expression of something which we all mean, which we know without giving ourselves an exact account of it—of something which has gradually become more and more explicit in the history of philosophy. The historical commentary would aid not a little towards disengaging what is essential in the doctrine from what in the exposition is inevitably special to the author of it, *i.e.* from what is transitory and irrelevant ; in other words, it would aid towards making it better under-

stood. I have not abandoned the thought of doing this, but I have been obliged to defer the publication partly from personal motives, but especially because I convinced myself that it was better to eliminate first of all not a few difficulties due to excessive conciseness and to some deficiencies of the *Great Problems*.

Some explanation can be found in a few other short articles by me, which refer to several points of the matter here treated, and which I quote:

*Tra Kant e Rosmini* in *Rivista di Filosofia*, I, n. 1, Modena, 1909;
*La Cognizione* in *La Cultura*, XXVIII, n. 3, Roma, 1909;
*Fisica e Metafisica* in *La Cultura*, XXVIII, n. 17-18, Roma, 1909;
*Sul concetto di realtà* in *Cultura filosofica*, IV, n. 1. Firenze, 1910;
*Cognizioni e convenzioni* in *Rivista di filosofia*, II, n. 3, Modena, 1910;
*Realtà e cognizione* in *Rivista di Filosofia*, II, n. 4, Modena, 1910;
*Moralità e ragione* in *La cultura contemporanea*, II, n. 8, Roma, 1910;
*Lo Spirito della filosofia* in *La cultura contemporanea*, II, n. 17-18, Roma, 1910;
*Das Subjekt und die Wirklichkeit* in *Logos*, Vol. I, n. 2, Tübingen, 1910;
*Cristianesimo e Morale* in *La cultura contemporanea*, III, n. 1, Roma, 1911;
*Sul concetto di verità* in *Rivista di filosofia*, III, n. 2, Modena, 1911;
*Dio e l' anima* in *Rivista di filosofia*, III, n. 3, Modena, 1911;
*In cerca d' una filosofia* in *La Cultura*, XXXI, n. 3, Roma, 1912;
*La possibilità dei fenomeni* in *Cultura filosofica*, IV, n. 1, Firenze, 1912.

# CONTENTS

|  | Page |
|---|---|
| INTRODUCTION | v |

## CHAPTER I
## THE FIRST PRINCIPLE

| | | |
|---|---|---|
| 1. | The abstraction of objective cognition | 1 |
| 2. | Philosophic problems | 2 |
| 3. | Philosophy and theory of knowledge | 4 |
| 4. | Continuation | 5 |
| 5. | What we can know | 7 |
| 6. | Self-consciousness | 9 |
| 7. | Consciousness and subconsciousness | 11 |
| 8. | Experience and thought | 13 |
| 9. | Thought and reality | 14 |
| 10. | Reality and the subject | 16 |
| 11. | Existence of the subject, and its self-thinking | 18 |
| 12. | Objections examined | 20 |
| 13. | Interpretation of subjectivism; its meaning | 22 |
| 14. | The empirical ego. The subject and the ego | 24 |
| 15. | Experience and cognition. Form | 25 |
| 16. | Objections examined | 27 |
| 17. | Continuation. Relations between subjects | 29 |
| 18. | Does a reality beyond phenomena exist? What it can be? | 32 |
| 19. | Phenomenal reality. Phenomena and self-cognition | 33 |

## CHAPTER II
## THE SUBJECT

| | | |
|---|---|---|
| 1. | Formation of the subject; the primitive particular unity | 36 |
| 2. | Development of the unity. The subject and the world | 37 |
| 3. | Characters of the primitive unity | 39 |
| 4. | Continuation. Consciousness and subconsciousness | 40 |
| 5. | Original multiplicity of primitive unities | 42 |
| 6. | Further remarks on the development of primitive unities | 44 |
| 7. | The dualities Peter-Paul and subject-object | 46 |
| 8. | Relations between subjects | 48 |

|     |                                                                                     | Page |
| --- | ----------------------------------------------------------------------------------- | ---- |
| 9.  | Higher unity of subjects; polycentric system                                        | 50   |
| 10. | Continuation                                                                        | 52   |
| 11. | Activity and cognition                                                              | 54   |
| 12. | Activity and resistance. Organisation of activity and of consciousness              | 56   |
| 13. | Reflection. Objective cognition of self                                             | 58   |
| 14. | Organisation of unextended (in the strict sense psychical) experience               | 60   |

## CHAPTER III

### REALITY

|     |                                                                                                                                       |    |
| --- | ------------------------------------------------------------------------------------------------------------------------------------- | -- |
| 1.  | Common concept of reality                                                                                                             | 63 |
| 2.  | Why it is necessary to discuss it                                                                                                     | 64 |
| 3.  | Unity of experience. Extended object, and sensation                                                                                   | 66 |
| 4.  | Existence of bodies; its meaning                                                                                                      | 67 |
| 5.  | Character of the physical sciences. The concrete and the abstract                                                                     | 68 |
| 6.  | Inseparability of extended experience from the whole of experience                                                                    | 70 |
| 7.  | How the subject constructs the external world, and at the same time organises itself                                                  | 72 |
| 8.  | Continuation. Reality and appearance                                                                                                  | 73 |
| 9.  | The two interpretations, scientific and philosophic, of experience. The philosophic interpretation does not introduce the "thing in itself" | 75 |
| 10. | Space and time as forms of reality                                                                                                    | 78 |
| 11. | The course of events, time, and spontaneities                                                                                         | 80 |
| 12. | Unity of the extended phenomenal world                                                                                                | 82 |

## CHAPTER IV

### FACT AND COGNITION

|     |                                                                                                                                  |     |
| --- | -------------------------------------------------------------------------------------------------------------------------------- | --- |
| 1.  | Judgment and cognition of the judgment. Facts                                                                                    | 86  |
| 2.  | Judgment; expression (of the judgment); sensation (on which the judgment is founded)                                             | 87  |
| 3.  | Reality, and the system of judgments                                                                                             | 89  |
| 4.  | Coincidence of reality and cognition. Concrete thought                                                                           | 91  |
| 5.  | Necessity as the condition of knowledge                                                                                          | 93  |
| 6.  | Experience cannot be resolved into pure rationality, i.e. into extra-temporal necessity. What is known, explicitly and implicitly | 95  |
| 7.  | In what sense reality and explicit cognition differ                                                                              | 98  |
| 8.  | Unknown reality                                                                                                                  | 100 |
| 9.  | Continuation                                                                                                                     | 101 |
| 10. | What is arbitrary in cognition                                                                                                   | 103 |
| 11. | Reality and knowableness. Externality and multiplicity of subjects                                                               | 105 |

## CHAPTER V
## THOUGHT

|    |                                                                                                                               | Page |
|----|-------------------------------------------------------------------------------------------------------------------------------|------|
| 1. | Thinking as a psychical process, and error                                                                                    | 108  |
| 2. | Truth and unity of the subject                                                                                                | 109  |
| 3. | The doing-thinking. Distinction between activity and thought. Necessity and unity of the subject                              | 111  |
| 4. | Objective value of subjective necessity                                                                                       | 113  |
| 5. | Necessity as founded on the unity of the real                                                                                 | 115  |
| 6. | How the two conceptions of necessity are identified                                                                           | 118  |
| 7. | Thought and Being                                                                                                             | 120  |
| 8. | Examination of some doctrines concerning Being                                                                                | 121  |
| 9. | Continuation                                                                                                                  | 123  |
| 10.| Abstraction in general; knowledge as a construction                                                                           | 125  |
| 11.| Of a knowledge which is at the same time the being of reality. Intrinsic truth and historical truth                           | 128  |
| 12.| Existence as a subjective-objective unity                                                                                     | 131  |

## CHAPTER VI
## UNITY AND MULTIPLICITY

|    |                                                                                                                                              |     |
|----|----------------------------------------------------------------------------------------------------------------------------------------------|-----|
| 1. | Definition of the theme                                                                                                                      | 134 |
| 2. | Explanations                                                                                                                                 | 136 |
| 3. | Concept of a system                                                                                                                          | 138 |
| 4. | System of cognitions                                                                                                                         | 140 |
| 5. | Relations—causal and rational; distinction                                                                                                   | 143 |
| 6. | Indispensableness of causal relations; impossibility of reducing causality to extra-temporal necessity                                       | 146 |
| 7. | Causality and succession                                                                                                                     | 148 |
| 8. | Relations and their terms; accidental and necessary relations                                                                                | 150 |
| 9. | Unity and multiplicity as reconciled by the necessity of relations. Difficulties which arise from accidental relations                       | 154 |
| 10.| Of physical determinism. Impossibility of excluding a certain indeterminism                                                                  | 156 |
| 11.| Connection between determinism and indeterminism                                                                                             | 158 |
| 12.| Our interpretation of the course of events                                                                                                   | 161 |
| 13.| Maintenance of it against common preconceptions                                                                                              | 165 |
| 14.| Philosophic doctrines founded on these preconceptions                                                                                        | 168 |
| 15.| Examination of them                                                                                                                          | 170 |
| 16.| Continuation of our interpretation; compare § 12                                                                                             | 173 |
| 17.| The universe as the unity of a multiplicity. The subject as the unity of the universe                                                        | 176 |
| 18.| Multiplicity of subjects and difficulties arising from it. Accidental manifestations of the subject                                          | 179 |

|     |                                                                                                                      | Page |
| --- | -------------------------------------------------------------------------------------------------------------------- | ---- |
| 19. | Accidental manifestations of the subject, and necessity                                                              | 182  |
| 20. | Reciprocal implication between spontaneities                                                                         | 185  |
| 21. | The common element as condition of reciprocal implication—Being                                                      | 187  |
| 22. | Concept and reality                                                                                                  | 190  |

## CHAPTER VII
## THE ABSOLUTE

|     |                                                                                                                                  | Page |
| --- | -------------------------------------------------------------------------------------------------------------------------------- | ---- |
| 1.  | Meaning of the doctrine expounded. The doctrine of phenomena, and metaphysics. Objection against metaphysics                     | 193  |
| 2.  | Philosophic agnosticism                                                                                                          | 195  |
| 3.  | Relativity of knowledge. Legitimate conclusions. The thing in itself                                                             | 198  |
| 4.  | Appearance and appearing. Common distinctions and limits of their validity                                                       | 201  |
| 5.  | Inseparableness of single phenomena from the unity-subject. One subject and another subject                                      | 204  |
| 6.  | The Absolute and Being. The Absolute and the phenomenal universe                                                                 | 207  |
| 7.  | Possibility of phenomena                                                                                                         | 209  |
| 8.  | Apparent contradiction in the concept of phenomena, and elimination of it                                                        | 212  |
| 9.  | Continuation                                                                                                                     | 215  |
| 10. | The phenomenal subject and the subject in itself                                                                                 | 217  |
| 11. | The unity of the universe as unity of one single (universal) subject                                                             | 221  |
| 12. | How the universal subject must be conceived                                                                                      | 224  |
| 13. | Identity of phenomena as included in the particular or in the universal subject                                                  | 226  |
| 14. | The particular or universal unity is not a resultant                                                                             | 230  |
| 15. | Intelligence and Being. The system of subjects; how it is intelligible without the hypothesis of a universal subject             | 233  |
| 16. | Difficulty arising from subconsciousness, and impossibility of eliminating it                                                    | 235  |
| 17. | The indispensableness of unity does not allow us to infer a non-phenomenal reality                                               | 238  |
| 18. | The universe as the result of a logical process intrinsic to Being                                                               | 241  |
| 19. | Extra-temporality of that process and temporality of the course of events                                                        | 244  |
| 20. | The Logical exigency and practical exigency. Finality. Has the universe an end?                                                  | 249  |
| 21. | Continuation                                                                                                                     | 252  |
| 22. | The beginning of the course of events as condition of universal finality. Condition necessary to the beginning of the course of events | 254  |
| 23. | The theistic and the pantheistic hypotheses; definition and meaning of them                                                      | 258  |
| 24. | Summary                                                                                                                          | 262  |

## APPENDICES

| | PAGE |
|---|---|
| Experience, religion, philosophy | 267 |
| Human knowledge | 275 |
| The *Great Problems* and its critics | 284 |

# KNOW THYSELF

## CHAPTER I
## THE FIRST PRINCIPLE

### 1.
#### THE ABSTRACTION OF OBJECTIVE COGNITION

We know things which we consider as altogether distinct from ourselves and, with regard to their being and their changing, not essentially connected with us. We have objective cognitions. These, setting aside accidental errors which can always be corrected, constitute a systematisation of experience, that is to say, of the impressions which we consider as produced in us by things, by reality.

In objective cognition, especially in science which is the most characteristic form of it, we pay attention only to things, to objects: we forget ourselves.

But we may also not forget ourselves. We may reflect that the experience systematised by us is *our* experience, that the systematising activity of experience is an activity of our own. Besides the known object, we then also take into consideration the knowing subject—the fact of our knowing. That, for purely objective cognition, the consideration of the subject to whom the objective cognition belongs is not necessary, is quite obvious; we have already said so: in objective cognition abstraction is made from the subject. As I breathe without reflecting that I breathe, so I abstract without reflecting that I abstract: the results of breathing, or of abstracting, are independent of such a reflection.

This reflection, the consideration of the subject, if it is not useful for the objective cognition—whether practical, or scientific in the narrow sense—is nevertheless legitimate. For—is it necessary to say so?—objective cognition is *my* cognition, cognition of an experience belonging to myself, and obtained by an activity of my own: it would not exist, if I did not exist.

Legitimate? The consideration of the subject is indeed necessary—not for building up objective cognition, but for understanding the value of it. If I limit myself to the objective view, I shut myself up in a field of which I do not even know in what way and in what sense it exists. How can I know whether the object exists independently of me, or what relation it has to me, as long as I limit myself to considering only the object?

2.

PHILOSOPHIC PROBLEMS

Besides the problems which can be solved by objective cognition, there are the philosophical problems, some of which are so momentous that their importance reveals itself immediately to the most modest reflection as supreme.

Let the problem, for instance, be: does God exist? Some people—too many!—will say: I do not care. If they really do not know the solution of the problem, and do not care to discover it, they are not reasonable. But there are some who say that they do not care about it, because they feel sure that God does not exist. This is well enough. But if we ask on what ground they feel so sure, we shall hear them answer more or less thus: God

## The First Principle

is an hypothesis which is useless to science, and which therefore, not being justifiable, must be given up. There cannot be worse reasoning. For science, or in general for objective cognition, God is not and cannot be established. Agreed. But, suppose He should be established for philosophy?

No one is obliged to occupy himself with philosophical studies. Indeed, all those—and they are so many!—who are wanting in aptitude, or preparation, or both, can never be too strongly recommended not to meddle with them. But not to occupy oneself with philosophical studies, and to presume at the same time that one possesses the rational solution of some philosophical problem, to know at least that a certain problem is insoluble, is absurd.

He who wishes to proscribe the study of philosophy, must proscribe philosophical problems. Now, to proscribe philosophical problems is quite easy, as long as we have to do only with objective cognitions; indeed, it would be impossible to do otherwise. But to proscribe them in practice as well, is impossible. I mean, impossible to a man who does not want to follow blindly the path on which he finds himself accidentally travelling, but to choose his path with full knowledge and consciousness. I also mean, to proscribe them really, for to say that we proscribe them, and then regulate ourselves as if one or other solution, positive or negative, were certainly true, is not to proscribe them. To think that one can regulate oneself in a way that is equally good, whether God exists or not, whether individual life lasts after the death of the body or not, is madness. Humanity cannot proscribe philosophical problems, which must therefore be considered as the supreme problems.

## 3.

### PHILOSOPHY AND THEORY OF KNOWLEDGE

Philosophy is built up by means of the theory of knowledge—that is to say, by studying knowledge in its complexity, in its factual reality, by considering also the subjective factor, which is altogether neglected in common or scientific cognition. What problems does objective cognition leave unsolved? Precisely those which do not concern the object of cognition itself, but cognition in so far as it is the systematisation of an experience of the subject, obtained by the activity of the subject.

Apart from the known object and the knowing subject, we have no other elements on which to reflect; the complete study of cognition, which in some way is the unity of the subject and the object, is therefore the only way to arrive at the solution of the problems which are not solved by objective cognition.

The fact of objective cognition implies the possibility of it; implies certain relations between the subject and the object; implies ... The theory of knowledge will explain what it implies. And when the implications of that fact have been made explicit, the problems of philosophy will be solved.

In fact, if what is not an objective cognition, was not even implicit in objective cognition, it could not be accessible at all, and there would be no possible reason for supposing its existence.

The theory of knowledge is a theory of the subject—of course, of the subject considered in relation to the object; but this relation is doubtless equally essential to the subject as knowing, and to the object as known. Objective cognition is the result of a matter which includes the whole of apprehended facts, and of a form which is the systematisation of such matter, made by means of our own activity. So that to study knowledge is to study the subject.

The possibility of constructing a theory of knowledge cannot be called in question. A doing of which we were unable to give an account, would be anything one likes, rather than a knowing. I know, means: I render myself, more or less clearly, more or less completely, conscious of the object. To suppose that such an operation takes place outside consciousness, that it is not itself a conscious operation, that the activity by which it is accomplished does not become conscious of itself in accomplishing it, has no meaning.[1]

4.

### CONTINUATION

By the precept which forms the title of the present book, Socrates laid it down that philosophy ought to be a theory of knowledge, and formulated the fundamental principle of the theory of knowledge.

The cognition of the object, in its own sphere, requires

[1] The act of consciousness is perfect transparency; it is clear to itself; in it intelligence is present to itself. That I may know, it is necessary that I should be conscious of my consciousness, that I should know that I know; an act of consciousness, which were to take place in the darkness of unconsciousness, would not be an act of consciousness. It follows that the act of consciousness proves the reality of itself and of the thinking subject, or rather is the reality of itself and of the thinking subject: in the act of consciousness, reality and cognition coincide. The act of consciousness is therefore an immediate, and consequently indubitable, revelation of the real, considered as a fact (the act itself) and as a substance (the conscious ego). The ego, in which being and knowing are one thing, is therefore the type of all substances. This is the doctrine which BONATELLI put forth long ago with much clearness and maintained with great force: see *La coscienza e il meccanesimo interiore* (Padova, 1872), especially pp. 45, 59, 63, 81 ff. On the points of agreement between his thought and my own, I think it useless to insist. Bonatelli, to whom I am united by family-ties and a life-long intercourse, has been for me a spiritual father. Incidentally I here remark that I have always asserted, even during what may be called the positivistic stage of my studies (see, for instance, *Scienza e Opinioni*, Roma, 1901, pp. 355-63), that the subject knows itself as it is, not only as it appears to itself, and that this self-knowledge is essential to it.

nothing else. But its sphere, although unlimited, is partial. The problems which have most importance for man as man, remain outside it. By means of objective cognition, the rational man brings his aid to the animal man; now, the rational man must provide also for himself, not only for the animal with whom he is associated. Objective cognition is not enough for him. To the end of procuring for himself that other cognition, which as a rational being he cannot do without, he must not indeed squeeze objective cognition dry in the hope to make it yield what it cannot yield, but must study knowledge itself.

The process of knowing, that is to say an activity which manifests or realises itself in a great number of acts; cognition, that is to say the totality of objective cognitions which result from these acts; the subject, that is to say the centre of irradiation, without which the acts would not be manifestations of one and the same activity; the object, that is to say, what in each cognition opposes itself as known to the subject as knowing; experience, that is to say the totality of facts which form the matter of the single cognitions—are elements of one unity, elements which we must distinguish, but not hypostatise.

Nothing justifies the assumption that the said elements are things which have singly a separate existence, and then meet together to form the unity. The elements exist only as elements of such unity; each implies the others and the system or unity; to consider one element apart is to abstract. That is to say, each element by itself alone is an abstraction; there is only one thing truly real, the unity of all.

This unity we must try to investigate. We can investigate it, because its existence is in the end nothing but the reality of knowing. Or we may also say: its existence is

## The First Principle

one thing with the existence of the subject, although not of the subject as opposed to the object, but of the subject as implying the object and implied by it.

To construct philosophy, to study reality in its concreteness, is therefore at once to construct the theory of knowledge and to develop the cognition which the subject has of itself.

### 5.

#### WHAT WE CAN KNOW

The theory of knowledge has to solve the problem, how a cognition of anything, on the part of a subject, is possible in general. That the sky is clear, I know, because I see; that somebody has knocked at the door of my house, I know, because I hear; the description of the processes of seeing, of hearing, etc., does not enter into the theory of knowledge. These and similar processes originate or constitute certain cognitions; but this is possible because I have the capacity of knowing. We must give ourselves an account of this capacity, we have to understand it. Such is the problem.

And here is the solution in general.

When the thing known is myself, the problem does not exist. I know that I am such and such, because I am such and such; or one might say—I am such and such, because I know that I am such and such. As it is a question of a conscious intelligent being, his being and his knowing himself strictly coincide. Of course, "I" here means the unity of which we have spoken above—a certain definite and concrete unity, not one or other of the elements which may be distinguished in it—a unity, the existence of which consists in its being present to itself.

When, on the other hand, it is a question of an external

thing, really external—of a thing which is not an element
of myself, the existence or non-existence of which has
essentially nothing to do with me, the changing of which
is not at the same time a changing of myself, then, and
only then, the possibility of my cognition of such a thing
is really a problem.

It is a problem which, in the form in which it has been
presented, is insoluble. I know a thing means, I am in a
certain relation to the thing. I can know the thing means,
I can enter into that relation to the thing. But the
possibility that two elements may become related, is
already a relation between the elements themselves. For
instance, two bodies can collide; but this is possible,
because they are both collocated in space—in a space
which is the same for both, and because one at least
of the two bodies is moving towards the other. Things
which I can know, are only those which are already
essentially in relation with me.

To conclude, the thing, known or knowable, is never
outside me in the sense in which outside is commonly
understood : it is an element of me, a constituent of my
self. My knowing this or that is always a distinguishing
between elements of the unity which is I. By distinguishing, some elements are collocated in space, and they are
bodies; amongst these there is my own body, and there
are others, collocated in space outside my body. Other
elements are not collocated in space, for instance, a pain
of mine, a recollection of mine. In this way that unity,
which is I, is organised, becomes distinguished into two
parts: what I call my self in the narrower sense, and
what I call the external world ; the two parts (connected
by what I call my body) become organised in their turn
each in itself, always by means of successive distinctions.
It is impossible to speak of elements which do not belong
to the general and primitive unity; the appearing in any

way of an element is nothing but the distinguishing it in the said unity.

Finally, I can never know anything else than myself. But from this it does not follow, that my cognition is necessarily limited. The true conclusion is this: I have no means and no right to assert or to assume anything which is not implicit in me. In other words, nothing exists which is not implicit in me: I am a centre of the universe.

## 6.

### SELF-CONSCIOUSNESS

But there are many people who think, that is to say, who believe that they think, in an absolutely different way. The ego, they say, is unknowable " in itself "; what we know of it, is simply what appears of it, the " empirical ego " (also called " phenomenal ").

Psychological observation shows that the child is not conscious of himself. Self-consciousness is the result of a process which is neither short, nor simple; therefore the opinion expressed by us, that self-consciousness is the first and necessary condition of every result, of every particular cognition, that it is inseparable from the act of knowing, would be inconsistent with the facts.

Our answer is that the child is certainly not self-conscious in the same way as the developed man; but we have not said, nor can it be inferred from what we have said, that he must be self-conscious in the same sense. The developed man is conscious of himself in the manner which is proper to him, inasmuch as he opposes himself to another man, and in general to the external world. The unity of my existence, the energetic unity of my will, inseparable from the unity of my knowing, only realises, only develops itself, in contrast with similar forces.

The contrast is, on the one hand, essential to me, as a particular being distinct from the other man and from the world; I act, only in so far as I overcome some resistence. On the other hand, the contrast, without which I could not be, constitutes an obstacle to my development, tends to impede it, to disorganise me, to suppress me.

It will depend on the greater or less energy, and the greater or less intelligence in my action (on my force of will and on my consistency of thought, which are one thing), whether the obstacles, though still remaining obstacles which I have to overcome with labour and with pain, shall serve as means towards the attainment of my end, which is that of asserting, of developing myself, of reaching the greatest fullness of my existence, or of my being conscious. I am self-conscious as a man, in so far as I set such an end before me; in so far as I do so with vigorous clearness; in so far as to set it before me is to will it and to know it, to will the means and to know them, or, briefly, to will myself and to know myself.

That the child is not conscious of himself precisely in the sense just explained, we are ready to admit. But the child arrives, or can arrive, at self-consciousness. Could he arrive at it, if he were not already, before and apart from any psychological process, a unity of consciousness? —a unity, in which all that will become explicit, is already implicit, and in which it cannot but be implicit? To suppose that the unity of the subject is the result of a coalescence of separate facts of consciousness, such as, for instance, according to the common point of view, the sensations of two other subjects, even if they were the parents of the subject concerned, is madness. That which develops itself, exists. The development of self-consciousness necessarily presupposes a primitive unity of consciousness,—a unity which exists in so far as it is not alien, but present to itself, or, in other words, in so far as it is, in an embryonic form, self-conscious.

## 7.

### CONSCIOUSNESS AND SUBCONSCIOUSNESS

The consciousness of the child, in comparison with the consciousness of the adult, ought rather to be called subconsciousness. But the unity of the adult itself implies a number of subconscious, and even very deeply subconscious, elements. Each of us is, not only that which he clearly perceives, but also that which he can remember, although now in fact he does not remember—and that which he will perhaps never remember, but which nevertheless is not entirely lost for him.

Indeed, according to Plato, to know is simply to recollect. I know, in so far as I make myself explicitly conscious of something which I must recognise to be implicit in me, which is a constituent of myself, if not as an animal, at least as a rational being. This means that I know, in so far as I know myself.

It is true that according to Plato ideas are external entities, which I have known in a former life, without being able to understand in what way I knew them then; reminiscence only explains objective cognition by means of another objective cognition. The Platonic solution is not only mythical, but incomplete.

But let us disengage it from its mythical setting, and consider it in its positive content. Into what does it resolve itself? Into the assertion, that the knowable, as a whole, is implied in the subject, is already known in a subconscious form; that knowing is never anything more than a self-developing of the subject; that in short the subject implies the universe, and that its knowledge of the universe is self-knowledge. And in this, which forms its positive content, the Platonic solution is satisfactory: compare the applications which Plato himself makes of it, for instance, in the *Meno;* or the more extensive applications which Galilei made of it in the field of physics.

To us adults, who have a clear consciousness, and who make use of it as a term of comparison, subconsciousness almost seems a zero of consciousness. But even the common man perceives that this is not true. Everyone knows the slow and painful process that is sometimes required for the precision of a recollection: we almost seem to feel the recollection gradually emerging out of the depths of subconsciousness, as if we could follow it in its passage from the darkest obscurity, through regions which gradually become more luminous, till it appears in the clearness of explicit consciousness. Nor is it necessary to mention Leibniz.

No doubt the man who sleeps deeply without dreaming is not dead. I mean, he is not dead as a man, that is to say as a reasonable, a self-conscious being; for, if he were dead as such, and only the animal were to survive (if subconsciousness were a zero of consciousness, then only the plant would really survive), the man would not come to life again, *i.e.* he would not awake.

The reason of the sleeping man is subconscious. And in the same way, the reason of the child is subconscious—more deeply subconscious, on the one hand, for the child needs much more time to become fully awake,—less deeply, on the other, for in fact the child feels, is happy, suffers, acts. And the way in which he acts, manifestly aims at overcoming certain resistances, at transforming them into means for intensifying, for developing, himself, for becoming himself.

It is the same process, by which we have seen the self-consciousness of the adult realise itself. This is no doubt

## The First Principle

the goal in which the process of infancy ends—a goal that is never attained once for all, must be attained again at every moment, and is attained in so far as it is transcended. Even the adult is never altogether self-conscious, if by self-consciousness we mean a process enclosed in the field of clear consciousness. Between the adult and the child the difference is one of degree—a remarkable difference, but only one of degree.

### 8.

#### EXPERIENCE AND THOUGHT

A further objection has its root in a vague and false conception of the relations between "experience" and "thought."

The unity, or let us say the constitutive activity of the subject, is not a datum of experience. Most obviously. The data of experience are apprehended as distinct, that is to say, as single concrete elements. A datum appears, then vanishes, another taking its place; in certain cases we may even follow the changes by which one datum is transformed into another. All this is a varying; but a varying of elements which have not in themselves, as empirical data, the reason of the varying. The causality underlying the changes, our activity as activity, and the resistances which oppose it as resistances, the doing or the interfering, are not data of experience. Hume's observations on the subject are decisive.

Activity and correlative passivity, and we may even add, all relations, are not given in experience, are not observed, but thought, introduced into experience by thought. They are only products of thought; and so also self-consciousness is only a product of thought.

These reflections, which are urged against us as objections, are even accepted by us, but we give a different interpretation to them. The difference between our opponents and ourselves lies in the meaning ascribed to the word "only."

We too say, that activity, passivity, relations of every kind, and self-consciousness, only exist in so far as they are thought. But by this we do not at all mean to deny their reality. They coincide with the cognition which we have of them; therefore (we say) there is, above or beneath cognition, no reality whatever which remains unknown. Activity, passivity, etc., are only products of thought; but the reason is that, if we take away thought, nothing remains of the things to which we refer by those terms.

On the other hand, according to our opponents, between our conception of activity, and the thing denoted by the name of activity (and similarly, between our conception of passivity, and the thing denoted by the name of passivity, etc.), there is only a correspondence. So, for instance, there is only correspondence between the number of this page, and the content of the page itself. By means of the numbers, we distinguish one page from another, and we can easily refer to any page we choose. This is no doubt useful; for instance, the reference, compare p. 13, is much shorter than to copy p. 13; but the undeniable usefulness of making a number correspond to a content ought not to lead us into the gross mistake of believing that the number as such can give us the knowledge of the content. So our opponents say.

### 9.

#### THOUGHT AND REALITY

Well (we say), that some of our conceptions, although useful to us for guiding ourselves amongst things, have no intrinsic cognitive value with respect to the things, do

## The First Principle

not constitute the character of things, is not denied by us, as shown by the instance alleged, to which it would be easy to add many others. But it does not follow from this that all our conceptions have only the non-intrinsic value of mere usefulness, of which we have spoken.

Let us take the former instance again. Between the number 13 and the content of page 13 there is no essential relation, but a simple correspondence—a correspondence, which has in it much that is arbitrary: it is enough to remark, that if the book had been printed in a different type, the number corresponding to the same content would have been different. Nevertheless, the conception of the special correspondence which has been established (has established itself in fact, though arbitrarily) between that content and that number, cannot be again an arbitrary construction, the meaning of which consists only in the utility derived from it.

In fact, 13 is the number which comes immediately after 12 and immediately before 14; so also, the content of p. 13 comes immediately after the content of p. 12 and immediately before the content of p. 14. Such an identity, between the order of the numbers and the order of the contents, is no arbitrary construction; it is indeed the condition without which the arbitrary denoting of the contents by means of the numbers would be of no use, indeed would not be possible at all.

There is a real correspondence between the numbers and the contents; both have an order which is the same for both. I say, a "real" correspondence. Certainly the correspondence only exists in so far as it is thought. But its existence is, nevertheless, existence. To assume a reality, unknown in itself, with which the conceived correspondence would have only a relation of correspondence, with regard to which the term of correspondence would only have a denoting value, would be (in this case) the maximum, not only of absurdity, but of extravagance.

Thus, what we admit to be true for some of our concepts is not true for them all, *i.e.* that they are "only" our conceptions, made by us to correspond to a reality, with which they have no essential relation. The concept of relation among others is not of this kind.

## 10.

### REALITY AND THE SUBJECT

It is not difficult to satisfy ourselves, that the same argument applies to the conceptions of activity (from which its correlative, passivity, cannot be separated,) and of self-consciousness.

We have no experience of activity as activity: to conceive something as activity is not to perceive by experience, but to conceive, to think. Every recognition is an effect of thought; of that which it may be possible to know without thinking, it is no use to speak. The point is that the work of thought must be thought, and that we must not be satisfied with phrases without meaning.

He who wants to show that the constitutive activity of the ego, *i.e.* the ego, is not knowable, has something else to do than to show the impossibility of having an immediate experience of it. Any kind of doctrine and the most common cognition presuppose experience as thought, and not merely immediate experience, if immediate means not-thought.

Experience may be resolved into a multitude of simultaneous and successive facts. Amid the multitude, the subject distinguishes certain manifestations of his own activity, and certain resistances which are manifestations of other activities. What value has this distinction?

The distinction, in the first place, is a manifestation of the activity of the subject—of a thinking, knowing activity. By making distinctions, I arrange my experience in a form, which it had not before; in reality, I make of it a different experience. I bring new facts into it, that is to say my distinctions; and, by means of these, I give the original facts a different organisation: I reorganise experience, that is to say, myself. The new ego, the ego so reorganised, exists in so far as it has reorganised itself, in so far as it is conscious of having so reorganised itself; to suppose that the reorganising activity consists in anything else than the consciousness of the reorganising, has no meaning.

Further, the arranging activity is not something different from what I have recognised in the process of distinguishing as my activity. In fact, there has never been and never is a moment, in which it would occur to me to think of reorganising myself, of constructing myself by ascribing to myself the character of a thinking being: a being who is not already a thinking being, cannot think of anything. The distinction goes on asserting itself step by step by means of my volitions, that is to say, of the manifestations of my activity. I distinguish myself as active from the resistances which I meet, precisely in so far as I am active, not in any other way.

The activity which organises, and which doubtless is activity, is one with that which after the organisation is recognised as activity. This means briefly, that the new self, which results from the organisation, is still the old self developed. The order which I produce by my action and of which I am conscious in so far as I produce it (for the activity by which I produce it, is an activity of consciousness), is not absolutely new: it is a work of mine, and therefore presupposes myself, presupposes an order similar to that which is produced.

That is to say, by arranging myself more and more consciously, I do indeed gradually transform myself, but this transformation of myself is a transferring into the field of clear consciousness of what was before in the field of subconsciousness, a making explicit of what before was implicit. It is no small task; the elements, by becoming explicit, enter into reciprocal relations, to which they were previously alien; consciousness is the stage and the factor of a much more varied and vivid becoming than subconsciousness. Still it is not less true, that consciousness is a development of subconsciousness; which makes the assumption, that the thing conceived as activity is, "in itself," something wholly different from activity, altogether inconceivable.

The assumption is as reasonable as if a person were to say: four is something corresponding to the legs of a horse; but what this thing is in itself, I do not know. Why! what do you imagine four to be, if not precisely the four of which you are thinking!

### 11.

EXISTENCE OF THE SUBJECT, AND ITS SELF-THINKING

What we have said about activity, is equally applicable to self-consciousness (and indeed, as we remarked, self-consciousness and the activity of the ego, that is to say, the ego itself, are all one).

Self-consciousness, in the developed form in which it presents itself in the adult, is, no doubt, conditioned by a process. This does not mean that it can begin absolutely. The ego is not a product; it is necessarily, in its most simple form, something original—something, however, which develops, and to which it is essential to develop. Self-consciousness, either develops, arranges itself more and more firmly, becomes more extended, grows in intensity, or else degenerates towards subconsciousness.

Self-consciousness, therefore, has its condition in a psychological process. But this is not the question. We ask: is self-consciousness, whatever the conditions of it may be, a cognition of the subject by the subject himself?

The negative answer is not justified by the fact that self-consciousness is conditioned by a process. By this process I come to know something which I believe to be myself. Whoever wishes to assert that I do not know myself "truly," must show that I am something different from that of which I attain cognition by means of the process in question. Such a demonstration necessarily presupposes the possibility of a comparison between that thing which is known to me and which I call myself, and the "true" self. It necessarily presupposes that cognition of the ego which is to be declared an illusion.

To get out of the difficulty, recourse is had to a device: the ego, which in self-consciousness knows itself, is "only" the empirical ego, not the true ego, not the deepest ego. The device (although it is connected with certain considerations, the value of which cannot be denied: compare below, §§ 13 and 16) is nothing but a makeshift.

It is quite obvious that, if the expression "non-empirical ego" had no meaning at all, the makeshift would only be a verbal one. But if that expression is not without some meaning, then we have a cognition of the non-empirical ego—a cognition which, like any other, will never be complete or incapable of development, but will still be a cognition, contrary to what has to be shown.

On the other hand, the non-empirical ego is an arbitrary and fantastic invention, brought forward with the sole object of saving the unknowableness of the ego in words against the fact—a fact essential to every cognition!—of self-consciousness. It is easy, in this way, to deny the light of the sun; the sun which you see, is not the true sun, it is only a phenomenal sun. Only! And who told you that there is a non-phenomenal sun? In the same way, who told you that there is a non-empirical ego?

The ego which has cognition of itself in self-consciousness, is the empirical ego; *atqui*, the ego is really nothing but the self-conscious subject; *ergo*, there is no other ego than the empirical ego.

### 12.

#### OBJECTIONS EXAMINED

It will be objected that innumerable facts show, that we do not know ourselves deeply; for instance, others know our defects better than we. And Socrates would not have been obliged to formulate his precept, if it were an easy thing to know ourselves.

We grant this. But we have already remarked that it is indeed essential to the ego to have knowledge of itself, but not that it should have a complete knowledge of itself, incapable of development. This point requires some further explanation.

The cognition which the ego has of itself, can grow: hence it is always imperfect. Nevertheless the growth and development of the cognition presuppose the cognition—an imperfect cognition, but a cognition of the ego.

Further, cognition, whatever degree it may reach, is always cognition of an empirical ego. The elements which are now included in it, and which before were excluded from it, were, even before, knowable. Cognition, as a state and as a development, gives no indication of any unknowable quid, which underlies the empirical ego. From the movement of a body we infer a space more extended than the body, not a hyperspace.

There is more to be said. The development of the

cognition which the ego has of itself, is precisely the development of the ego. As self-consciousness the ego coincides with the cognition which it has of itself. I am that which I know myself to be. The cognition extends as far as the ego extends.

But how far does it extend? Clearly, to the animal which is always conjoined with the ego, and which is the true substratum of the ego. That the ego exists, means that certain constitutive elements of the animal subject are so organised that the consciousness of their unity is superposed on the unitary consciousness of the elements.

The development of the ego is a conquest over the associated animal—it is an extension of the organisation in which self-consciousness consists to elements of the animal, which were not yet included in the said organisation.

My knowledge of myself is small: "men and years will tell me who I am." That is to say, I know but little of the animal associated with me, am but a small part of it. My further development, what I shall do and what I shall be, will depend in great part on the potentialities of the animal, and also on circumstances. I know explicitly what I am actually; but to know what I am potentially, it would be necessary that I should have already organised in me the elements, which I have not yet been able to organise; it would be necessary that my potential capacity should become actuality.

Moreover, what men and years may tell me of myself, belongs, though actually unknown, to the phenomenal, empirical ego—to the range of what is observable. To pretend that what cannot be observed can ever become the content of an observation is nonsense. The future phenomenon cannot be foreseen except in a very vague way, not because it is non-phenomenal, but because it is future.

## 13.

### INTERPRETATION OF SUBJECTIVISM; ITS MEANING

The impossibility, for the particular subject, of knowing himself as he is (of knowing his own noumenal reality), besides being maintained on the psychological grounds which we have examined and discarded, is however also maintained on grounds of another kind which we have still to examine.

We represent to ourselves time under the image of a line, as drawn by us. Without this operation of drawing (without motion, not in so far as it is observable from without, but in so far as it is an operation of the subject), we should not have the concept of succession. Hence, we arrange the psychical facts which we call internal in time, in the same way in which we arrange the data which we call external in space. Consequently, if space is simply a subjective form, time also will be no more than a simple subjective form; and the subject will know itself only as a phenomenon.[1]

This doctrine we propose, not to refute, but to interpret —to interpret it in its true and only meaning.[2]

Is space simply a subjective form? No doubt; but in this sense, that outside the subject, independently of the subject and of the spatial form which is a constituent of it, there would be no reality,—and not in the sense that the subject apprehends spatially, as if this were his way of apprehending a reality in itself non-spatial, or of apprehending the impressions which he receives of it.

Space means that which the subject represents to himself and knows as space: it means nothing more. To assume a space in itself, the existence of which does not

---

[1] KANT, *Critique of Pure Reason*, § 24. I have not transcribed, but recapitulated him.
[2] We claim to understand Kant "besser als er sich selbst verstand."

consist in my representing it to myself, which is not the form whereby I represent to myself external reality, is to suppose that the space of which I am speaking, is not the space of which I am speaking.

But what has been said of space, applies also to existence, which is, though not a representation of mine, a concept of mine. Existence is my way of conceiving all that I conceive; to assume it to be something else is to assume that the existence of which I speak is not the existence of which I speak. I say: reality exists. These words, either have no meaning at all, or else mean this, that the existence of reality consists in its being conceived by me as existence.

The same may be said of time. It is not permissible to assert that the understanding, applying itself to the manifold of apprehended facts (apprehended externally or internally), "finds" temporality in it: since temporality is nothing apart from the intellectual operation by which we arrive at the discovery, it is properly not found, but "created" by the operation itself.[1]

With this we agree. But it is incredible, that the understanding creates temporality in the same way in which, for instance, the sculptor creates the statue—by impressing, upon a matter which was already there, a form which was not there before. Matter too is a creation of the understanding, for what we call its existence is really nothing but an operation of the understanding: to assert existence is to apply a category.

Things have no kind of existence but objective existence. Objective existence is such only in relation to the subject. And the existence of the subject is nothing but its appearing to itself. The contrary supposition is altogether gratuitous; and, on a deeper examination, it turns out to be hopelessly contradictory.

[1] KANT, *loc. cit.*

## 14.

### THE EMPIRICAL EGO. THE SUBJECT AND THE EGO

The empirical ego, we have said and we repeat, is real. Underlying this, and as its support, there is the animal—a unity of consciousness. It is necessary to distinguish between self-consciousness and the simple unity of consciousness, although it is true that every unity of consciousness implies at least an embryonic self-consciousness. And under the unity of consciousness there is the world; a system, and in its turn a single system, of unities of consciousness. There is nothing non-empirical, except a higher self-consciousness—God—which is the condition of the world as a system, and of it we have nothing to say at present.

There is nothing non-empirical; and yet it is true that self-consciousness and the unity of consciousness are not something given in experience. It seems as if we were affirming and denying at the same time; but it is not so. Only facts of consciousness are given in experience and can be experienced: we may call them contents of consciousness, although to call a feeling a content may give rise to misunderstandings. Now a fact is experienced only in so far as it is included, and can be experienced only in so far as it can be included, in a definite unity of consciousness or self-consciousness. This unity is not what is experienced or can be experienced; it is the act of experiencing.

Unity is a form; every real or possible content of experience is matter. The form, as such, cannot be experienced, for it is not matter. I say, for instance, this is a book. The book, as a concept, is the form of this thing; and certainly I neither see, nor touch, nor in any way experience the book, the concept; I simply experience this thing; but this thing experienced by me is nevertheless a book: matter does not exist without a form.

Vice versa, the form exists only as the form of some matter. The form, therefore, although it cannot be experienced, is not outside experience of which it is the order—an order which absolutely cannot be wanting. A subject, it matters little whether animal or man, apprehends something: a certain matter becomes included in the unity of its consciousness. It is included there along with that form which is inseparable from it; for instance, it is impossible to apprehend two facts, without apprehending them together or successively.

All the difference between the simple subject and the ego lies in this, that in the consciousness of the subject the form asserts itself only as implicit in the matter, whereas the ego thinks the form explicitly. The dog sees, smells, etc., his master in the thing which he sees, smells, etc.; the master can say explicitly, this is my dog.

By asserting that there is nothing non-empirical, we do not therefore exclude, nor do we neglect, the irreducible difference between matter and form, between fact and concept, between the *a posteriori* and the *a priori*, between sense and cognition, between the simple subject and the ego. We only refrain from unjustified hypostases which dissolve the unity of the real and tend to deny the true worth of rationality by exaggerating it.

15.

EXPERIENCE AND COGNITION. FORM

To conclude from the fact that form, as pure form does not admit of being experienced, that form is not knowable, would be worse than a mistake, it would be an extravagance. Certainly, the thought of pure form is no cognition of reality. When we reflect on certain forms, in abstraction from the matter with which they are, and cannot but be, associated, we know very well that we are not considering realities, but simple possibilities. But, most obviously, without abstractions it is impossible to reconstruct the order implicit in the matter of life; it is impossible to know reality.

To know reality, it is necessary not to float in the abstract, but at the same time not to shut oneself up in the concrete. It is necessary to refer the concrete to the abstract, as we do in a judgment. It is necessary to rearrange the concrete consciously according to certain laws or forms, which, no doubt, are laws or forms of the concrete, but which we should not be able to render explicit, to recognise as laws or forms of the concrete, if we had not before separated them from it by means of abstraction.

Form is knowable, just because it cannot be experienced, not in spite of this. To experience means to live through a number of facts. Form is neither a fact, nor a number of facts: it is the order, whereby a complex constitutes a system, it is life. And to know a fact, a complex of facts, is to put it again consciously in the place which belongs to it in the order—is to mark distinctly, to render explicit, the form implied in the matter. The unknowableness of form would imply the impossibility of knowledge.

If this is true of every form, it is true *a priori* of self-consciousness. For, while every other form is something knowable, self-consciousness is the act of knowing. The objection is made that for this very reason it cannot be known: the eye does not see itself. The comparison, so often repeated, shows that this agnosticism (a theory of knowledge, which presupposes the unknowableness of knowledge !) has its only foundation in a meaningless hypostasis.

Knowing, self-consciousness, is not a thing, which knows

other things placed before it. It is a form or supreme further organisation of these other things; with regard to them to be known means to be so organised—to be arranged in a system, the existence of which, as a system or form or organisation, consists in being transparent to itself, in possessing itself, in being at the same time and necessarily a knowing of itself and a knowing: a knowing of itself in so far as it is a knowing, a knowing in so far as it is a knowing of itself.

To conceive cognition in any other way is to give the name of cognition to that which is not, and cannot be, cognition.

### 16.

#### OBJECTIONS EXAMINED

But this is not all. Let us return to some considerations, of which no one will deny the importance, and which, at first, seem to prove that our thesis is mistaken.

I, as I am present in this moment in the clearness of my consciousness, am not the whole of myself. In fact, I continually appeal (so to speak) to my past, to my future, and also to something which in short I still consider as a present essential constituent of myself, but which nevertheless is hidden in a depth, to which my consciousness does not penetrate. I could not affirm or deny anything confidently, nor even formulate a serious doubt, if I had no recollections and no expectations capable of being used as a rule for estimating the present, or for abstaining from such an estimation. And I not only use actual recollections and expectations. I tacitly imply, I assume, in the present and in the future, a reality and a possibility incomparably more extended, more varied, than what can be contained in the actuality of any recollections and expectations. Yet I know, and if I did not know this I could not know anything, that reality and possibility, although they extend so far beyond the range of my consciousness, are subject to certain laws which I can formulate.

Further, I appeal continually to other subjects, which, though I oppose them to myself as distinct, as others, I cannot but consider as like myself. Between the experience of these other subjects, and my own, I recognise certain differences, indeed great differences; yet, in every act of mine, and in every reasoning of mine, it is presupposed, that possible experience is the same for the others as for me—that the subjects, all of them, live in the same world, and that the world in which we all live is regulated by the same laws which are essential to any subject.

Man lives psychically, intellectually or morally, only in relation with his fellow-creatures. Spirituality means intercourse, communion of spirits: such is its essence. The relations which Peter and Paul have with each other, may be accidental; but the possibility that any two subjects will enter accidentally into certain relations, is a relation which conjoins all men and is an essential constituent of each man. Plato wrote even for me; the Dalai Lama and I have never had, and probably shall never have, anything to do with one another, but, if we were to converse, after having overcome the material difficulty of language, we should understand each other.

The reason with which each man is endowed is one in all. And its value extends, not only to all men, but to everything. That to which reason denies existence is outside existence; in fact, existence is strictly nothing but a form of reason—a human thought.

From this it is concluded that in each man it is necessary to distinguish a particular or subjective phenomenal ego, and a universal noumenal ego, which is the same in all.

I exist in a double sense. I am here, now, as a certain empirical unity of consciousness. But I am also, something else; I am that universal ego, or unity of apperception, which creates phenomena and the order of phenomena.

I, as a particular, empirical subject, have before me an external reality, the laws of which are independent of my caprice. But, vice versa, reality is in me in so far as I can know it—its laws are identical with the rationality which is a constituent of myself. Hence, besides being a particular empirical subject, I am also a universal subject, which creates and governs the world ; and, as a universal subject, I am identical with every other man.[1]

### 17.

#### CONTINUATION. RELATIONS BETWEEN SUBJECTS

The doctrine recapitulated above does not seem acceptable to us ; for, although implying some obvious truths, it draws consequences from them, which are not included in the premisses. The question must be presented under a somewhat different aspect.

We commonly represent to ourselves a man, in presence of another man and of external reality, under the form in which we represent to ourselves a body in presence of another body. The pen and the inkstand are, according to common opinion, two wholly separate things, which indeed have accidental relations to each other and to other things, but without any essential relations either with each other or with other things : the rest of the world might even vanish away, without any change having necessarily to take place either in the pen or in the inkstand.

---

[1] ROYCE, *The Spirit of Modern Philosophy*. I have in part transcribed, but in part I have paraphrased freely, without changing the sense of the doctrine.

Such a conception, false even with respect to bodies materially considered,[1] is altogether absurd with regard to man.

The world which I, not without reason, call external to myself, is partially known to me, and the cognition which I have of it can be increased indefinitely. It must be therefore connected with myself in a much more intimate way than appears at first. If it were only accidentally placed before me, like the pen before the inkstand, I should know nothing of it, I should not be able to know anything of it. Its appearing to me as placed before me, is really nothing but its being an object of my cognition.

The world which I know, is not, and cannot be, anything but precisely the object of my cognition; it is therefore essential to the world to have that relation with myself, in virtue of which it is knowable by me. On the other hand, the same relation is equally essential to myself, who am the knowing subject, who would not exist if I were not such.

I have spoken of myself as a knowing subject; what I have said about myself, is therefore true of every knowing subject, supposing that there is more than one.

There is more than one. The process by which I arrive at a knowledge of the world consists in a series of external manifestations of that conscious activity, which is myself—manifestations which imply similar resistances, that is to say, other conscious activities. This is not all. The same process consists in part (not wholly, but the other parts of the process imply this part) of the revelation to me of some portion of the contents of the minds, different from mine, which constitute the activities opposed to me. To know myself, to know the world, to know that the

---

[1] Each body gravitates towards every other, and has therefore a relation to every other, which is constitutive for each.

world presupposes a multitude of subjects, separate from me although similar to me, are different expressions for one and the same process.

The world, we have said, presupposes a multitude of subjects. But, if we do not wish to assert more than we know, if we do not wish to hypostatise materiality, in which we have to recognise a subjective phenomenon,[1] we ought rather to say that the world is resolvable into a multitude of subjects, more or less developed, perhaps more or less capable of development, but none of which falls short of that character which constitutes a subject as such, *i.e.* the character of being essentially related to all others.

Hence, each subject presupposes all the others; it exists in so far as it presupposes all the others. We may even say that each subject exists in so far as it acts, in so far as it evolves itself; but its evolution, by overcoming the resistances caused by the evolving of the other subjects, is precisely a presupposing of the other subjects. And its evolution, or presupposing of the other subjects, *alias* its existence—an existence, which is a being-related to the others—is fundamentally a knowing. It is a knowing at once of itself and the others—a knowing which has not always the clearness and distinctness characterising the developed subject, but yet remains a knowing: to deny that subconsciousness is cognition means to make all cognition impossible.

As every subject is essentially implied by every other, the totality of the subjects constitutes a system of which each subject is the unity.

Will it be possible to go beyond this conclusion, which makes us conceive truly of "spirituality" as a "communion of spirits" (that is to say, as the unity of many)? We have only touched on the question; we have still to

[1] Compare below the chapter on *Reality*.

penetrate into it. But if we are really to penetrate into it, we shall have to take it up in the form to which we have been able to reduce it. The rest of the present work will aim, almost exclusively, at justifying that form with some developments.

18.

DOES A REALITY BEYOND PHENOMENA EXIST?
WHAT IT CAN BE?

That there are many subjects, each of which is conscious on its own account separately, since the consciousness of one subject, under any of its forms, cannot be *eo ipso* the consciousness of another, is too obvious. That the many subjects constitute a system, and that each subject is the unity of the system, is equally obvious.

A system: that is no doubt to say a unity, but a unity which implies a multiplicity, a unity of multiplicity; —a multiplicity; but a multiplicity of elements, none of which is outside the system, each of which implies the others, and therefore constitutes the unity of the system: —this is what absolutely cannot be denied; this is, in substance, what we all understand by the name of reality, if we try to explain what we think to ourselves. To suppress the many is as reasonable as not to recognise the unity. In both cases the system, that is to say reality, vanishes away.

All that remains to be known, all that we shall come to know, but perhaps not so very soon (I, in particular, have no great confidence in my powers, and should be satisfied, if I were able to co-operate in some small degree towards the solution of the problem), is only this, whether the system, as we have briefly delineated it, is self-sufficing or not.

Let us admit, that the system is not self-sufficing. What

would this mean ? It would mean that the unity of the system, the mutual implication between its many elements, or between its many particular unities of consciousness, requires a higher unity of consciousness in which all that is implicit in any particular unity, *i.e.* all that is real, is contained explicitly.

Note, that the higher unity, granting it to be unavoidable, must be a unity of explicit consciousness, or completely self-conscious unity; in fact, if it were simply an implicit (subconscious) unity, it would coincide with the unity of the system, as already recognised; it would not be the condition of that unity.

The higher unity can be nothing but God.

According to the theistic hypothesis, each subject and the system of subjects, or universe, exists in so far as God knows or determines their existence. But it does not follow, that the particular subject can be resolved into an appearance. The particular subject appears to God. We mean that the whole content of the consciousness and subconsciousness of the subject is in the perfectly clear consciousness of God, and that if it were not so, the subject would not exist. Still the consciousness of God includes not only the appearance of the subject to Him, but also its appearance to itself. The particular subject only exists in so far as it is thought by God; but God, in thinking the subject, thinks a particular being which in its turn thinks itself and other particular beings.

### 19.

#### PHENOMENAL REALITY. PHENOMENA AND SELF-COGNITION

He who suppresses the particular thinking beings, also suppresses divine thought; professing to resolve all thinking beings into one alone, he suppresses every thinking being, every thought. It is impossible without a paralogism to deny what we all commonly call reality without denying all reality and all appearance. And this, for a very simple reason.

All our possible constructions presuppose a concept which is absolutely inconstructible—the common concept of reality, or of Being. If this concept has not the value commonly ascribed to it, if the *true* concept of Being is not the *common* concept of Being, all our constructions, including that which would lead us (as it is said) to the *true* concept, which is also necessarily founded on the *common* concept, resolve themselves into dreams—dreams which, if the doctrine were true, could not have been dreamt, for there would be no dreamer.

The considerations recapitulated above (§ 16) have, as we have said, an indubitable value—but a value, into which it is necessary to inquire deeply; not even here, indeed here much less than in other places it is allowable to judge by appearances. Those considerations are just; but what has seemed the only possible interpretation of them to others, is so only in relation to a certain historical development which has to be transcended, which ends in the transcending of itself.

We are not beginning anew what others have done, under the pretext of doing it better; we are interpreting their finished work, and interpreting it by means supplied by that work itself.

The thought of the particular subject (there is no known thought which is not the thought of some particular subject) is not confined within the particularity of the subject. Even the subject, particular as it is, is not confined to its particularity. And there is no contradiction at all between its not being so confined and its being particular. Each subject is a particular subject, in so far as it is a particular unity of the multiplicity of subjects; the unity is particular, although it is the unity of the whole multiplicity; for each element of the multiplicity is in turn the unity of the others.

From present clear consciousness we are necessarily led to past, and also to future—to recollections and to expectations; we are led to recognise a sphere of subconsciousness inexhaustible in its depth. Consciousness (together with subconsciousness, from which it cannot be separated) is a form, a law—form and law, at the same time, of strictly subjective particularity (of myself, in so far as I am different from every other person) and of the whole—form and law which would not be form and law of myself, if they were not *eo ipso* form and law of the whole, and vice versa. I only exist in relation to the whole; and the whole only exists in relation to me.

All this becomes obvious to any one who has attained a clear notion on the matter. To construct metaphysics means simply to become well acquainted with what has been said, and to develop, it may be, that which is implied in what has been said. In substance, metaphysics is constructed by penetrating into the cognition which we have of ourselves;[1] it has self-consciousness as its presupposition, though not a self-consciousness incapable of development, which indeed would not be self-consciousness at all.

Know thyself: this is the starting-point, and must be the goal.

[1] ROYCE, *op. cit.*, P. I.

# CHAPTER II

# THE SUBJECT

## 1.

### FORMATION OF THE SUBJECT; THE PRIMITIVE PARTICULAR UNITY

MAN is something very complicated; he is, even psychically, an organism. He is a being, not a collection of beings; but his unity is not the empty and abstract unity of a mathematical point, it is rather the unity of conscious life—a full and concrete unity, implying a multiplicity which characterises it and of which it is the unity.

Obviously, that constituent of ourselves which is the psychical organism, did not exist always. None of us was aware of the moment in which his own psychical organism had its beginning. What others tell us of our infancy, and that which we ourselves remember, in a vague and fragmentary way, of our infancy, or which we infer from our observations on the infancy of others, exclude an absolute and sudden beginning. But everyone may confidently assign a time in which his own psychical organism did not yet exist.

The psychical organism, the present ego with its extreme complexity, with the multiplicity which it includes, is not something original: it is a formation. Rather, it is always in course of being formed; therefore it changes unceasingly. Besides being the result of a process, it consists in a process. We are continually organising and reorganising ourselves : he who does not organise himself, disorganises himself.

How is the formative process possible ?

A sucking babe knows at first neither itself, nor physical reality, nor other subjects : it knows absolutely nothing. And nevertheless it has (it is usually said) confused sensations, perhaps even vivid but obscure feelings, blind tendencies. We may say more exactly : the babe is the unity of those sensations, of those feelings, of those tendencies, in general of those facts, which, just because they are associated in the same unity, are its own facts. It is a unity of consciousness. The unity of consciousness is implied by every process by which we imagine it to be constructed ; therefore it is primitive and original : it has always existed. The origin of man, and of every individual subject, is to be sought for in the development of the primitive unity of consciousness. It would not be possible for us to expound in detail the process of development, and it does not matter. It is enough, if we show the possibility, or rather (given certain conditions) the necessity of development, and if, from the concepts of unity of consciousness and of development, we draw those few but certain deductions which are absolutely required for obtaining a general conception of the universe.

### 2.

#### DEVELOPMENT OF THE UNITY. THE SUBJECT AND THE WORLD

The subject is certainly, therefore, a primitive unity of consciousness—a centre, into which all the facts without exception which constitute its experience, flow together and interfere. The subject, in this sense, is a form, or rather the essential or fundamental form of experience.

No doubt, if the whole experience were to vanish away, even the unity of it would disappear. Experience, and consequently also the matter of experience, is therefore essential to the subject: it is a constituent of it. We may say that the ego is one and the same with experience, or with its own world. In fact, if that of which I am aware changes, I change. (We do not consider ourselves as changed by every minimal fact of the external world: this depends on certain further distinctions.)

But, while I am not separable from the universe, the universe also (as known to me) is not separable from me: we are co-essential to each other. If I were to vanish, my experience also would vanish. Although it is true that in a certain sense I am one with the universe, even materially considered, it is more exact to conceive the relation between the universe and myself, as that between matter and form (primitive, essential or fundamental, form).

I am the centre of my world, and consequently I imply the world. On the other hand, my world implies me, as the centre of it.

To recognise in oneself, by reflection, with explicit clearness, the character above indicated, of being the unity or centre of one's own experience, or of one's own world, a process is required which never goes on rapidly, and which many people never bring to completeness.[1] But it is only a defect of reflection. A man, however obtuse he may be, cannot believe that he does not see while he is seeing. The ego of which we are now speaking is never wanting. Not only does it exist, but it knows of its existence; for its existence is to have that unitary experience which it has —to know of its existence. This is true, although, reflect-

---

[1] Some persons probably have not understood my explanations, and would not understand any kind of explanations.

ing on this knowledge, he misunderstands, and gets lost in perplexities which appear to him inextricable.

The developed ego is much more complicated than the primitive unity of consciousness of which it is the development. But the unity, which is the essential, fundamental constituent of the developed ego, is, as unity, nothing but the same primitive unity. The developed ego is the development of this unity—it is the primitive unity with a content more vivid, more varied, and therefore distinct and organised in itself.

### 3.

#### CHARACTERS OF THE PRIMITIVE UNITY

The primitive unity (the undeveloped subject) is not a distinct element in the field of that experience which is unified in it; nor is it even a distinguishable element. It is not a part of experience which may become an object of cognition. But it is that which knows: the unity without which there would be no distinguishing, by which cognition is made possible, by which cognition is constituted. From this it does not follow that the primitive unity does not know itself: its knowing itself consists in knowing. Nor can it consist in anything else, for the primitive unity is simply the unity, that is to say, the cognition of the elements which are unified in it.

But it is necessary not to be ambiguous. Primitive consciousness cannot rise above our subconsciousness—that relatively obscure region of consciousness, in which the "small perceptions" so well brought to view by Leibniz, and the possible but not actual recollections, and even something else are contained together. Indeed primitive subconsciousness has to be considered as inferior to our own; for the latter is a complicated organism, while the former is relatively inorganic—a uniform aggregate, in which there are no distinctions. However this may be, the little which has been said (and to which very little could be added) is sufficient to make us understand that the primitive unity—

(1) differs from the developed ego; we cannot ascribe to it those forms of cognition, which we consider as specially important: concepts, judgments, explicit reasonings;

(2) is not, nevertheless, something heterogeneous to the developed ego, and to the cognition (properly so-called) which is the most intimate and most vigorous life of the developed ego, so that the possibility of deriving the latter from the former is out of question.

To primitive consciousness we must evidently ascribe those characters which must be recognised in our own as primitive, that is which it cannot have derived from any process, and which are rather the condition of every process. And we must ascribe to it no other characters: that which is referable to a process, has to be referred to the process—cannot be considered as primitive. The primitive characters of our consciousness, and consequently the characters of primitive consciousness, are three: the cognitive, the emotional, the active.

The unity of primitive consciousness is, therefore, in an involved form which we should try in vain to represent to ourselves with clearness, cognition, feeling and activity, essentially connected and inseparable from each other.

### 4.

CONTINUATION. CONSCIOUSNESS AND SUBCONSCIOUSNESS

It is important that we should understand each other; therefore it will not be useless to repeat the same things with some difference of words.

In the particular subject we have recognised two

## The Subject

unities: a fundamental one, original or primitive, and a secondary one, the result of a formation (that which more properly is called the subject).

Each of us speaks of himself and of others, knowing, at least to a certain degree, what he is saying: he distinguishes himself from another subject, and two other subjects from each other. Such distinctions are distinctions between secondary unities. The primitive unity remains outside common reflection; only philosophical reflection arrives at it, drawing it as a necessary conclusion from the secondary unity, as its condition.

The secondary unity is not something which is added from the outside to the primitive one, but it is simply a development of the latter.

All my cognitions, all my facts, which have any value with regard to knowledge (my apprehending, under whatever form), imply the primitive unity, but they imply also that development of the primitive unity which is I, in the sense which this pronoun commonly has. Primitive unity is not that being aware which is our common awareness, for it falls short of that internal complexity to which our awareness is subordinate, in which our awareness consists.

But it does not follow, that primitive unity is not awareness. Consciousness, awareness, has many degrees; there is the consciousness of the man awake and in full possession of himself, that of the man about to fall asleep, that of the feverish man, that of the child, etc. Subconsciousness means consciousness with a minimum of organisation.

The development of a primitive unity into a secondary unity, of subconsciousness into consciousness, is a process of organisation.

And the process of organisation, which implies a minimum of primitive organisation, is at once a breaking up and a connecting again of that which is in process of organisation.

The chicken has tissues, members, viscera, nerves, which were not in the egg. It is intrinsically more varied, less uniform in itself, less one, than the egg. But just for this reason, it is in another sense more one. Without the diversity of parts, there would not be the new higher unity of the whole; although it is true that the new whole would not be one, if the different parts were not the product of the differentiation of a pre-existing whole pre-existing as one.

The life of the egg is certainly life, although it is not the life of the chicken. And so, the primitive unity is not unconscious, although it is not conscious in the way which is proper to the secondary unity: we call it subconscious. It falls short, not of all organisation (the primitive unity is unity), but of complexity of organisation.

The appearing to a subject of an object, of several objects, the distinction of one object from another, of the distinguishing subject from every object which is distinguished by it, the reflection of the subject on itself, etc., are extremely complicated psychical processes; as those of which the life of the chicken is the result, are extremely complicated physiological processes. The secondary unity is the higher unity of a complex whole, and is conditioned by a primitive whole which has broken up and at the same time become united again in itself.

### 5.

#### ORIGINAL MULTIPLICITY OF PRIMITIVE UNITIES

There are evidently several secondary unities. The question is, whether each of them is the development of a particular primitive unity, or whether all of them are the result of the development of only one and the same primitive unity. The problem is of the greatest importance. The solution which we accept has already been previously indicated: the primitive unities are as many, irreducible to each other, as the real or possible secondary unities. To show the correctness of the solution accepted by us is one of the principal objects, if not the principal object, of the present book.[1]

As we have already said, the primitive unity, although it falls short of that organisation which is a development of it, and which gives rise to the secondary unity, cannot be wholly inorganic. In this case it would be no unity, but a heap. And a heap of facts of consciousness, or of subconsciousness, is an absurdity. A pure heap can only be formed of things independent of each other, for instance, of stones; now, the hypothesis that facts of consciousness (or subconsciousness) are independent of each other, has no sense: it would be the same as to suppose that I can throw away, transfer to somebody else, or put into my pocket, a headache of mine.

Subconsciousness must be understood as a more simple kind of consciousness, not by any means as something opposed to consciousness. Therefore the primitive unity, however simple it may be, is in any case something organic. It is comparatively homogeneous, but one. We may compare it, very roughly, with a sphere; the sphere would not be such, if it had no centre. The elements of which the primitive unity is the result, are, as constituents of that unity, grouped in such a way as to have a centre common to all, essential to all. Or, in other words, those determinations of subconsciousness which we call the fact A, the fact B, etc., are determinations of one and the

[1] Here, the proof can be only prepared; to become satisfied that our solution is the true and only one, indeed to understand the problem and the solution well, it is necessary to read the whole book, and study it with diligence.

same subconsciousness : the sameness of subconsciousness is the primitive unity.

The primitive unity develops itself. Well, it is easy to understand how a unity, being developed, will become, at the same time and in consequence of the same process, more varied and more one : the comparison of which we have made use above, and which is more than a mere comparison, with the egg and the chicken, removes all doubt on the subject. The same process, while it increases the internal complication by making the unity intrinsically more varied, establishes also at the same time a more intimate connection between the constitutive elements—makes more intense the character of unity in the unity.

## 6.

### FURTHER REMARKS ON THE DEVELOPMENT OF PRIMITIVE UNITIES

But the process, by which a primitive unity is developed and becomes more complicated, cannot give rise to the formation of two separate secondary unities, such as are two subjects (taking the word subject in its common meaning).

Let us consider a man asleep who is gradually waking.

A man asleep is a subconscious unity.[1] The process of his awakening consists in his subconsciousness becoming more complicated—in a complication which is at the same time, as complication, a more firm and close rejoining together (and is therefore like the process, by which the primitive unity changes into a secondary unity).

Now, a man, when he has awakened, is still *one*, as when he was asleep ; or rather, the awakening is a becoming one in a higher degree.

---

[1] He is not a primitive unity, but this matters little ; our reasoning is necessarily analogical, but not less instructive for that reason.

Scissiparous reproduction proves nothing against us.

An organism which reproduces itself by fission, may be a subject or not; let us admit it to be one. A body A, which is the body of a subject, breaks up into the bodies B and C, which are the bodies of two subjects, separate like the bodies. What must we conclude ? That the body A did include not only one primitive unity, but two if not more.

The *absolute* beginning of that unity which is the subject, is possible as much by means of fission as in any other way. It is impossible in any way, as absolute beginning. The expression—a subject begins, means— a process begins, by which a primitive unity evolves into a secondary unity. It cannot mean, it cannot pretend to mean, anything else. The particulars of the process have, with regard to the present matter, no importance at all. Scissiparous reproduction is neither easier nor more difficult to understand than any other form of reproduction.

The beginning and continuation of the process be which the subject is formed, is absolutely conditioned by a unity which exists before the process, and which persists as long as the process lasts. The unity constituting the subject formed, is nothing else but the unity conditioning the formative process—is still the same unity, together with the complication added by the process.

Hence, a primitive unity in course of evolution, evolves into a necessarily single subject; and the existence of several subjects implies the existence of as many primitive unities.

Let us suppose that the development of a single primitive unity gave rise to two subjects. Then, either one of the two subjects was absolutely created, or else the primitive unity, breaking up into the two subjects, has ceased to exist. Neither one thing nor the other is possible. The unity can neither absolutely begin, nor absolutely end. It may develop, and may even (we say) envelop itself again—proceed from subconsciousness towards consciousness (as when we awake), and relapse from consciousness into subconsciousness (as when we go to sleep). It can have no other history; and this for a very simple reason : the history of the unity presupposes the unity of which it is the history.

### 7.

#### THE DUALITIES PETER-PAUL AND SUBJECT-OBJECT

We have to distinguish two different dualities : the duality subject-object and the duality Peter-Paul.

The duality subject-object[1] is still a unity. Or rather, it is a higher unity, more organic, more truly one, as being clearly aware, conscious of its being conscious. I distinguish myself from my inkstand. The inkstand, nevertheless, is seen and touched by me ; in so far as it is apprehended by me, it is not outside that unity which is I; its being outside me, in the sense in which I can and do say that it is outside, is its way of being included in the said unity.

This unity, in the form under which it presently exists, in its reality and its awareness, has not existed always ; it has formed itself. Its self-formation can be nothing else but the development of a primitive unity, which has organised itself, has become what it is now, by an internal process of distinction and reunion. All that which I apprehend in any way is something which I apprehend : and this proves, to any one who is merely capable of reflecting, that the primitive unity exists always in the

[1] There is no need to remark that each of the two terms of this duality implies a multiplicity.

actual one—that the actual coincides with the primitive, plus the organisation.

The duality Peter-Paul is, obviously, different from the duality subject-object. When Peter falls asleep, that is to say vanishes, although temporarily, as a developed subject present to itself with clearness, everything which was for him an object, vanishes at the same time ; whereas (as every one knows) the falling asleep of Peter does not imply at all the falling asleep of Paul.

It may be said that the falling asleep of Peter does not imply the vanishing of those things which were objects for him, and does imply the vanishing of Paul also as Peter's object. We agree to this. But this remark, which is doubtless just, does not eliminate the difference above indicated. Paul is another subject : his existence is not identical with his being Peter's object ; as such, he persists even when Peter falls asleep. With the falling asleep of Peter, the two subjects Peter and Paul remain two subjects, one of which has become subconscious ; whereas the duality subject-object implicit in Peter vanishes in so far as Peter's object as such vanishes together with Peter (with Peter's waking consciousness) ; for it matters nothing whether it preserves, as Paul does, any other kind of existence.

The difference between two subjects cannot be absolutely resolved into the difference between subject and object as the two essential constituents of one and the same unity of developed consciousness. That the (developed) subject and the correlative object inseparable from it are formations implying one and the same primitive unity is, in fact, necessarily inferred from the inseparableness of the (developed) subject and the correlative object—from the fact that the unity of both can still be noticed in the developed form of consciousness.

On the contrary, that a developed subject is a constituent of another developed subject,[1] is evidently not true. The two consciousnesses are distinct, are two, not as constitutive parts of one and the same consciousness, but as consciousnesses. Therefore, the same reasons, for which the duality subject-object must be resolved into a primitive unity, require that the duality Peter-Paul should be recognised as primitive.

And it is useless to add that the undeniable distinction between the developed consciousnesses of Peter and Paul, considering the one and the other both in their subjective and objective elements, is true also of the respective subconsciousnesses. My possible recollection is as much my own, and as exclusively my own, as my actual suffering. The developed subject is the development of a primitive subconscious unity. If the primitive unity was common to both, an identity which nothing authorises us to admit, or rather which we are of necessity obliged to exclude, ought to exist between the subconsciousnesses.

### 8.

#### RELATIONS BETWEEN SUBJECTS

Certainly subjects are not absolutely separated from each other. One subject is not another; but this distinction, this otherness, does not exclude, or rather implies, mutual relations, essential to each. Peter knows of the existence of Paul, and has to do with Paul in a thousand ways. It is quite manifest that the process by which a subject, gradually and slowly, has developed itself from primordial subconsciousness up to clear and distinct consciousness, could not have been brought about, nor have had a beginning, without mutual actions, without

---

[1] Note, that we are speaking of developed subjects, in so far as they are developed.

relations, between the primordial subconscious unity and other subjects already developed. A subject presupposes certain parents and some kind of education.

The process to which Peter owes his being may be said to be complete, in the sense that Peter is now a developed subject, but not in the sense that the process has ceased to evolve. It is impossible for Peter to make abstraction from the other subjects, to detach himself entirely from them; if he were to do this, he would at once cease to exist. A subject can never be resolved into a mere aggregate of sensations and physiological feelings. Even these facts require as essential to them certain relations with something else, *i.e.* at least indirectly, with other subjects; but it is useless to insist on the matter. A subject is never without affections (even hatred is an affection), without preoccupations, without thoughts; and the affection, the preoccupation, the thought, imply another subject.

I am not, explicitly, consciously, related to every other subject. But there is no subject, with which it would be for me intrinsically impossible (here we are not speaking of physical possibility) to acquire an explicit and conscious relation. Now, as we have remarked in another place, the possibility of entering into (explicit, conscious) relations is already a kind of (implicit, subconscious) relation. No doubt, all existent and possible subjects form a system—a system without which there would be no subject, that is to say a system which is an essential constituent of each subject.

Even the conflict, sometimes of an extreme violence, which breaks out between one subject and another, and by reason of which the one wishes and indeed tries to obtain the elimination of the other from its own field, the destruction of the other, are, for any one who reflects, an indubitable evidence of the system—of the fact that the whole sum of subjects is an essential constituent of each. A conflict between disconnected forces is not possible, just as there can be no conflict when there are not several forces.

But the system, the mutual co-essentiality of the subjects, becomes especially manifest in rational necessity. A reasoning, if it is necessarily conclusive for me, is necessarily conclusive for everybody. "You speak well in your own way; but I speak differently." Phrases of this kind, far from implying the denial, imply on the contrary the acknowledgment of a common rationality, absolutely, numerically one. You speak well in your own way, means, you speak well in my way too; I speak differently, means, I do not accept your premises.[1]

### 9.

#### HIGHER UNITY OF SUBJECTS; POLYCENTRIC SYSTEM

The subjects form a system, essential to each. In other words, besides those many particular unities which are the subjects, there is a higher universal unity which contains, includes them all,—and which is contained, included in each, as its constituent. It would seem therefore (in opposition to what we have concluded,) that the subjects are, all of them, particular formations within one and the same primitive unity—within the universal unity. This would unfold, without being dissolved, into

[1] Failure to understand one another is, at bottom, equivocation, as if, for instance, the "fummo" (instead of *fumo*, smoke) in Dante's *Inferno VII*, 123, were considered as a verb. And we equivocate, because the variety of words in a language is much smaller than the variety of thoughts. That community of actual thought, which is established by the community of language, does not exclude diversity. But diversity is in any case diversity in actual thought; it does not concern the possibility of thought. For Peter it may be very difficult to think what Paul thinks; the difficulty may be such as to be called practically an impossibility; for instance, it would be impossible for me to learn Chinese. But pure theory need not take account at all of a mere practical impossibility.

the multitude of particular secondary unities; its unfolding, still without being dissolved, or rather by being reconnected and intensified (by rising up to consciousness from subconsciousness), ought to be understood, more or less, in the same way in which we have interpreted the development of each of our many primitive unities.

Let us discuss the question.

We too recognise the higher universal unity. For we have recognised it as essential to each particular primitive unity to be related to all the others, to imply all the others. Each of our unities is therefore the unity of the system; it is not only included in, but includes, the universal unity. The system is one, as much for us as for our opponents. But it is, for our opponents, essentially monocentric, while for us it is essentially polycentric, and its unity consists precisely in its polycentricity.[1]

The polycentric doctrine offers an indisputable advantage over the monocentric.[2]

The superiority of the polycentric doctrine is shown, first of all, from what we have already seen (§§ 4–8). One single unity, in course of development, accounts fully for the duality subject-object, since the consciousness of that duality is still one consciousness. But it does not account for the duality Peter-Paul, for, although Peter and Paul are inseparable (and the polycentric doctrine

[1] The system is one, in so far as every centre is a centre, and implies the others; evidently, it is not possible to imply that which does not exist.

[2] Note, that we do not mean to exclude absolutely the existence of one single higher centre. Indeed, we think that its existence must be inferred from certain considerations different from those made till now, and which we will make later on. But, to assume above the many particular centres one single universal centre, and to resolve the multiplicity of particular centres into the unity of a higher centre, to consider each of the former as a development of the latter, are two different things. Whether there is or not a higher centre, in the sense in which we assume it (a question which at present must be left aside), we maintain that the universe has many particular centres (each centre is particular, although it is the centre of the whole universe, for the centres are many); that the particular centres are primitive, are not the result of any process, and that each subject, such for instance as a man, is the result of a definite particular centre.

accounts perfectly for their inseparableness), it remains true that Peter's consciousness is different from that of Paul. Peter and Paul may see the same things; but the seeing of Peter is not the seeing of Paul. They both think according to the same laws; but the thinking of the one is not the thinking of the other.

## 10.

### CONTINUATION

Further, a development implies, on the part of the developing being, a doing which, in its turn, implies certain resistances, *i.e.* implies a doing on the part of some other being.[1] Given certain actions and reactions (the reactions are essential to the actions), given a multiplicity of facts which are connected according to laws not exclusively logical, it becomes necessary to assume a multiplicity of beings which act on each other and resist each other. The varying of experience [*l' accadere*] which would be no varying if it were not temporal, implies of necessity something not exclusively logical,—cannot be resolved into a logical process, for the logical process is essentially outside time; therefore, the varying of experience implies of necessity a multiplicity of beings.

We mean a connected multiplicity, as we have already remarked more than once; therefore a multiplicity which is recomposed into a higher unity. But this higher unity must be the unity of a system, not mere and simple unity, for mere and simple unity, as such, accounts for logical necessity, not for temporal succession.

Each developed subject is a unity of consciousness—unity of facts of consciousness, that is to say, of a varying. Let us suppose that in the beginning one only subject

[1] On the general way in which the primitive unity develops itself, compare below.

existed, as a unity in the sense in which each developed subject is a unity, and that the many developed subjects were the result of the development of that single original conscious or unconscious subject. It is easy to perceive that such an hypothesis is absurd. For that single original unity could never give rise to any variation. In consequence, the said original unity could neither determine in itself a multitude of developed subjects, nor even develop itself into what is commonly called a subject (not even into a single developed subject); for both forms of development imply a varying which would be impossible.

The development, any kind of development, of a primitive unity requires that besides the evolving primitive unity, there should be something else. It is indeed true that this other thing must be connected with the unity, for, otherwise, its existence, with regard to the development of the unity, would be quite the same as its non-existence. And to understand how a thing may be at the same time different from the unity and nevertheless connected with the unity, seems difficult or even impossible.

But the difficulty vanishes, if we assume the existence of a number of primitive unities, as distinct from each other, though subconscious, as the consciousness of a developed subject is distinct, different, from the consciousness of another developed subject, and implying one another precisely in the same way in which a developed subject evidently implies other developed subjects.

A man is different from another man, and nevertheless implies the other man. Not one of us would be what he is, if he had not been generated and in some way educated by other people, if he had not the power (I do not say, the physical possibility) of entering into relations with anyone else. In this sense each man implies the others; the implication, as appears manifest, not only does not exclude, but requires otherness. Each man is a unity of facts which would not happen if there were no other men, no other distinct unities, different as unities from his own, and nevertheless not segregate, not independent, but connected into a system essential to each.

To understand life and consciousness in general, we have only to generalise these simple results of observation on the life and the consciousness of man. And it appears manifest from what we have above observed, that life and consciousness absolutely cannot be understood in any other way. There are primitive (absolutely primitive) unities of consciousness or, more exactly, of subconsciousness; there are many of them, not independent of each other, for on the contrary each of them exists only in so far as the system of all exists, but, as unities, mutually co-ordinated and capable of developing through their reciprocal actions and reactions.

We do not pretend, nor will anyone pretend, that our doctrine should be from this moment entirely clear and complete in every part. Can reality be resolved into the system of primitive unities, or is such a system integrated by something else, and by what else? This and other such questions we shall answer by degrees, as the opportunity will present itself. We think that we have said even more than was necessary to justify us in going further.

## 11.

### ACTIVITY AND COGNITION

Cognition implies an object, that is to say something which is not outside cognition, which indeed is an essential integrating element of cognition, but which at the same time is opposed to it—which opposes it in the act of becoming associated with it, and becomes associated with it in the act of opposing it.

## The Subject

Activity exists, as activity, only in so far as it manifests itself in actions. And each action implies a resistance which is opposed to it. Obviously, the resistance is not outside the action, it is an essential integrating element of the action, but is at the same time something which opposes the action—which opposes it in becoming associated with it, and becomes associated with it in opposing it.

Activity and cognition both imply in the same way a relation between the primitive unity and something else. This something else has a relation with the primitive unity which is an essential constituent of that unity, for without an object, without a resistance, the unity would be neither cognitive nor active unity, that is to say, would not exist. The other is, at once, essential to the primitive unity and other than the primitive unity.

Feeling is associated with action, and is a constituent of action, as action is a constituent of feeling. The character of feeling is determined by the relation between action and the resistance which opposes it. According as the relation established is favourable or unfavourable to a further development of the activity according to certain special laws, the feeling is agreeable or painful. But, although feeling fulfils an important function in the organisation of the primitive unity, it has as such no relation (although it has one indirectly, in so far as it is inseparable from activity, and also from cognition) with anything else.

Activity and cognition are on the contrary related to something else : to what ?

They will be both related to the same things, for both in the end can be resolved into the same thing. Activity is conscious activity : its acts are acts of cognition. And consciousness is activity : to know means to do. (We, developed subjects, distinguish the doing from the knowing without being able to separate them; but we distinguish them by means of secondary formations, which are wanting in the primitive unity.)

The resistance which opposes activity, becomes known at the same time with it: it also is an object. And the object is a resistance: we see what we can, not what we wish to see.

We have not said, (it is to be noticed,) that the "other" to which the primitive unity is essentially related, exists only as resistance-object; we have said simply this, that what is opposed as resistance, is opposed at once as object, and vice versa. What the "other" may be, we shall establish more exactly in the sequel. Meanwhile, for us the "other" is often another subject; it is easy to infer from this, that the primitive unity is essentially related to other primitive unities, but whether to other primitive unities only, remains to be known.

### 12.

ACTIVITY AND RESISTANCE. ORGANISATION OF ACTIVITY AND OF CONSCIOUSNESS

To have identical feelings is almost the same as to have none.[1] For, between identical feelings no distinction can

---

[1] This acute and obviously true reflection comes from Hobbes; the meaning of the "almost," which we have introduced into it, will be explained by what follows. To have identical feelings is to have feelings—it is a form of psychical life, which cannot be identified with the absence of life. But it is a subconscious life. If Peter were to lose for ever his clear and distinct consciousness, if all his psychical states were to become subconscious, would he be alive no more? Would he no more exist? For the sense in which the being of a subject and its life are commonly understood, certainly not. But, if we wish to express ourselves with exactness, we ought to say that he would still exist, that he would still be alive, with a subconscious life. That subconscious life is not the same thing as the absence of life, we have a thousand proofs, on which it is no use to insist. Conscious life (the life of clear and distinct consciousness) can be only understood, absolutely, as the luminous flame, inseparable from the oil dark in itself which nourishes it. Consciousness implies subconsciousness, of which it is a formation.

be made ; and, no distinction being made between the feelings, even the other facts, which become distinguished through the feelings with which they are associated, remain undistinguished. And consciousness degenerates into subconsciousness.

To meet resistances may not be, on the part of the primitive unity, the same thing as to have feelings like our own ; in any case, it is to have those feelings of which the primitive unity is capable. Therefore, a primitive unity, the relations of which with the " other " are uniform, or almost uniform, since it does not distinguish between the resistances which it meets, will not even be able to distinguish between the resistance which is opposed to its own act, and its own act ; nor will it distinguish, in this act, what we call action, from what we call cognition, nor from what we call feeling.

Under the said conditions, the primitive unity distinguishes nothing of the external world, nothing in itself —cannot distinguish (as we do, with clearness) itself from the external world. Its life is an entirely subconscious life, a kind of very deep sleep. Of course, such a life, however inferior to ours it may be, is life all the same, infinitely remote from death : subconsciousness is no absolute unconsciousness.

But let us suppose that a primitive unity be closely bound to a particular system, well connected in itself, of " other " elements,—to a system the structure of which makes possible and requires a vigorous and various exchange of actions between that unity and the other elements of the system. We shall have, in the unity, a multiplicity of different feelings, which will make a psychical development possible. Distinctions will take place ; and the life of the unity, which before flowed uniformly, will break up and become internally complicated ; in other words, it will become organised.

I distinguish myself from the external world, that is to say from a system of resistance-objects; and, both in myself and in the external world, I subdistinguish many elements. Therefore I am no longer merely (although I am still in great part) subconscious: consciousness in its true and proper sense has superposed itself on subconsciousness. The primitive unity which persists, (if it did not persist, there would be nothing,) includes everything, or rather is everything, is the whole life in its variety; but in its variety there is a distinct and dominant, a central nucleus—I, in the most usual and proper sense of the word. Confronting the ego there is the external world, and, mediating between them, my own body.

To this last we have manifestly to ascribe a remarkable part in the said organisation. My body is precisely the system of which we have spoken, which makes it possible for a unity occupying a dynamically central situation in it to obtain a sufficiently varied and rich content.

### 13.

#### REFLECTION. OBJECTIVE COGNITION OF SELF

The primitive ego, that is to say the primitive unity, is no particular distinct, or distinguishable, element in the field of experience; it is the unity of experience—not an object of cognition, but the knowing being, or we may say, the act of knowing. On the other hand, the ego more properly so called, which is a formation, is a particular distinct element; and it can be known, more or less deeply, as well as any other distinct element—with this difference, that the cognitive activity forms a part of itself.

This gives rise to the antinomy so often noticed: I, who am the subject, ought not to be able to know myself as object; nevertheless, I know myself, in great part, precisely as object. And this cognition which I have of myself, is always incomplete, and evidently cannot but be incomplete; while a knowing being which does not know itself, is nonsense.

Everything becomes simple, if we distinguish the primitive ego, the self-knowledge of which consists in the act of knowing, and the secondary ego, which is no longer the pure knowing being, but a compound resulting from the knowing being and something knowable; which last, like any other knowable thing, can be actually known only by means of a process which is never exhausted.

The former is never known as object, but is always completely, integrally known, that is to say, known in the indivisible unity of its being, as knowing; for its existence consists precisely in the unity of knowledge, or self-knowledge. It is known, that is to say, it knows itself, in so far as it is always present in every act of cognition, and in every system of cognitive acts, or in so far as it is the condition of knowledge—that which gives the character, the value, of cognition to an act, to a system of acts.

Every element of the complex ego, of the ego more properly so called, being a determination, a realisation of the primitive ego, is immediately conscious, just as a realisation of the primitive ego. But it may become also the object of another determination of the primitive ego, and so be known in a different way, that is to say reflectively. That the elements of the complex ego cannot be exhausted by means of reflection, that therefore the (complex) ego appears always to reflection as something which in part, for the most part, escapes it, will be now understood without difficulty. But my inability to give myself in reflection a sufficient account of myself, in so far as I am a complex ego, does not suppress the immediate consciousness of the primitive ego, nor even of the complex ego in so far as it is a system of determinations of the primitive ego.

Reflecting, by a particular act, on another particular act, I recognise in this particular act a determination of the primitive ego, that is to say, I recognise that the act on which I am reflecting, as well as any act on which I may reflect, and so even the act by which I am reflecting, would not exist, if it were not connected with the others in one and the same unity of consciousness—if it were not something apprehended, which is at the same time an apprehending, and always the same apprehending.

So I arrive by reflection at the primitive unity. Still I arrive at it, not as something which is outside reflection, but as something which is the soul of reflection—as something which is the reflecting. The reflection which recognises the primitive unity, is the primitive unity which, by reflecting, makes its own consciousness of itself more intense.

### 14.

#### ORGANISATION OF UNEXTENDED (IN THE STRICT SENSE PSYCHICAL) EXPERIENCE

The physical world is (as follows from what has been said, and as will be made more clear below; compare the next chapter, §§ 1–4) a distinct element, admitting again of further distinctions, in the field of total experience. We shall have to say the same of every definite unextended psychical fact, of every element of the complex ego, and also of the complex ego.

A man is affected by the recent loss of some person dear to him. No one, who does not wish to change the usual value of words, without motive or reason, will say that the suffering is not real. But the suffering is

## The Subject

real as a distinct element in the whole of experience ; it is not absolutely separable from the whole of experience.

The man suffers, but at the same time remembers. And his recollections are not all intrinsically painful ; indeed, among those which come back to him more vividly, some, or many, had for him, some time ago, a very marked positive value. Now, even these are painful ; but they are so through their connection with other painful recollections, through their contrast with a present which is painful in consequence of the contrast itself. The pain would not exist without the recollections. (It seems a paradox, and nevertheless it is true, that without recollection even physiological pain would not exist : a pain the duration of which were infinitesimal would be no pain at all.)

The man will have moreover some indifferent recollections and some indifferent actual sensations, also some agreeable actual feelings. All this will be only slightly noticed by him, but to be slightly noticed does not mean not to be noticed at all. The confused mass of psychical facts only slightly noticed, or even altogether subconscious, constitutes, we may say, a psychical materiality, without which there would be no life, and consequently no suffering. We admit that life, under the pressure of a dominating pain, is in some way entirely suffering, but the dominated mass and the dominating pain are not one.

The pain itself (besides including elements which have a positive worth, as we remarked,) has also, as pain, a positive worth. Man is not disposed to get rid of it as of an inconvenient burden ; he suffers from it, but it is dear to him ; he understands how that suffering constitutes for him a real increase of value. Tender memories are so much purer and higher, when they are associated with anguish ; and to bear pain with firmness is a most essential part of virtue. (Respect is due to sorrow—to that of others and to our own, although it is true that sometimes we are partly induced to respect it by sentimental, morbid elements, which ought to be eliminated.)

We have shown, perhaps too fully, that pain is not something subsisting by itself. It implies other psychical facts; and since these in their turn evidently imply the totality of experience, so even pain implies the totality of experience. It is not the less real for that reason, we said; and here we add, it is real just for that reason. Just because it is nothing outside the whole of experience, pain constitutes a disturbance of the whole of experience; it is something deeply rooted in reality; hence, its indisputable importance.

We have alleged only one instance; it seems useless to allege more. Psychical experience in the strict sense, non-spatial experience, is, equally with spatial experience, a distinct element in the field of total experience; consequently every psychical formation resolves itself into a distinct element in the field of psychical experience, and therefore of total experience.

We have seen that even the subject, in the most common meaning of the word, the developed subject, is a formation, a distinct element in the field of total experience, although it is at the same time a development of the primitive unity of that same experience.

# CHAPTER III

# REALITY

### 1.

#### COMMON CONCEPT OF REALITY

BODIES exist, and facts happen. The former are connected with each other, the latter with each other, the former with the latter, by relations, so as to constitute a system—the universe. The happening of facts is a varying; every body varies; even the relations between bodies, between facts, between bodies and facts are subject to variation. It seems certain that the unceasing varying of the universe implies a permanent substratum.[1]

There are living bodies, organisms,—and facts, or functions to which only living bodies give rise. The name physical reality is given to everything else. The relations which arise between the elements of physical reality can be expressed by mathematical formulas. Therefore physical facts are rigorously determined.

Organisms also, although they have special properties and correlatively functions distinguished from physical facts, give rise to physical facts, for instance, to the facts of gravity. And, in general, organisms do not escape physical determinism: life cannot arise, nor continue except under certain physical conditions.

Both materially and dynamically, life is nothing but a

[1] The hypotheses which are made about the nature of the substratum are not to be taken here into consideration.

minimal part of the universe—minimal and negligible. Most physical facts, if not all, and especially astronomical facts, which are the grandest and also the most decisive with regard to the physical conditions of life, are altogether independent of life.

Among organisms, some have a very singular property: they become aware, in some way (the ways are extremely various), of certain acts of their own and of certain impressions which they receive from the outside. This being aware, whatever the manner of it may be, is no physical fact—nor is it even a simple organic function: many functions (in many organisms all) remain unnoticed. Therefore we ascribe to those organisms which become aware, a soul as well as a body. To be an organism associated with a soul means simply this, that the psychical fact, the fact *sui generis* of awareness is associated with some of its functions.

Although a psychical fact is neither the corresponding function, nor the awareness of the function (to see is not to be aware of the visual physiological processes), it is inseparably associated with organic function. In what way it becomes associated is a mystery. Psychical life, or consciousness, develops, becomes more complicated and connected in itself, correlatively with the improvement of the organism. Man's reason is the highest form of it—the highest of the forms reached so far, known to us.

### 2.
#### WHY IT IS NECESSARY TO DISCUSS IT

We have summed up the essentials of the common concept of reality: a very old concept, which modern science has modified in many particulars (not noticed here) making it more perfect, but leaving it intact, or rather confirming it, as concerns essentials.

## Reality

Let us discuss this concept. There is an obvious reason for discussing it. This concept can be considered, by one who accepts it and does not wish to contradict himself, only as a human construction. And man, always according to the same conception, is a product of reality—a product which is a mystery, for we do not know, nor can we imagine in any way how he has been produced. If man is such, is it possible to believe, or even simply to suppose, that such a concept, a human construction, a construction made by a mysterious product of reality, is conformable to reality, is true?

The question is reasonable; let us search for the answer.

A body is never seen alone, nor in all its parts, nor always under the same form, of the same size, of the same colour; even the other sensations, which we receive from it, vary in the same way. Nevertheless, we ascribe to the body both existence and properties which are invariable within certain limits. Obviously such judgments are founded only on the order of spatial experience; they can be considered as true only in so far as they express the order of spatial experience. A body with certain properties is a distinct element in the field of ordered spatial experience.

The ordered experience of which we are speaking is not only that of a definite subject; it includes the experience of each definite subject; it is common experience. I, here, see this; another person, there, sees that. But I, there, should see (at least, nearly so) what the other sees; the other, here, would see what I see. And, instead of seeing, I might sleep; but, if I were to look, I should see this and this. Various circumstances make the actual experience of each of us much less complete than possible experience. But each relies on possible experience, which he infers from his own actual, ordered experience, and from what he knows of the ordered experience of others.

F

## 3.

### UNITY OF EXPERIENCE. EXTENDED OBJECT, AND SENSATION

The whole spatial experience is nothing but a distinct element in the field of a wider experience.

I see, and I remember. Recollection is a non-spatial, internal fact—a psychical fact. And vision also is a psychical, although spatial, fact: I am aware of seeing. I distinguish between what I see, a coloured form, with a certain collocation among other coloured forms, and my seeing. I do not see, unless I see something; the psychical fact of sensation without the object (without the content) is impossible. But the object is seen and, in so far as it is seen, it implies of necessity my seeing, the sensation. The object and the sensation, although distinct, or rather because they are distinct, imply each other: they are as inseparable as form and colour. The whole constitutes the datum, a determination of my conscious life; in other words, a psychical fact. The object is simply one of the elements of that fact, and therefore cannot be considered as something non-psychical. We are speaking of the object as object, of the content; of nothing else. We are enquiring precisely, whether there be any reason for assuming anything else.

Experience is all a tissue of psychical facts. It is distinguished into internal and external experience. But the external is itself psychical, and would not exist without the internal, in the same way as the latter would not exist without the former. They are not two kinds of experience, but two distinct elements in the field of one total experience.

A fact of external experience, we were saying, is a distinguishable, but not separable, element of a more complex fact, of which the other element is a fact of internal experience. Further, the facts of external experience depend also on those facts of internal experience, which would seem to be without an external object (and the latter on the former). I do not see while asleep. When awake, I see what I can, not what I wish to see. But, within the limits of my power, my visual perceptions depend on my general state, on my feelings, and even on my caprices. A discourse attracts me; I care for nothing else, and I am hardly aware of anything else. The world which presents itself to me in my room, tires me; I have only to go down into the street: the scene changes.

### 4.

#### EXISTENCE OF BODIES; ITS MEANING

The conviction that a body has an existence and properties independent (within certain limits) of other bodies and of physical change is founded, as we remarked (§ 2), on the order of external experience. The conviction that the physical world is, with regard to its existence and its varying, independent of internal experience, is founded in the same way on the order of all experience. Correlatively to the varying of my internal experience, the external varies in such an irregular way that I should know nothing of an external reality, if I had no other information about it. But I combine (with great quickness, for I am in the habit of doing so,) the actual external experience with the corresponding recollections, with the actual internal experience and the corresponding recollections, and with what I know of the experience of others; so I am able to order the chaos of actual external experience; I form a complex representation, a collective conception of the physical world.

The system of judgments by which I express my concept

has a foundation, and is true, in so far as it sums up the distinctive process above indicated, and formulates the result of it. It is not permissible to interpret it in any other way; that is to say, the system is no longer true if we ascribe to it another meaning. The reality of the physical world is simply its being a distinct element in the field of total experience.

He who speaks of something of which he is not aware— of something which neither to him nor to others appears positively certain, and cannot even be inferred from what is positively certain, speaks without knowing what he is saying. We distinguish external from internal experience; and we ascribe to external experience (I do not say to external experience only), in so far as it is distinguished and as distinct, an intrinsic order. We do all this by means of a process which, although made easier to each of us through his living with people who have already accomplished it and who speak to him, requires a considerable time. Our cognition of the external world is cognition, in so far as it is justified by the process; it is cognition (to say the same thing in other words), in so far as the external world is a construction of the process itself. Therefore, the hypothesis that the external world is something more than a distinct element in the field of experience, that it is outside the process and the cause of the process, is not justified. The causes of experience (of which we are not now speaking) are not to be confused with the content, which is on the contrary one of its elements.

## 5.

### CHARACTER OF THE PHYSICAL SCIENCES. THE CONCRETE, AND THE ABSTRACT

So, (it will be asked,) physics is an imaginary science? Physics (we answer) studies a group of facts, which cannot be separated from the whole of experience, but are distinguished from it. As distinct, the group can be studied in itself, without its being therefore necessary to represent clearly to ourselves the whole in which it was distinguished. A watchmaker uses the known order of certain facts to secure that other facts shall take place according to a pre-established order. He is working on a distinct element. This element would not be such if it could not be considered and elaborated apart; but it would not admit of being elaborated or considered, if, instead of being a simple distinct element, it were outside total experience.

The physicist does in substance what the watchmaker does. He studies a group of facts, and cares about nothing else. The essential inseparability of the group from the whole of experience is the condition *sine qua non* which makes his study possible, but is neither element nor object of study. By asserting the inseparability, we take away nothing from physics; by denying the inseparability (if it were possible to deny it), nothing would be added to physics. Both the assertion and the denial fall outside the field in which physics does its work.

That which can be distinguished in the whole of experience, is real, precisely because it is included and can be distinguished in it; although, just for that reason, it is not a reality subsisting by itself, an absolute real. Therefore physics is no imaginary science, but an abstract science, for it studies separately something which has no separate existence.

A carriage which runs over me, is no abstraction. But remove the harm which it may cause to me, and you will remove the importance of the fact; remove also the feelings, and tell me, who will still be able to assert the reality of the fact. As distinguishable elements in the whole of experience and as constituents of it, bodies and physical facts and the whole physical world are reality. And so, the form of the inkstand, the number of sheets of the booklet, as constituents of these bodies, are as real as those bodies. But they become abstractions when we consider the form of the inkstand without the matter, the number of sheets without the sheets of which it is the number. In the same way, bodies and physical facts and the whole physical world become abstractions if they are considered outside the whole of experience in which only they are real, as distinct constitutive elements of it.

### 6.

#### INSEPARABILITY OF EXTENDED EXPERIENCE FROM THE WHOLE OF EXPERIENCE

Abstraction takes place when a thing which is essentially related to another is considered without reference to the other. We cannot avoid making abstractions; nor is it easy to see why we should abstain from it, even if we could. But if the absence of reference in considering things is interpreted as a real absence of relations, abstractions become hypostases. That such hypostases ought to be avoided, is indubitable. But, when we have to do with abstractions, we may easily happen, if we do not always bear their abstract character well in mind, to convert them inadvertently into hypostases.

It happens that Peter considers a definite body; for instance, this stone. Perhaps he will not formulate, but he certainly tacitly implies the judgment: this stone exists. As he is not addicted to philosophy, it does not cross his mind to ascribe to the stone the character of being separable from his total experience; it does not even occur to him that there is a total experience. He may think about the single stone, for the stone is a distinct element; and he thinks about nothing else, for at that moment he cares about nothing else. So far there is no harm.

But let us suppose that Peter afterwards comes back to his judgment with a speculative aim, and tries to analyse it. There is no word in it of anything but the stone, as if there was nothing else in the world. And existence is predicated of it—not some kind or other of existence, but existence *sic et simpliciter*. Now, existence, understood in this sense, outside all relation[1] is absolute existence. . . .

A stone is a body so manifestly dependent that any one who by his own reflections is led to consider it as self-subsisting will directly recognise his mistake. But, suppose the discourse, instead of being about a stone, or any definite body, should fall on the ultimate substratum of bodies, on matter? (In whatever way matter may be then conceived, for in this respect the atomic or the energetic or any other hypothesis are equivalent.) The mistake, in this case, is no longer so easy to recognise. And from the judgment—matter exists, the legitimate consequence is drawn—matter is the absolute, is God.

The consequence (let us be clear) is legitimate and necessary; but only for the man who does not reflect, that "matter" is simply (like the stone) a distinct element in the field of experience, and that, consequently, to consider matter apart from the whole of experience, to speak of matter alone, is to abstract. An abstraction, when it is not apprehended as such, transforms itself, for speculative thought, into an hypostasis. And the consequence, the deification of matter, becomes inevitable.

[1] Peter's discourse implies certain relations; but these, not being expressly stated in it, easily remain unnoticed.

## 7.

### HOW THE SUBJECT CONSTRUCTS THE EXTERNAL WORLD, AND AT THE SAME TIME ORGANISES ITSELF

Now, my total experience is my own total experience: it implies myself. It does not imply however the complex ego of which I am clearly conscious, and which, in the clearness of my consciousness, I oppose to other like subjects and to the physical world; the complex ego, as we saw (in the last chapter), has also been formed in the field of total experience. The ego, implied by my own experience, is simply the primitive unity—that unity which, organising correlatively itself and the content of its own experience, has developed so as to constitute the complex ego, which is now contending with itself.

The experience of the primitive unity, as we have seen, is formed in so far as the primitive unity manifests its own activity externally by overcoming certain resistances opposed to it. Among the resistances opposed to it, some are no doubt to be referred, as we remarked, to the external activities of other primitive unities. We must now add that the resistances are all of this kind; in other words, that there are no other activities but those which are manifested by the primitive unities.

Besides the resistances coming from more or less rational animals, we have also to overcome those opposed to us by inorganic bodies and by the forces inherent in the latter.

But physical reality as a whole is a phenomenon; it is, as we have seen, the result of a process of distinction. The process implies a multiplicity of facts in a single consciousness, which form various groups, become more complicated, combine into an order, and so build up physical reality. The facts (of which any body is simply an element inseparable from the others), which arranged and variously grouped constitute physical reality for the primitive unity (which has at the same time become organised in itself, and in this way developed), imply certain factors. These are—the primitive unity, and certain activities which are opposed to it. To suppose that the second factor can be resolved into bodies and their dynamical properties (impenetrability, gravity, electricity, etc.), while bodies and their properties result from the interference of the primitive unity with the other factor of which we are in search, is absurd.

After having eliminated physical forces, which have no right at all to be considered here, for their field is the physical world, and here we are asking in what way the primitive unity builds up its physical world and develops itself at the same time, the other factor concerned can only consist in other analogous unities, primitive or developed. The above discussion does not allow us to assume, or accept, a different solution.

### 8.

#### CONTINUATION. REALITY AND APPEARANCE

Consequently, the essential constitutive elements of the world are primitive unities, each endowed with consciousness (cognition), activity and feeling.

But we must not think, that all the rest is simple appearance. Every fact is real, although certainly not a self-subsisting reality. Every fact is an appearance, that is to say consists always in some form of consciousness—a form, which is not separable from the unities of which we are speaking (whether they be in their primitive condition, or developed); they in their turn are not separable from the facts of which they are the unities. A fact is real in so far as it is an appearance: its reality consists in its appearing to some, embryonic or developed, subject.

Such—it may be objected—is your conception of reality; you have to show, that your conception is true.—But you on your side ought rather to expose the reasons which lead you to assume, to suppose, another conception of reality. I do not a priori exclude a non-factual reality; indeed it is quite clear that the primitive unities, which are neither formed nor dissolved, although variable cannot be resolved into mere variation; they are inseparable from facts (each from its own varying and the varying of the others), but are no simple facts. Granting that there are reasons for admitting a reality superior to facts and to the primitive unities, we shall naturally admit also the higher reality. But it does not appear, why the admission of a higher reality should be a rejection of the lower one. It is we, lower realities, who admit the higher reality; if we, being of a lower order, were no reality, not even our admission, not even our conception of a higher reality, would be real; and consequently there would be no higher reality. To speak of a hierarchy of realities, and to deny the reality common to the elements of the hierarchy, is a contradiction.

Every fact is real, we were saying: without excepting those which we call only apparent, as for instance the bending of the oar plunged into the water; without excepting dreams and hallucinations. In the distinctions which we draw between reality and appearance, there is always necessarily implied a common conception of reality, which is predicated of everything, and also of appearance.[1] That last night thieves entered my room, was a dream. That is to say, it was a fact, the relations of

---

[1] In other words, the above distinctions, usual in common speech and in science, imply a conception of reality which is applicable to what is usually called appearance, as well as to what is usually called more properly reality.

which to other facts were not those imagined in my dream : the lock is intact, the watch and the purse are in their place, etc. But while the fact had no such relations, it was related to the rest ; like any other, it is a distinct element in the field of experience. It is an irrelevant fact ; but just its irrelevancy implies its reality.

The external world and the internal world, which I have built up myself little by little, are real, just because they are factual, because they are certain constructions made by me.

What I more properly call myself, is also a construction, inseparable from the other construction which is my external world. So, I exist only in appearance ? Certainly, my existence is nothing but an appearing of myself to myself, my being conscious. Certainly, the appearing of myself to myself is conditioned by the primitive unity, and by the process by which the latter has developed. But to recognise this is not to recognise that I do not exist ; it is precisely to recognise the way in which I exist.

9.

THE TWO INTERPRETATIONS, SCIENTIFIC AND PHILOSOPHIC, OF EXPERIENCE. THE PHILOSOPHIC INTERPRETATION DOES NOT INTRODUCE THE "THING IN ITSELF"

We must distinguish two conceptions of reality : the common or scientific (reduced, of course, to its general outlines, and setting aside more definite characteristics, which vary greatly with the varying of objective cognition), and the other which we have built on it. Both are interpretations of experience, but different interpretations. The second is superior (at least in our opinion) ; it is according to truth. The first is according to appearance. By distinguishing between the two conceptions, do we therefore distinguish between reality as it appears to us, and reality " in itself " ?

We answer no. In fact, we also have remained within the bounds of an interpretation of experience; only, we have taken into account also the subjective factor of the latter—a factor, which certainly is not unknown to anybody, and is as essential to every systematisation of experience, as to experience itself; but which, in the common or scientific systematisation, is not taken into consideration, in so far as it is not among the elements to be systematised, although it is the indispensable instrument of systematisation.

What we have done is simply to have noticed, that the instruments of systematisation cannot be left outside a complete system. The conception which we have reached is therefore nothing but a development of the common conception, although it is a development of it in a wholly different direction from that obtained in building up the science of nature.

Certainly, another subject is no simple distinct element in the field of my experience, for it also, like myself, possesses an experience. The knowing, the doing, the suffering of the other man are not my own knowing, doing, suffering. What we say of a man with regard to another man, is to be said of every primitive unity with regard to every other. All primitive unities are centres of one and the same universe, that is to say, of the same system of primitive unities; but each of them is a different centre from every other. Each is something more than a phenomenon appearing to another: it is something in itself.

It is impossible to proscribe an " in itself " in this sense. It has however nothing to do with an " unknowable " in itself. In fact—

First, the reason why neither of two primitive unities

A and B is a simple phenomenon of the other, consists precisely in the fact that each of them is a primitive unity, and that in this sense (I do not say, in every sense), both are mutually co-ordinate. Now, the character of primitive unity is immediately known (setting aside the difference between clear consciousness and subconsciousness) to each primitive unity, in so far as it is a primitive unity, a unity of consciousness (or of subconsciousness).

Second, each primitive unity is a (subconscious) activity which becomes manifest in so far as it meets certain resistances, opposed to its manifestation by the manifestations of those other activities which are the other primitive unities. The action which overcomes a resistance, or is overcome by it, is correlative to the resistance, and presupposes it : it implies the resisting activity. Each of the primitive activities implies others—implies, at least indirectly, all the others, the system : it is the unity of the system.

Further, the action is conscious (subconscious). It is, as action, a knowing itself which exists in so far as it knows, in so far as it apprehends the actions opposed to it as resistances. The primitive unity, the existence of which consists in its self-knowledge, knows itself only in knowing something else. Therefore to the primitive unity to be known is not less essential than to know itself. To say that the existence of A and of B consists in their self-knowledge, while it is essential to the self-knowledge of each to know the other, is the same as to say that it is essential to the existence of each to be known by the other.

We shall have later on the opportunity of developing with more clearness what we are obliged here to point out briefly. But what has been said, is sufficient to exclude the unknowableness of that in-itself, which we have in a certain sense recognised. The in-itself of known things is not at all external to the in-itself of the knower: both are in the end nothing but one and the same in-itself.

## 10.

### SPACE AND TIME AS FORMS OF REALITY

Accordingly, space and time are to be considered as belonging to reality. The arguments by which it is proved that space and time are no realities in themselves, being simply forms through which a subject (any subject) builds up its own phenomenal world,[1] have an indisputable value; we admit them. But, on the other hand, there are no reasons for assuming a reality different from that which can be resolved into the matter and the form of experience; the subject and the primitive unity itself, the original germ of the subject, are forms of experience. We reject the view that space and time are merely subjective; for the "merely" has no meaning, unless we suppose that there are non-subjective elements. And we reject the view that there are non-subjective elements, not because the subject can go out of itself, and make sure that there is nothing outside; but because the subject, never going out of itself (not even when it recognises the other subject, for the subjects imply each other), has not the smallest indication, direct or indirect, of anything outside itself.

The primitive unity (the same applies to the developed subject) is, although not divisible into parts, as extended as the universe. To make it easier to understand what seems an extravagance, it will be useful to reflect that a body, in the sense in which common people and physicists use the word, fills up the universe with itself by its own force of gravitation, however small the space may be to which its other more evident properties extend.

[1] KANT, *op. cit.*

I see Sirius distinctly; the space to which my clear consciousness extends, is therefore already very great. I can see through a telescope stars immensely more remote; the space to which my subconsciousness is extended, is therefore infinitely greater. There is no difficulty in convincing oneself that it cannot be limited. For space is not something which subsists outside the unity of my consciousness, and through which the unity of my consciousness must pass, as a body would pass through it. I pass through space in so far as I am a body, that is to say, a certain group of elements, constitutive of myself as a developed subject, and capable of occupying various positions in space; but space, and precisely the space in which bodies have a place and movements occur, is all included in the unity of my consciousness, as it is included in the same way in any other unity of consciousness (or of subconsciousness).

What we have said seems paradoxical, only because we are not able to rid ourselves of the old prejudice that the world, and consequently even space, subsists outside the subject, which thus would have merely accidental relations with the world; whereas the subject is the unity (although not the only unity) of the world.

The unity, as a unity of something extended, is itself extended; but not therefore divisible (*qua* unity). In the same way, the gravitational force of a body fills space; but we cannot therefore divide it, except in so far as we can divide the body. This inkstand, by its gravitational force, extends as far as Sirius (and everywhere); but it is not therefore possible to cut its gravitational force into portions, and separate the portions from each other.

## 11.

### THE COURSE OF EVENTS, TIME, AND SPONTANEITIES

To deny the temporal character of reality, to resolve into appearance the varying [*l' accadere*] which is the matter of experience, is to resolve into appearance the very forms of experience themselves. So we arrive at an absolute agnosticism which, to say no more, is without meaning. After having found a refuge in the darkness of an unknowable reality, after cherishing the illusion of having transferred ourselves outside time, temporal appearance, which has now become incomprehensible, remains before us, and we must resign ourselves to accept it.

By suppressing the reality of variation, without solving the real problems which press upon us, we add to them other fictitious problems; and in the end we become aware of having done nothing but change a word.

We have to understand the possibility of variation. The course of events is composed of facts connected with each other according to necessary laws. The possibility of it therefore implies a principle of necessity; it implies the systematic unity of facts; for only unity can be the principle of necessity. But the possibility of variation implies moreover a principle (I do not say, a beginning) of variation. The necessity of the connection, or unity, makes us sure that, *if* certain facts happen, they will be necessarily followed by certain others, and so on; but it is not a reason, *why* facts happen. The reason why facts happen, the principle of variation, can only consist in a multitude of spontaneities. The concept of spontaneity coincides in substance with the true concept of activity; that principle is spontaneous which gives rise to absolute beginnings, to facts which do not imply other facts, which are not the necessary result of others having taken place. And the spontaneities must be many; for, as we have already noticed, unity alone, by itself, is the principle of necessity; it cannot give rise to variation, if a varying is not already implied.[1]

To clear up the matter, the following example may be of some use. Let the formula be—

$$ay = x^2$$

We may interpret it, either as the equation of a curve in orthogonal co-ordinates, or (if we choose suitable units of measurement) as the law of the fall of heavy bodies. But the formula knows nothing about our interpretations. It is a relation—between the values, whatever they may be, of $x$, and the corresponding values of $y$: a merely logical relation, absolutely outside time. The geometrical interpretation does not deprive it of this its essential character, but the mechanical interpretation does so, and misinterprets the relation altogether. In the mechanical interpretation we consider the different values of $x$ as successive, *i.e.* as the successive values of a time calculated by starting from a given origin; and we consider the corresponding values of $y$ as successive, *i.e.* as the distances from the starting-point, at which a moving point will gradually arrive. But these successions are foreign to the formula, with regard to which the possible values of $x$ are all simultaneous (as it appears also from the geometrical interpretation), and all the corresponding values of $y$ are also simultaneous. If we had to draw the notion of variation from the formula, we should not arrive at it to all eternity. We can interpret the formula as a law of variation; but the reason is that we possess the notion of variation from other sources. The logical deduction of variation, even of an apparent, illusive variation, is a hopeless undertaking.

[1] The above reflections were developed by me a little more fully in *Massimi Problemi* (Milan, 1910; Eng. Tr., *The Great Problems*, 1914).

The many spontaneities, in which the principle of variation consists, are evidently the activities of primitive unities; each of which, consequently, will vary in a double way. That is to say, in the first place, on its own account. It changes its own mode of being, without any reason, without any determination; merely, for the sake of changing it; for, spontaneous variation is its character, its essential constituent. It changes, in the second place, because its mode of being or of varying is determined, in consequence of its necessary connections with other unities, by the interference of its spontaneous varying with the spontaneous varying of the others.

In every variation we have therefore an element of spontaneity and an element of necessity. A variation appears mainly spontaneous, or mainly necessary, according to the various combinations of the two factors. In the facts which we call physical, necessity is far more predominant, so that spontaneity escapes observation. On the contrary, in the actions of developed subjects spontaneity becomes manifest.

### 12.

#### UNITY OF THE EXTENDED PHENOMENAL WORLD

Facts are therefore to be ascribed to the activities of primitive unities, which evolve because of their spontaneity, and in their evolution interfere with one another because they form a system, a higher unity. It is impossible to dispense with these sources of motion; to introduce others is to build up hypotheses which can in no way be justified, and which are not even intelligible: of other variations and of other causes, nobody would know anything even if they did exist.

To construct a doctrine of variation on such foundations is not the office of philosophy, but of science, of psychology and of physics. Both psychology and physics have still to do with facts of consciousness, connected in the unity of subjective consciousness and in that vaster unity, which is the system of subjects; nothing more is required to be certain that both are occupied with the field assigned by us; although the one as much as the other, and especially physics, can, as objective disciplines, make abstraction from the true notion of the field with which they are concerned.

We shall briefly mention a question which, although philosophically of secondary importance, is not without some fineness: is the external phenomenal world the same for every subject, or has the world of one subject nothing in common with that of another? The solution, which I gave on another occasion,[1] seems to me to be correct: the phenomenal world is fundamentally one only; although, since the subjects are variously placed in the system containing them all, (that is to say, since the relations of each to the rest are not the same for all,) the fundamental unity does not exclude a variety which may even be remarkable.

The facts which we call external, or physical, result from the mutual interfering of the activities manifested by primitive unities. To be more easily understood, let us schematise. The primitive activities (or unities) A and B unfold themselves and interfere with each other, giving rise to a fact $a$. That $a$ is a fact of consciousness, let us say a sensation, of A as well as of B, is quite obvious. The happening of $a$ is the realisation of a fact of consciousness of A, and of a fact of consciousness of B; but not of the two facts, as if each one happened independently of the other. Each of the two facts takes place, only

[1] Compare *The Great Problems*, the chapter on *Sensation*. What is said in that chapter must be taken together with what is said in another place (in the same book) about the activities of the monads. The doctrine has not been, in general, well understood; perhaps, for my own fault.

in so far as it interferes with the other; the real fact, of A as well as of B, is the interference, the unity of the two activities; in substance, only one fact is realised; as, to use a gross example, when a rope is stretched, the existence of the traction at one end is the existence of the traction at the other end. Consequently, only one fact $a$ takes place, which is at the same time a becoming aware on the parts both of A and of B; A and B have (are) distinct consciousnesses of one and the same content.

The matter takes on a somewhat different aspect, if, instead of two primitive unities in the immediate interfering of their manifestations, we consider two developed subjects in their respective relations to facts external to both. The process may be schematically represented as follows.

A particular limited system S of primitive unities, which may be relatively (never absolutely) considered as closed, gives rise to a fact $a$. Each of the subjects A and B interferes with S, coming so to apprehend $a$ in some way. The following is the reason why we say " in some way." Since S is, though only relatively, closed, we must believe that the interfering with A and with B has introduced into it only a minimal change; for instance, the light of the sun is not perceptibly modified by the fact that Peter and Paul see it. But while the fact $a$ may be said to be independent of the interfering, the modification of consciousness which the interfering produces in A and in B, is not independent of such interfering; it will depend, partly on the invariable $a$, which both for A and for B is one and the same; but partly also on the structures of those systems which we call A and B. And as the systems A and B are different, and differently collocated with respect to S, it may be, or rather it is not improbable, that the respective modifications of consciousness, the ways in which A and B apprehend $a$, will differ. So, for example,

Peter and Paul see an obelisk differently, for they look at it from different places; and Paul, if he were to go where Peter now is, would see the obelisk differently from the way in which Peter now sees it, for his sight is better or worse (perhaps also, because a cloud throws a shadow on the obelisk, which it did not throw before, etc.). The notion that the phenomenal world is strictly the same in so far as it is apprehended by different subjects, for a blind man and a seeing man, for an Eskimo in Greenland and a creole in Peru, is a grave mistake; but a mistake which I have never made, and which is no consequence at all of my doctrine.

Nevertheless it remains true, that by means of sensations we come into relation with facts which are facts of consciousness, as our sensations are facts of consciousness;—that the constitutive consciousness of the facts to which we become related in the way mentioned, is not our personal consciousness; whence it does not follow that it is a consciousness " in the air " : it is the consciousness of other subjects, or in general of other primitive unities; —that feeling, although it is no simple and mere inclusion of what is felt within our personal consciousness, implies and is such an inclusion : what is felt becomes included, although the inclusion is generally accompanied by some modification;—lastly, that the phenomenal world is fundamentally one and the same for all men, notwithstanding the differences, relatively of secondary importance, which may be found between the phenomenal world of one and that of another. Common sense has always felt sure of this conclusion; and neither physicists nor psychologists have ever succeeded in opposing to it any doctrine, which was not grossly agnostic.

# CHAPTER IV

# FACT AND COGNITION

## 1.

JUDGMENT AND COGNITION OF THE JUDGMENT. FACTS

I THINK a judgment; I formulate it, perhaps without either assenting to it, or dissenting from it. I say something, and I know what I am saying. In other words, in formulating a judgment, and in consequence of my formulating it, I know the judgment which I formulate.[1]

A judgment formulated by me, considered in the fulness of that act which is my formulating it, is a reality of fact—a reality which is at the same time, necessarily, my cognition of the said reality.

Sometimes, while I am convinced of knowing a datum of fact, I am mistaken. I believe, for instance, that this ring is of gold; the ring on the contrary is simply gilt. The judgment—this ring is of gold—is not a cognition of the ring. It is however a cognition of itself. I am in error, if I assent to it; but if I limit myself to pronouncing it, I know.

The formulated judgment, and the cognition of the formulated judgment, are *unum et idem*, numerically one thing. My act is cognitive in so far as real, real in so far as cognitive; it has in itself its own justification. I know

[1] "A proposition present to my spirit may be also called a cognition, in so far as I apprehend and know that proposition" (ROSMINI, *Nuovo Saggio*, etc., Sect. VI, P. I, Chap. III). Any proposition or judgment which I pronounce even mentally, which I think or formulate, is present to my spirit.

# Fact and Cognition

for certain, necessarily, that reality, that fact, which is the judgment formulated by me.

Can I know any other kind of realities?

I wish to satisfy myself whether the ring is of gold. I rub it on the touchstone; I wet the streak with nitric acid: the streak persists; I say, giving this time my assent, the ring is of gold. A fact has given me a cognition which is no longer a simple cognition of the judgment, but of the ring (of another datum of fact).

But of the fact which has furnished me with that cognition, I have given to myself an account by means of a judgment: I see, etc. Of what use would the persisting of the streak have been to me, if I had not become aware of it? That awareness which is mere seeing, would have been as useless to me in so far as I am a reasonable person, to me who wish to judge about the ring, as the absence of all observation. The consequence drawn by me is a judgment; the premiss from which I draw it, can be only another judgment.

It is usual to say of a man who does not yield to evidence: that man would deny even the light of the sun. Certainly, the fact, meaning of course the apprehended fact, is undeniable. Precisely, the undeniableness of the apprehended fact proves that the way in which we, reasoning men, apprehend a fact, is the judgment which serves to express or assert the fact.

## 2.

### JUDGMENT; EXPRESSION (OF THE JUDGMENT); SENSATION (ON WHICH THE JUDGMENT IS FOUNDED)

We do not mean that the fact and the apprehension of the fact can be resolved into the judgment in so far as it is simply formulated, or thought. We mean this: the reality of the fact, the reality of the sensation by which

I apprehend the fact, and the judgment by which I express and know the fact, constitute together one unity. The elements of the unity are distinguishable from each other; they can be, also by abstraction, thought of separately from each other; but they are not really separable.

The judgment is not always wanting where the expression of it is absent. We may pronounce the words by which a judgment is expressed; we may, without pronouncing them, represent them to ourselves distinctly one by one (which is itself, for us, the same as to pronounce them). We may also represent them rapidly, as a complex and confusedly. And, for us, it will be almost like pronouncing them; on condition that the general and confused representation be sufficient to make concrete, to fix, that definite act without which not even the words pronounced would have any meaning at all.

Between thought associated, and thought not associated with a distinct representation of words, there is, even for a thinking being, a difference. When it is a question of analysing a judgment, of establishing exactly the relations between several judgments, distinct representations are useful or indispensable. Without language, we cannot succeed in developing a connected series of thoughts (indeed, sometimes to speak is not sufficient, and it is necessary to write). The deaf-mute cannot develop his own thought, not only because he cannot profit by that of others, but because he cannot express it to himself.

But let us limit ourselves to the essential. An impression on my body would be for my knowledge as if it had not taken place, if it determined or constituted no fact of consciousness. And the fact of consciousness would be as if it had not taken place, if *per impossibile* it remained entirely separate. My seeing, in order that

## Fact and Cognition 89

it may render possible or constitute a knowledge, must call back to mind some reminiscence, must occupy a place in a complex of representations.

The act which gives a place, and therefore a meaning, to each psychical fact, is precisely the essence of the judgment—that essence, which will receive from the expression the refinement indicated, but does not consist in the expression, for the expression alone would mean nothing, and would not exist.

A sensation apart from judgment, if it can be realised (we do not raise this question), has no value for thought; it is as if it did not exist. A judgment is never founded on a sensation which is external to it, which confronts it as one body confronts another: the sensation which justifies a judgment and the judgment which is founded on the sensation, are distinguishable, but not separable.

### 3.

#### REALITY, AND THE SYSTEM OF JUDGMENTS

Is it possible to compare with each other these two things: the fact in its reality, and the supposed cognition which a particular subject has of the fact?

The stuff which you have before you seems blue to you. Still it might not be blue; its colour may be altered, here, now, by a reflection, by a contrast. Go to the open air, to the full light, where there are neither reflections nor contrasts. If the stuff even there seems blue to you, it is blue—supposing, of course, that you are not colour-blind. In any case, not everyone is colour-blind. If the stuff, seen in normal circumstances by one who has normal eyes, seems blue, it is blue. We may compare different visions with each other; but we cannot compare the vision, the colour seen in any way, with the colour in itself, for colour " in itself " is a chimera.

So, we can refer one judgment to another, to several others; we can build the frame of a universal system, in which every judgment must have its place. A judgment, of which it is assumed that it ought to be in a given relation with certain other judgments, but which turns out not to be so related to those others, is called false, unless indeed the falsity is ascribed to the assumption in question itself. The ultimate test is the possibility or impossibility of placing a judgment, a particular system of judgments, in the frame of the universal system. A judgment, a particular system of judgments, which cannot be an element of the universal system, is called false. The concept of falsity is nothing but the concept of the impossibility of inclusion in the universal system.

But to compare together, on one hand judgments, on the other hand facts supposed to be in themselves foreign to every judgment, is as possible as to compare with each other the colour seen and the colour in itself.

We can connect our judgments so as to form a system, rejecting as false those which prove incapable of being connected; we can, at least, build up what we have called the frame of a universal system—a frame, which comes to be the ultimate test of truth.

It is impossible to assign any means for going beyond the system of judgments. Whence some might infer, (not a few have inferred), that man is shut up within the system of his own judgments, as in a cage with huge walls; about what is outside the cage we can neither know nor conjecture anything; cognition has absolutely insuperable limits.

For the hundredth time we again assert that such an inference is a gross mistake. It is a judgment which cannot become an element of the universal system of judgments (and which consequently is false); the system, in fact, is closed, and we are enclosed in it; whereas, by that very inference, we go beyond it, for we assert an outside. The legitimate, and true, inference is this, that outside the universal system of judgments there is nothing. The cage in which we are enclosed constitutes the whole of reality, exhausts every possibility. We cannot go beyond it, not because the means fail us, but because a beyond does not exist. In fact, to assert something beyond is to consider it as something on this side,—is to make it be on this side.

### 4.

#### COINCIDENCE OF REALITY AND COGNITION. CONCRETE THOUGHT

In the sense indicated by us, reality of fact and cognition coincide : they are absolutely one.

But cognition, if it is to be identified with factual reality, must be considered in its concreteness. I look out of the window ; I see that it is raining ; I say : it is raining ; I might even say (I have said implicitly) : I know that it is raining. As we have remarked in another place, we have here a strict unity : self-consciousness ($I$ know), cognition (it is raining ; in which we have to sub-distinguish the judgment in so far as it is simply formulated, and the assent), sensation (the apprehension of the fact), the fact (in so far as it is apprehended, and in so far as it is apprehensible), are elements of one and the same whole —elements which we can distinguish, which it is useful to distinguish, because they are distinguishable, but which it is not possible to separate : if separated, they would no longer be the same as before. To separate them, that is to say, to consider them as separate, is (as we have said) to abstract.

Physicists abstract the fact, the content ; and they examine it. They examine it, of course, by means of cognition. But they do not concern themselves about the impossibility of separating the fact from the cognition which they have of it, and into which they try to penetrate. As physicists, they have no need to be concerned about it. But, if they consider their abstraction as a reality subsisting of itself, if they directly ascribe a philosophical value to the results of a physical inquiry, they are mistaken.

Logicians abstract the judgment, the form. And it is manifest that the judgment as such, independently of its connections, which are however essential to it, with a reality of fact, may become an object of study. But when we say that reality coincides in the end with cognition—that nothing exists or happens independently of all judgment, we do not mean to speak of abstract judgment, of form as pure form. We mean, that there is no matter without form; not, that the existence of matter can be resolved into the existence of form; form is indeed a necessary condition of the existence of matter, but the latter is in its turn a condition of the existence of the former; while there is no matter without form, reciprocally form is always the form of some matter.

He who should presume to identify reality with abstract cognition (or, more exactly, with abstract judgment, which, so abstracted, is no longer cognition), would fall, by the opposite way, into the same error as those physicists who imagine themselves to have built up a system of philosophy, whereas they have simply constructed a physical doctrine.

The doctrine of reality (philosophy) can be constructed only in its general outlines; it can be resolved into what we have called the framework of the universal system of judgments. The framework cannot be constructed by means of the artifices of formal logic alone; although of course it does not follow that the laws of formal logic have to be violated in order to construct it.

If we wish to philosophise, we must think concretely. We all think concretely in so far as we really live; but mere living is not yet philosophising. In order to philosophise we must re-think that concrete thought which is the life, or the being, of ourselves and of things—re-think it in such a way as to reduce it to a system, but without divesting it of its concreteness, without limiting ourselves to systematising the mere form of it. And to do this is not easy. For, any other branch of knowledge is knowledge in so far as it is abstract. Philosophical knowledge must be knowledge, and nevertheless must not be abstract. The difficulty which so far has not been entirely overcome, but which is being overcome little by little, consists in ridding ourselves, in learning, of the habit of abstraction which seems to be essential to knowledge.

### 5.

#### NECESSITY AS THE CONDITION OF KNOWLEDGE

As we have lately noticed, reality of fact and cognition are identifiable only if we take into account subconsciousness, which is an inevitable constituent of the subject.

An apprehended fact is always apprehended together with other facts, with which it forms in some way a system. Yet the whole of the facts apprehended in the clearness of consciousness, even when integrated by clearly conscious recollections,—what is usually called the present reality, never constitutes a complete, self-sufficient system: it is but a fragment of a system. The actuality of clear consciousness implies subconsciousness; only the unity of consciousness and subconsciousness is systematic; while in the latter we must also include its most hidden depths which perhaps will never come to light, but are all necessarily implied by what takes place in the light of consciousness.

The system in its indivisible integrity, the constitutive totality of the unity of the subject, with the intrinsic necessity of its connections : such is true rationality, *i.e.* the character, on account of which such a system of reality of fact can and must be called a system of cognitions, or a truly unified cognition—a cognition, which for each of us, particular subjects, is always for the most part implicit. We can make explicit some parts of it, more or less extended, but always limited to ourselves, although the process by which they are made explicit has no definite limits.

A complex of explicit cognitions can be arranged in such a way as to be relatively (never more than relatively) self-sufficient; so we have the single objective sciences. In the intrinsic order of a science, we can recognise a relative necessity; this is especially manifest in mathematics.

But the necessity which is recognisable in the intrinsic order of each science, is always, without excepting mathematics, merely relative. In mathematics, the dependence of a theorem on the premisses which serve as its foundation, is no doubt necessary. But by retrogression we arrive in the end at premisses which mathematics can only assume (for the attempt to penetrate into them would be a departure from the field of mathematics), and which therefore, however evident they may seem, cannot be called necessary. We cannot but assume them, if we wish to construct mathematics; mathematics cannot justify them in any other way. And that there are good reasons for constructing mathematics, is indubitable; but mathematics can give no account of these reasons.

Further, mathematics is nothing but a system of abstractions, certainly not useless, not gratuitous, but which are no cognitions of reality. The other sciences are less abstract, though still abstract, as we have already noticed; conversely, the advantage which they offer from this point of view has its own compensation: the less abstract a particular science is, the more remote it is from the necessity of intrinsic connection.

The possibility of constructing any science implies a universal, necessary order of reality. Now, no science lays hold of this universal order—not one, except mathematics which by its extreme abstractions gets almost entirely rid of reality, can fail to take into account contingency. And not one can justify its assumption of a universal order—not one is able to reconcile the necessity of order with the unavoidableness of contingency.[1]

### 6.

EXPERIENCE CANNOT BE RESOLVED INTO PURE RATIONALITY, I.E. INTO EXTRA-TEMPORAL NECESSITY. WHAT IS KNOWN, EXPLICITLY AND IMPLICITLY

Experience cannot be reduced to mere rationality, cannot be resolved into a logical process, for it implies absolute beginnings, essentially a-logical spontaneities. Nevertheless experience is deeply impregnated with rationality; it is in fact one experience, which is as much as to say, necessarily or logically connected within itself.

We were saying lately that a judgment, at least an implicit one, a judgment in which there is always something implicit, is an essential constituent of fact; so that

---

[1] "Die mathematische Naturwissenschaft... ist das Erzeugniss der neuern Zeit; das Wahrzeichen derselben; der eigentliche Mittelpunkt der modernen Kultur sofern ein solcher in der grundsätzlichen Methodik allein zu erkennen ist"; so says H. COHEN, *Logik d. rein. Erkenntniss*, p. 221 (Berlin, 1902). In this, together with some exaggeration (for another characteristic of our time is the historical doctrine), there is much truth. But it does not appear that the method of the "mathematische Naturwissenschaft" can be advantageously applied to philosophical inquiry. The assumptions of objective cognition are of more importance to philosophy than the method. The method varies and has greatly improved: the assumptions remain the same.

the mere fact as such, independently of the judgment, is an abstraction, while the mere judgment as such, independently of the fact, is also an abstraction.

True reality is the unity of the two elements which can be distinguished in it, fact and judgment—a unity, which is the unity of experience, or of the subject considered in the indivisible complexity of its existence. And in this sense, reality and cognition coincide. But they coincide only in this sense, *i.e.* in so far as the existence of experience (of the reality of fact) and the existence of cognition are the existence of the subject which is one although infinitely complicated.

The subject of which we are speaking, is the particular subject; that is to say, one of the many particular subjects co-ordinate with each other;[1] we shall wait to assume a subject which is not particular, till we have recognised it to be implicit in the particular subject. Now, the particular subject is not entirely and altogether a clear and distinct unity of consciousness; its unity is

---

[1] It will be well to make a remark, simply to avoid possible misunderstandings. One subject is not another; therefore every subject differs from every other, essentially. But not every difference excludes co-ordination; otherwise there would be no co-ordinate elements. It remains to know whether the differences which we must recognise between primitive unities are such as to allow or to exclude a rigorous co-ordination of them. The present writer thinks the second hypothesis probable, if not certain. But he cannot now develop his own thought with clearness and exactness: the question does not seem to him ripe, and perhaps it may never ripen (during the short time which remains to him for making it ripe). Founding ourselves on observation, we must say that a very great number of subjects are co-ordinated with one another, and that not all subjects are co-ordinated with one another. But the different importance in a hierarchy (and so, the existence of several hierarchies, arranged again hierarchically) can be recognised, through observation, only between developed subjects; we can refer it to the conditions of development, which no doubt co-operate in determining it, even if they do not determine it by themselves alone. I think that this point is clear. By saying that the subjects are co-ordinate, I do not deny that among their original differences there may be some inconsistent with absolute co-ordination; I express myself somewhat crudely, for I cannot go more deeply into the matter now, nor is it of any importance to the limited object of the present work that this point should be more fully explained. But we must be careful not to consider as closed those questions, which in reality are still open; it was my duty to warn the reader against this.

indeed chiefly (let us say, for the most part) subconscious, for clear and distinct consciousness is nothing but a relatively secondary and minimal formation within subconsciousness, although it is true on the other hand that subconsciousness is not unconsciousness : to us, developed subjects, it seems to be such only by comparison with consciousness. Reality and cognition are therefore identical, but only in the field of subconsciousness.

Of course, their identity in the field of subconsciousness is necessarily inferred from what we apprehend as positively certain in the field of consciousness. We seek the reason of a judgment which we have formulated and to which we assent, because we have formulated it, because we have given our assent to it, because we feel certain of it. The reason, when it is found (and we can always find it, if only we search for it long enough), always implies something which appears to consciousness from the depths of subconsciousness. Subconsciousness cannot be denied, without denying consciousness; it can only be conceived, if we do not wish to deprive consciousness of its evident rationality, as a rational organism, as an implicit system of possible judgments. He who wishes to give to himself an account, which will really be such, of any judgment, is led again to acknowledge what we have called the fundamental framework of that system.

In conclusion, anything new which we may know, is new only in relation to explicit consciousness : implicitly we already knew it. The whole universe is implied by us : observation, reasoning, are simply means, by which some part of what is implicit becomes explicit. There is nothing of what can be known as real which is not implicit in our subconsciousness; on the other hand, what is implicit becomes manifest by means of judgments—becomes manifest under the form of cognition; therefore, the essence of the reality implied by us, the essence of any reality, consists in its knowableness.

### 7.

#### IN WHAT SENSE REALITY AND EXPLICIT COGNITION DIFFER

If cognition is considered under its explicit form, its difference from reality, the impossibility of identifying it with reality, become manifest. There is no reason to be astonished at this. Clear consciousness is precisely the field of distinctions—a field, which is constructed by means of distinction.

Now, we cannot distinguish one thing from another, and at the same time, by means of the process of distinction, identify it, consider it as numerically one with the other. Implicit reality coincides with implicit cognition and with the (subconscious) subject; the process by which we make our consciousness of implicit reality or implicit cognition explicit, ends in the formation of explicit consciousness only in so far as it resolves the subconscious unity into a triplicity: the knowing subject, the known reality, the cognition.

This triplicity is, under one aspect, undeniable. I know my inkstand. Just because I know it, I assert that the known inkstand, I who know it, and the cognition which I have of it, are not one; to say the contrary would be to deny my cognition. But, from another point of view, the same triplicity is embarrassing, or altogether contradictory. What I call my cognition, how can I call it cognition, if it leaves out (nothing less!) the reality of the known thing, if it is almost a kind of utensil, by means of which I arrive at the thing, but with which the thing as such has essentially nothing to do? I say: the cognition is present to me; as I say: the thing is present to me. Now, if the cognition is merely present to me, it will be once more a thing, and will not be known to me, except by means of another cognition, which in its turn will make it known to me only from the outside, that is to say, will not make it known to me at all. . . .

All these difficulties, which we have simply mentioned, vanish when we reflect that the triplicity is a triplicity of distinct elements, and not of separate realities. In the unity of subconsciousness the elements are inseparable; they are not three, but only one, they are the unity of subconsciousness. The act of distinguishing them loses its meaning and its value, becomes absolutely unintelligible, absurd, unless we consider it in correlation with the fundamental indistinct unity—unless we recognise in it the process by which the unity manifests externally its own content and the order intrinsic to its content.

Above is not below; therefore, there is an above, and there is a below. But the above is such only in relation to the below, and vice versa. There is therefore properly neither an above nor a below; and yet it is impossible to deny either the one or the other. How these apparent difficulties are to be solved is clear to everyone. In a body, let it be for instance a tree, we distinguish an above and a below; but the above and the below exist only in so far as they are distinguishable in it. If we hypostatise what are simply the results of a distinction we fall into an absurdity, and so also if we deny the distinction. But if we ascribe to the distinction the value of a distinction, if we recognise the distinct terms without hypostatising them, then all becomes plain—so plain, that some will be astonished to see us waste time on such trifles.

Cognition properly so called (explicit cognition) and reality differ in so far as they are two distinct elements, and not one alone; but even this difference of theirs (as two distinct elements, not as two separate entities,) implies a deeper unity which we have to recognise, unless we wish to exclude the very distinction, which at first seems to be inconsistent with unity.

The consequences at which we have arrived are further borne out by any but the most superficial study of cognition as distinguished from reality.

## 8.

### UNKNOWN REALITY

It is usual to say: facts have happened, do happen and will happen, without my knowing anything about them. This assertion, if we interpret it strictly, cannot be maintained. I *know* that facts have happened and do happen and will happen, of which I know nothing else, except what I have said; but what I have said, I know. What I know about them, is very little; it is nothing definite; but yet it is something.

To assert the reality (it does not matter, whether past, present, or future) of a fact, and to assert at the same time one's own complete and absolute ignorance of the fact, is a contradiction in terms. Therefore, no facts happen or are possible, absolutely outside our knowledge.

No doubt facts happen, of which no man knows all the determinations. Indeed, there is no fact, of which all the determinations are known. The determinations which are known, may either be so many, that we do not inquire further; we then say that we know them all; but even then a more extensive and more accurate observation, a riper reflection, leads to the discovery of determinations which had escaped us;—or they are few, in comparison with those which we are accustomed to consider as constituting the full cognition of the fact; we shall then say, that we are little acquainted with the fact. We go even so far as to say that it is altogether unknown to us; but such a formula is true only in a practical and relative sense.

We all know the meaning of the expression: a fact. A fact of which we know nothing else we represent confusedly to ourselves as a distinct element in the field of total experience. We know that, under favourable circumstances (of time, of place, etc.), we should be able to distinguish it in that field effectually. We know that a fact is fully determined, and therefore in every case exceeds our cognition of the same fact, which is never completely determined. We know that every fact is related to other facts, to all other facts; that it cannot transgress certain necessary laws; in other words, that it forms a part of a rational, universal order.

The propositions above mentioned, which are true without exception, constitute together a cognition, however incomplete, of any fact whatever. And we infer from them, not only, as we have already said, that no facts take place or are possible, which are absolutely outside our cognition; but that it is possible to each of us to obtain a cognition of every fact, capable of an indefinite development or integration.

It is almost useless to observe, that the possibility of which we have spoken is a simple logical possibility. My knowledge has limits which I cannot practically exceed; but the great deal which practically remains, and will always remain unknown to me, is theoretically just as much knowable, as the very little which has become known to me.

### 9.

#### CONTINUATION

It is necessary to distinguish between the fact and the (explicit) cognition which I have of it, for the former has certain determinations which are no determinations of the latter. Partially, however, fact and cognition are identical: certain determinations of the cognition are also determinations of the fact, although they are not the only determinations of the fact.

It will be asked, how we know this. If we denote the cognition by $CC_1$, the fact ought to be (on our theory) denoted by CX. The assertion that the element C is the same (one and the same) both in the fact and in the cognition, implies the impossible comparison between the fact in itself and the cognition. And vice versa, the assertion of the element X, foreign by hypothesis to the cognition, appears to be unjustifiable and intrinsically contradictory (it is not allowed to assert that of which one is ignorant; and it is absurd to assert one's own ignorance while the assertion is made). It is necessary to make a reply.

I say: a fact (any fact) happens. This judgment made by me is a cognition of my own, but an extremely indeterminate cognition; the fact might be the fall of a stone, or the death of a man, etc. Can the fact, of which I say and know something, be indeterminate? No. And how can I satisfy myself that, besides the determinations of my cognition, the fact implies other determinations?

I satisfy myself of this, not indeed by instituting an impossible comparison between the fact in itself and the cognition, but by reflecting on my cognition—that is to say, by reflecting on the whole of my cognitions, for a cognition separated from the whole vanishes.

Each of the facts which I distinguish, occurs with certain determinations of place, of time, etc.; every fact is a distinct occurrence in the field of total experience. A fact, which could be resolved into mere indeterminate change [*l' accadere*], is a distinct occurrence which is not distinct: an empty jumble of words. That the fact cannot be indeterminate, results, not from the comparison of my cognition with the fact, but from my cognition. I know of it only the indeterminate element constituted by the change. The fact, therefore, surpasses my cognition.

In what way does the fact surpass it? This we have to investigate, instead of sitting in judgment, easily but inconclusively, on a word of which we are obliged to make use, but which must not be understood in the common sense. The fact surpasses the cognition, just in so far as the cognition surpasses itself.

Last month I saw my friend in F. This morning I meet him in the street in R. I conclude that he has come from F. to R. on a day which I cannot exactly tell, but which can no doubt be marked in the calendar. A man would have to be either very subtle or very simple—I hardly know which—to doubt that my conclusion is sound. Now, this conclusion of mine, this cognition of mine, constitutes the act by which the fact surpasses my preceding cognition. I know that my friend has been travelling without my having known it. And really there is no mystery in all this.

I never know, with strict exactness, all the determinations and circumstances of a fact; but I know that the fact implies determinations and circumstances of which I am ignorant, for I infer it with certainty from the rest of my knowledge concerning that fact and other facts and the whole of experience.

### 10.

#### WHAT IS ARBITRARY IN COGNITION

Some determinations of cognition are also determinations of fact. This assertion, as well as the preceding one, is founded on anything rather than on an imaginary comparison between the fact in itself and the cognition. The fact of which we are speaking, is a phenomenon, a distinct occurrence in the field of total experience, and would not be such, unless what we are saying about it were a constituent of it. What appears explicitly in consciousness, leads us necessarily back to something which is only implicit in subconsciousness; but the explicit part, and the implicit part which is connected with it and implied by it, constitute a unity. The explicit is the implicit become partially explicit; and if it were not so, we neither should be able to recognise what is implicit, nor would there be anything explicit.

What is recognised by me as a fact, is, first of all, a fact. And what is recognised by me as yellow, is yellow, and can be nothing else. The physical arguments by which it is supposed to be proved that yellow is simply a psychical fact, to which in "reality" certain ethereal vibrations correspond, have been already examined and put aside. (We have discussed no physical doctrine in particular; we have denied that physics is a doctrine of reality in itself.)

It is true that the same sheet of paper, which now seems yellow to me, seen under another light would seem to me of another colour; in the dark it would not appear to me. Therefore, if I assert that the sheet will seem yellow to me under all circumstances, I fall into error; but the possibility that the colour will change with circumstances does not prove that in the present circumstances, among which the state of the organism itself has to be reckoned, the colour is different from what it appears.

The process, by which cognition is built up or by which the implicit content of subconsciousness is made explicit, is voluntary; hence, in cognition there are certain determinations, those above denoted by $C_1$, which might have been different, without depriving it of the character of cognition. And it is to be noticed that, in consequence of the dependence of everyone on the society in which he lives, arbitrary conventions become with time consolidated, so that everyone in particular must adapt himself to them. When we say " the 21st of April " we make use of a convention, from which, however arbitrary it may be in its origin, it would not be easy to escape.

The characters which cognition derives either from personal volition, or from that system of volitions which constitutes for every one the intellectual and moral environment, are not to be identified with those characters which cognition has in common with the known fact. But the distinction, although not always very easy, is never impossible.[1] On the other hand, while those characters of cognition which we may call conventional have no absolute cognitive value they, with regard to fact, have a cognitive value in relation to a certain state of civilisation, not to add that they make us acquainted with just the particular determinations of the civilisation in which we live, or of another.

We do not think it necessary to insist on this point.

## 11.

### REALITY AND KNOWABLENESS. EXTERNALITY AND MULTIPLICITY OF SUBJECTS

A fact appears to me; I know it. That is to say, I distinguish the fact; I distinguish it in the field of experience, and from every other fact which I distinguish in the same way. In order to distinguish it, I must know some of its determinations. The determinations which I know, belong to my cognition, certainly; but at the same time, or rather just for that reason, they belong to the known fact.

[1] On some philosophical mistakes, to which the failure to distinguish has given rise, compare below the note on *Human Thought*, and the note *Thought and Reality* in *The Great Problems*.

And what about the determinations which I do not know?

First of all, my not knowing them is not absolute. I know that they exist; I know that, together with the known determinations, they are constitutive of the fact (of that certain fact); and in general I know other characters of it, although they are insufficient to give me a precise cognition of it. Referring to the journey of my friend, of whom I have spoken above, I know that the journey was effected during the interval between the last time that I saw the friend in F. and this morning; even this is something.

Moreover, I know that I might become acquainted with each one of the determinations actually unknown. I do not say that I am able to know them all; but there is not one, among the unknown ones, of which I can reasonably assert the absolute impossibility of my knowing it. To say that there is, in the fact, something absolutely impenetrable by my cognition, is absurd. For to say this is to predicate something of the said something—it is to predicate of the said something: (1) its being impenetrable by my cognition; (2) its being a determination of the fact. But that, of which something is predicated, is known, and not impenetrable by cognition.

In conclusion, fact, both with regard to that part of it which I know, and with regard to that which I do not actually know, is of the same nature as cognition. What belongs to cognition, belongs (with the exception noticed above) to fact; and what belongs to fact, can belong, even if it does not actually belong, to cognition.

Or in other words, fact results from elements which are all, without exception, knowable, elements of cognition; its occurrence, its reality, coincide with its knowableness. Between fact and cognition we can, indeed we must, distinguish; but to distinguish is not to separate. At the end of a rather lengthy but not a vicious circle, we come back to a point at which we had already arrived; when we distinguish between fact and cognition, the fact so distinguished, as well as the cognition so distinguished, resolve themselves into abstractions. And a philosophy which hypostatises such abstractions, is out of the right path.

Only comprehensive experience, the whole of experience, or the subconscious unity, in which fact and cognition are inseparable, is real, in the true sense of the word. Fact is matter, and cognition is form; the form is form of the matter; the matter is matter of the form. Matter by itself is not more real than form by itself.

In relation to actual or explicit cognition, fact is, in a certain sense, although not absolutely, something external and independent. The possibility of surpassing actual cognition proves at the same time, both that the externality of fact is not absolute, and that a certain externality is not to be denied.

Obviously, externality is to be derived from the multiplicity of subjects, for the clear consciousness of one subject is different from the clear consciousness of another subject. And the non-absoluteness of externality is to be derived from the consideration that each subject as subconscious, each primitive unity, implies each of the other subjects, of the other primitive unities—implies the universe.

# CHAPTER V

# THOUGHT

## 1.

### THINKING AS A PSYCHICAL PROCESS, AND ERROR

I think. That is to say, I judge and reason, I connect several judgments so as to make one system of them. My judging, my reasoning, are facts of internal experience. But in reasoning a necessity becomes manifest of which experience as such gives no account.

No doubt, experience is not chaotic, and therefore implies a necessity. But I do not foresee what the aspect of the sky will be an hour hence; while I know, that no one, under whatever circumstances, will ever discover a fraction having 2 as its square, nor will ever be able to think two contradictory propositions, both of which should be true, or of which neither should be true.

Further, the necessity implied by experience can be only a law (or a system of laws); and a necessary law is nothing but a necessary thought. The necessity of thought cannot be reduced to that of simple fact; for the necessity of fact is necessity of thought.

But, on the other hand, our actual thinking, thinking as a psychical process, is not subject to what we have called the necessity of thought (logical or rational necessity). We think, as a psychic fact, even what is absurd. We can deduce legitimate consequences from absurd presuppositions (Euclid often makes use of such a proceeding); we may by incorrect reasoning, deduce from legitimate presuppositions absurd consequences, which to us seem legitimate.

There are, therefore, in fact, both a legitimate thinking and an illegitimate thinking. In what do they differ?

He who lies, asserts something with regard to himself, and denies the same thing—he himself denies it—with regard to others. By his lie, he disturbs the unity of his consciousness. But not all mistakes are lies.

A grain of corn, sown in the ground, may sprout or not; if it sprouts, it will produce a tiny shoot of corn. A boy has to solve a problem; the solution of the problem is implicit in the enunciation: it must be made explicit. Let us suppose, that it could become explicit by itself, as the grain can sprout by itself; that, which had become explicit, would obviously be the true solution. But the boy, in order to arrive at the solution, has to do something himself. He does something, that is to say he makes use of his freedom of action; the result at which he arrives, may not be, let us suppose that it is not, the development of what was implicit in the enunciation: here is the error.

In the same way as lying, error can be resolved into an internal conflict, with this difference, that in error the conflict is between consciousness and subconsciousness, in lying it is between consciousness and consciousness. But subconsciousness is a constituent of the subject just as much as consciousness. That thinking, therefore, is illegitimate, by which the unity of the subject is disturbed.

2.

TRUTH AND UNITY OF THE SUBJECT

The conflict, the disturbance of unity, due to the will which, making use of its power, evades in some way the bond imposed on it by the essential unity which is a constituent of it, becomes manifest when the consequences of the act are realised. What was implicit in me, very often becomes, sooner or later, explicit. Then the unity of my being recognises itself as broken up into two parts, which tend to exclude each other without success; the uneasiness which thus arises is then experienced by the subject as a pain. But the pain, the explicit apprehension of the conflict, is an accident. Error consists, not indeed in the explicit apprehension of the conflict, but in the conflict itself. The life of the subject consists in spontaneity which, in order to exist, requires a field, within the limits of which it may unfold itself without any restriction. But the unfolding of spontaneity is a vital act, a development of the subject, only in so far as spontaneity unfolds itself within that field. The spontaneity which in unfolding itself goes beyond the field assigned to it by the constitution of the subject, succeeds only in struggling against itself: such an unfolding of it tends, not to develop the subject, but rather to destroy it by dissolving its unity.

This, with regard to the self-conscious subject. The not-self-conscious subject, or the subject in so far as it is not self-conscious, will suffer from an apprehended conflict; but suffering is not destructive of the simple unity of consciousness, at least when it does not go beyond certain limits.

On the contrary, the self-conscious subject which is reduced to say at the same time and in the same sense: I know and I do not know,—in so far as he is reduced to enunciate together the two judgments, kills self-consciousness. He is not simply a subject standing in opposition to himself; he is a subject, in which the act of living is resolved into creating the impossibility of that act. The subject perhaps will not even become aware of this evil; perhaps even, becoming aware of it, he would not care about it. But whether he becomes aware of it or not, whether he cares about it or not, it remains true that such an opposition to himself is the destruction of self-consciousness.

We mean, of course, a destruction *sicut et in quantum*. The man who has made a mistake, is not resolved into the act in which the error consists; he is a complex being who may continue to live, notwithstanding the germ of death which he has made for himself and inoculated into his own system. In the same way as suffering for an animal, so error may perhaps even be for man an occasion of something better, by exciting attention, by inspiring a less exaggerated self-esteem, by provoking an increase of activity—of course, on condition that the error be eliminated. Nothing of all this is denied; nor do we wish at all to ascribe to error an excessive importance. Our object has been simply to exhibit the real nature of error. Error, by itself, is an element which tends to dissolve self-consciousness. It does not succeed in dissolving the latter, because it is never complete; it exhausts some parts of life, not all of them. But, although it does not dissolve self-consciousness, it tends to dissolve it; and this tendency is what characterises it. *E converso*, legitimate thinking is that in which self-consciousness asserts itself, or in which self-consciousness consists. For man, to be in the truth means, in the most exact sense of the word, to exist.

### 3.

THE DOING-THINKING. DISTINCTION BETWEEN ACTIVITY AND THOUGHT. NECESSITY AND UNITY OF THE SUBJECT

The real activity of the subject is rigorously one, not the combination of separate or separable elements. It is conscious, self-conscious activity—a doing-thinking, let

us say : a doing which is a thinking, a thinking which is
a doing. But two elements are to be distinguished in it :
one theoretical, the simple thinking ; one practical, the
simple doing.

In study, the element of thought predominates ; in
those actions, which being habitual are accomplished
irreflectively, the element of doing predominates. But
learning implies a doing, which for its own ends makes
abstraction (if I may so express myself) from itself. And
even subconscious actions imply an organisation, which,
if we render ourselves conscious of it, we recognise to be
an organisation of thoughts. Unity always exists, with
everything which we can distinguish in it ; but all that we
can distinguish in it, is not always distinguished with
clearness, explicitly.

The construction, or even the reconstruction of a
doctrine (to study it, meditate on it, possess it) are
thoughts and operations—thoughts which are operations,
operations which are thoughts : the unity doing-thinking
here appears manifest. But the doctrine is still something
in itself (it was formed, and we wish to possess it, or we
possess it). It is something in itself ; that is to say, we
may make abstraction from the doing which is necessarily
implicit in it. Then, the doctrine comes to be considered
as a system of thoughts alone ; and in itself (in so far as
we consider it in itself, or distinguish it) it is a system of
thoughts.

We mean a system, the unity of which as a system
consists in its being intrinsically connected by rational
necessity. Now it is already evident, that rational
necessity is the condition of the doing-thinking, the
constitutive law of the doing-thinking, or of the subject
which does and thinks. And the law constituting the
doing-thinking, or the subject, is nothing but the unity of
self-consciousness.

The subject is spontaneous. It is an activity which, within certain limits, can unfold itself, independently of any law. Within those limits, it can do anything—except destroy itself, for in destroying itself it would do something, that is to say, it would exist, it would realise itself. But it can even go so far as to attempt its own destruction—that is to say, accomplish certain acts (it matters not with what intention) which, although they do not destroy it, diminish it by disturbing its unity—acts of such nature that, if its acts were all of the same nature (which cannot be, for the field of spontaneity is limited), the destruction of the subject would be inevitable.

The unity of the subject is preserved only in so far as the acts which tend to disintegrate it are in some way abolished, dropped, surpassed. In like manner, a complex of acts, including some of those acts independent of law just considered, which are in opposition to the rest and to each other, cannot constitute, within the unity of the subject, a more circumscribed distinguishable unity, a connected system. It cannot therefore constitute a doctrine. A doctrine is built up only by those acts which are not contrary to the unity of the subject, which do not disturb it but develop it, which are manifestations of life, useful to life, and not germs of death.

That which in the doctrine considered in itself appears to us as rational necessity, has its true root in the unity of the subject; it is required by the unity of the subject; indeed, it is nothing but the unity essential to the subject.

### 4.

#### OBJECTIVE VALUE OF SUBJECTIVE NECESSITY

Although essentially subjective, or rather because it is subjective, necessity is however at the same time objective also. The object is that which confronts the subject—

that which is considered, thought by the subject. No object exists but for the subject. Therefore, the object necessarily yields to the requirement of the subject: something, which did not yield to the constitutive requirement of a subject, would be no object for that subject.

That which I denote by the name of object, and that which I denote by the name of reality (external with regard to myself), are not identical. My object is what is thought by me; external reality is an aggregate of other subjects. And the thinking of another subject is not my own thinking, although the thing thought may be common to both. So, the spontaneity of another subject is not my own spontaneity. That is to say: the other subject is another subject; its existence cannot be resolved into my thinking it as another subject.

The object is reality in so far as it is known to me. Now, reality is certainly known to me; but its existence cannot be resolved merely into its being known to me; it implies cognitions different from my own and other spontaneities besides my own. Whence it follows that I cannot construct the object for myself a priori, by my own thinking only; the object does not admit of such a construction, precisely because my construction of it is an overcoming of certain resistances.

But I know on the other hand, that the object, and the resistances by means of which I construct it for myself, that is to say reality, cannot contradict the a priori laws of my thought. In fact, the resistances which I overcome, which are opposed to me, are implicit in me, in so far as they are opposed to me, are essential to me (for my spontaneity is an overcoming of them). They are therefore a constituent of me; as such, they are not, and it is impossible that they should be, outside that unity which is Myself, and in which the a priori laws of my thinking have their root, or into which they can be resolved.

## Thought

The spontaneities of the other subjects, although each of them has a field of action, within which it evades all law (whence the essential indetermination of variation, and the impossibility of constructing the object a priori), as necessarily included in the unity of my being must yield to the order established by the unity of my being, to the order consisting in that unity.[1]

[Let us notice to avoid misunderstandings, that not even for me—not even for the subject considered, not as an element of reality, but as that which knows—does unity imply absolute determination. This does not destroy its character of being an absolutely inviolable law. I may err, although it is not possible that my thought should be resolved into mere errors. Law exists in as much as the field of action of every spontaneity is limited. Law implies spontaneities—elements, which are absolutely subject to it outside certain limits, precisely because they are not subject to it within the same limits.]

### 5.

#### NECESSITY AS FOUNDED ON THE UNITY OF THE REAL

We have expounded a doctrine of the necessity of thought and the value of such necessity in relation to reality, which may be called subjectivistic, in so far as it resolves that necessity into the unity of the knowing subject. It is not difficult to recognise that this doctrine may be presented under another, apparently but only apparently contrary, aspect: rational necessity is founded on the unity of reality, it is the unity of reality. The

---

[1] "The principle of the synthetical unity of apperception is the highest principle of all employment of the understanding." And the unity of apperception consists in the "I think," in an "act of spontaneity," or in "self-consciousness"; KANT, *op. cit.*, I, §§ 17, 16; *cf.* the whole *Transcendental Analytic of Concepts, passim*. I have made use of the interpretation, which Royce has given with great clearness (*op. cit.*) of Kant's doctrine; of course, I do not accept Royce's doctrine, although I recognise its value as an interpretation of that of Kant. My brief references have the value of simple explanations.

doctrine may, or rather must, also be called realistic. And it is realistic in so far as subjectivistic, subjectivistic in so far as realistic.

In order that all this may be clear, it does not seem out of place to repeat a few things already mentioned.[1]

A particular subject is not the only particular subject.

If there were no other activities, opposed to that which constitutes it, different from that in which the real thinking or the existence of the particular subject consists, such a subject would not be particular; it would not recognise those limits to its field of action, which in point of fact it recognises. Its field of action, in fact, is limited only in so far as it is limited by the fields of action of other opposed activities. It appears moreover manifest from what has been previously established, that the opposed activities, those other activities, are each of them a doing-thinking, in the same way as the activity which recognises itself to be limited by them is a doing-thinking: an activity which could not be resolved into a doing-thinking (more or less subconscious) is nothing but a meaningless word.

Further, a unique subject would not even be spontaneous, that is to say, it would not exist. Spontaneity and particularity (the being one of many connected with each other) are one. To do is simply to overcome resistances; but resistances exist only for him who acts. We do, in so far as we react; the doing implies, both a determinate element (determinate with regard to him who acts), viz. the resistance, and an indeterminate element, the doing, the reacting: the former external, the latter internal, but each correlative to the other. Suppress spontaneous action, and you will have made determinate variation impossible, as we have seen. Inversely, suppress

[1] The reader who does not like repetitions may pass on to the next paragraph.

determinate variation, the resistance, and you will have made spontaneous action impossible.

A particular subject therefore is not the only particular subject. Its existence implies the existence of other particular subjects. And consequently, of the particular subject it cannot be said that it has an absolute existence in itself. The consciousness which the subject has of itself, and which is one with the existence of the subject, implies a reality, which is, in a certain sense, external to the subject itself. The particular subject which denies external reality, disowns its own particularity, disowns itself; it thinks in opposition to that law, which is its own essential constituent: it denies explicitly what it asserts implicitly—that, without which there would be neither its own asserting nor its own denying.

It is clear, in what sense reality is called external. Each subject is particular: the consciousness of one and the consciousness of another (we are speaking of consciousness, not of its content,) are two. Therefore, the other subject is outside me, as to that which constitutes its own particularity. Still, the activity of the other subject is neither segregate nor capable of being segregated from my own, for my own would not exist without the resistance opposed to it by the activity of the other. And the activity of the other implies my own, in the same way as my own implies the activity of the other; that is to say, that which I have considered as another subject, is another subject; and my knowing it to be another subject is as essential to it as it is essential to me to be known as a subject by the other subject.[1]

[1] Obviously, the cognition which one subject has of another is in general only implicit and subconscious and always limited; as particular, each subject has something of its own, which cannot be in the consciousness of another subject. My thinking is not the thinking of Peter; but I know this; and my knowing this is precisely my knowing that Peter is a subject like myself, another subject. For subjects imply each other, both with regard to their existence and with regard to their knowledge.

## 6.

### HOW THE TWO CONCEPTIONS OF NECESSITY ARE IDENTIFIED

Thus reality can be resolved into a multitude of subjects (and, of course, of their actions or manifestations, which are a doing-thinking, generally subconscious). But it is no simple multitude, no chaotic multitude : it is a system, a unity of subjects. The unity consists in the inclusion of each subject in each of the other subjects ; the reciprocal inclusion of the subjects, the fact that each subject is the condition of the existence of every other, and its limit—this is what makes a system of the multitude.

The unity of one subject, therefore, is also the unity of all taken together, the unity of the whole. This is the indubitable ground of the subjectivistic doctrine. But this is at the same time also the ground of the realistic doctrine.[1]

In fact, reality is related to me, exists for me, only in so far as it is implicit in me. That reality, of which I can in any way assert the existence, is as such necessarily subject to the unity of myself, for I am the unity of it ; the forms or laws, which are consequences or expressions of the unity of my thinking, just because they are laws or forms of my thinking, are laws and forms of reality. Vice versa, I exist only in so far as I am the unity of that reality, of which I can assert the existence, or in so far as I imply reality. That which implies cannot subsist without that which is implied. And the implicit factor is not, in this case, absolutely dependent on the implying factor ; for

---

[1] I have opposed (and every one will see that it is no real opposition) "realism" to "subjectivism," not to "idealism." Having clearly explained the meanings of the terms which I use, it seems to me that I have done enough to be understood by any one who does not wish to misunderstand. As to the misunderstandings to which the extremely intricate common terminology (granting that there is a common terminology) may give rise, I am not to blame for them. Whoever finds an amusement in quarrelling about words, may amuse himself with words.

it can be resolved into subjects, each of which is an implying factor, as I am, and in each of which I am implicit.

Consequently, we can and must say that the unity of the subject and the necessity of its thought constitute the unity and the necessity of reality, just as we can and must say that the unity and the necessity of reality constitute the unity of the subject and the necessity of its thought: the subjectivistic and the realistic doctrines can be deduced reciprocally from each other, and coincide.

I have spoken of "that reality, of which I can assert the existence." There is no other; he who assumes another, must, contradicting himself, assume that this other exists.

Necessity can be resolved into the unity of the subject, that is to say, of every subject, for every subject recognises necessity in consequence of the unity which is essential to it. On the other hand, a necessity which held good for one subject and not for another, which were not universal, would be no necessity. Therefore, if we once recognise (and we cannot but recognise) the subjective character of necessity, we must then also recognise that subjects have essentially something in common.

One identical element, numerically one only, must be constitutive of every subject, and must be the foundation of necessity. On the other hand, necessity is the law of spontaneity; it would not exist without spontaneity, that is to say, without the many spontaneities. We find before us two principles, which seem antithetic, and which nevertheless imply each other. It is impossible to reconcile them, without recognising that the subjects are many considered as spontaneous, and that the existence of each, the spontaneity of each, is conditioned by the existence of every other. Each one includes the totality of them all, just in so far as it is different from every other: the common factor could neither exist without the particular factor, nor the particular without the common.

## 7.

### THOUGHT AND BEING

The totality of the subjects and of their manifestations or of the facts to which they give rise, is implicit in each subject. I know very little, both about the universe and about myself (that is to say, about that particular organism of facts which I call, in the more proper and stricter meaning, myself). My definite cognition is extremely limited. Nevertheless, there are no things the cognition of which is impossible to me because of an absolute and essential impossibility. And every new cognition, which I may in any way obtain, is the actuation of a potentiality which I already possessed; it is the development, in the clearness of my consciousness, of something which was already before in me in a subconscious and involved form. Therefore we must say that the totality is implicit in the subject; but, *as* a totality, only implicit.

The totality, as implied by the subject, can be resolved into the concept of Being (quite indefinite Being: this adjective must always be tacitly understood). In other words, there is no subject which does not think Being more or less clearly or subconsciously. The totality is implicit in me, in so far as I think Being. Or again, my thinking of Being, my having the concept of Being, is nothing but my being (in so far as I am at least a subconscious subject, capable of knowing,) essentially related to the totality.

There is nothing of which I must not say that it is a Being. Of nothing can I say anything, unless I say first of it : it is a Being. I know only determinations of Being.

Even the distinction between being and change can be
resolved into a determination of Being : there are some
beings which endure, and some which pass away : fact is
a Being, the existence of which consists in passing away,
in change. Moreover, all that which I know about anything, that is to say, about any determination of Being,
is again a determination of Being.

Obviously, the indeterminate exists only in its determinations. This I know, for when I think the indeterminate I simply make abstraction from determinations ;
the indeterminate is therefore nothing but an abstraction,
a concept which would not exist without a thinker. But
abstraction, on the other hand, is possible. The indeterminate therefore does not exist in itself ; but neither
do determinate and single realities exist each in itself,
separately : they exist only in so far as they have in
common one and the same indeterminate ground—Being.
Reality is one and manifold—one in so far as manifold,
manifold in so far as one. Its existence consists in the
existence of a multitude of elements, which however do
not subsist each by itself, for the existence of each consists in its being an element of reality.

### 8.

#### EXAMINATION OF SOME DOCTRINES CONCERNING BEING

On the contrary some maintain that the Being posited
(predicated) when we say "this is" is not real, but is
simply an *ens rationis*, a bond of concepts, a subjective
copula.[1] The concept of Being, although it is the *primum
cognitum*, in the sense that nothing can be known but by
means of it, is merely a collective concept, a kind of
receptacle of all others. Being is not a genus, for there
are no differences outside Being ; the unity of Being is

---

[1] SERTILLANGES, *S. Thomas d'Aquin* (Paris, 1910), Vol. II, pp. 182-3.

nothing but an analogical unity; that is to say, all things which we can designate exhibit, in so far as beings, common properties, and have real relations with each other, but without constituting for that reason a real unity which would be something more than a collection.[1]

But collections, and the corresponding concepts, have no doubt a *ratio essendi*. The *ratio* sometimes is to be ultimately referred simply to an act of choice. Peter, for instance, says about certain money: it is my own. He says so on the ground of a civil order, not capriciously; anyhow, the order which serves to him as ground, cannot be conceived independently of the forms in which humanity has historically developed. We are, in this and similar cases, within the field of choice. Here, however, it has to be noticed that the choice of man and the history of man still belong to reality; not even in such cases is it right to speak of collective concepts without a corresponding reality.

In other cases, although a certain influence of choice (and of the historical conditions from which it is impossible to separate it,) may still be recognised, it is necessary to recognise also, in arbitrary formations, a corresponding reality altogether independent of choice. For instance, a

---

[1] *Op. cit.*, Vol. I, pp. 27–8. The reason why Being comes to be considered simply as a collective concept ("une simple accolade," SERTILLANGES, *l.c.*) is the fear of otherwise falling into pantheism. This we shall discuss later, when we shall have to speak of God; at present, Being is for us the foundation common to all particular subjects. But it is well to notice the following passage of S. Thomas: ". . . ea, quae de Deo et rebus aliis dicuntur, praedicantur . . . analogice, *hoc est secundum ordinem* . . . *ad aliquod unum.*" (The italics are mine.) "Quod quidem dupliciter contingit: uno modo, secundum quod multa habent respectum ad aliquod unum, sicut secundum respectum ad unam sanitatem animal dicitur sanum ut ejus subjectum, medicina ut ejus effectivum . . .; alio modo, secundum quod duorum attenditur ordo . . . non ad aliquid alterum, sed ad unum ipsorum. . . . Hujusmodi igitur nomina de Deo et rebus aliis non dicuntur analogice secundum primum modum"; and therefore, *according to the other of the two ways!* Compare *Summ. c. Gent.* Lib. I, c. XXXIV. Mr. SERTILLANGES, *l.c.*, in the note, quotes S. TH. *c. Gentes.* c. XXXII, XXXIV and XXV, without specifying the book.

dolphin is a mammal according to naturalists, and a fish according to fishermen; the difference between the two concepts proves that in both there is something arbitrary; it cannot however be denied, that the dolphin is in some characters like a horse, and in some others like a tunny.

Finally, in other cases the influence of choice on the mental product, on the concept, cannot be in any way admitted. Certainly, to have a concept is to think in a definite way; and to think means to act, implies the spontaneity of the subject. But it implies spontaneity (in the cases to which we refer,) in so far as it is arbitrary thinking or not-thinking about certain things, not in so far as there may be something arbitrary in the way in which we think them. We believe, for instance, that the horse has four legs. Nothing has forced us to count the legs of the horse, it is true; but, supposing that we have counted them, we could only conclude that they are four.

9.

#### CONTINUATION

It is needless to stop to demonstrate that Being is a concept of the last kind. Indeed, this character belongs especially to it. Whoever was not certain of the existence of a horse, and of the existence of its legs, could not say that the legs of the horse are four; he who had no concept of Being, would have no concepts of any kind; he would not even be able to construct those which we have recognised to be arbitrary formations.

To suppose that the unity of Being is nothing but a collective unity, is the same as to break up reality into a multitude of elements having no essential reciprocal relations. But such a reality would not be conceivable by any subject (supposing but not granting, that subjects still existed) not even as a disintegrated multitude.

I construct arbitrarily for myself a collection of things which, outside my arbitrary construction, have to each other none of the relations which I afterwards recognise in consequence of that construction; for instance, I put in a bag clothes, books, etc. This I could not have done, unless, before my action, independently of my action, I had been already related to those things in certain ways. As they were all related to me, the things had already, at least indirectly, a relation to each other—a relation which is not an arbitrary product of mine, since it is the condition of my arbitrary act.

A real unity of all the elements which for any reason are called real, is the necessary condition, nor only of any doctrine, but also of any conception, even the crudest, of any action. Real unity can be constituted only by something, which is common to all real elements; and it is indeed difficult to understand what these elements can have in common, if we deny that Being is a character common to them all.

"But Being is not a genus, for there are no differences outside Being." True, Being may not be a genus. But to infer from this that Being is only a collective concept, is not to reason with strict logic. We have recently seen that the concept of mammal is partly, although not entirely, arbitrary; and the same can be said of any generic concept. In so far as it is arbitrary, the genus can and must be called collective, at least in some way.

However, it matters little whether the genus be collective in this way or in that, or not collective at all. What it is impossible to doubt, for the doubt itself implies the assertion doubted, is this, that Being is no collective concept. And what kind of concept will it be, if it is not collective, nor yet generic ? It will be a concept *sui generis*, irreducible to the usual classes of the usual formal logic. This can be no cause for astonishment: Being, presupposed by every psychical formation, and therefore also by every classification, must elude classification.

"There are no differences outside Being." Just so: Being is not subject to specification, but to concretion; it does not receive differences, which are added to it from outside; it develops into determinations, which are intrinsic to it. If concretes did not exist, Being also, which is their common ground, their unity, would have no existence: but if Being did not exist, there would be also no concretes; for concretes imply each other, that is to say, each concrete exists in so far as the rest exist, in fine, every concrete exists only as implied by the totality, by the Being of which it is a determination.

### 10.

#### ABSTRACTION IN GENERAL; KNOWLEDGE AS A CONSTRUCTION

Therefore, the abstraction by which we think Being, differs profoundly from that by which we think any other concept. I should have none of the other concepts, unless I had the aptitude to think; but I should have no aptitude to think, unless I thought Being at least implicitly; by recognising that particular beings, however they may be distinguished and however active, have all one common ground, I make myself explicitly conscious of that which is the indispensable condition of any reality, including my own thinking.

The other concepts are constructed by me; although it is true that none is entirely constructed by me, for each of them implies Being and also determinations of

Being which cannot be reduced to mere externalisations of my spontaneity. My spontaneity can never be separated either from the system of all, or from the partial limited systems which are nearest to it (I am a child of my times and of my people; I have formed myself in a certain environment of culture, etc.); notwithstanding all this, I still remain a particular spontaneity. All my thinking consists in a manifestation of my spontaneity, which, while it unfolds itself among others through a process of adaptation, manifests its own activity, does something of its own. In this sense, every concept of mine is, though not exclusively, a construction of my own.

We must except the concept of Being. For, unless I thought Being at least implicitly, I should not be spontaneous and should not exist. Of course, the Being implicit in me does not become explicit without action on my part; even my explicit idea of Being is a product of my spontaneity. But the function of my spontaneity, with regard to it, is not in the least degree constructive, but merely recognitive; I do not create, nor share in creating, Being: I simply make explicit to myself, or recognise, the Being implicit in my particular spontaneity, and in all things.

All that is necessary in the varying of reality, can be resolved into the unity of Being. But in the varying of reality not everything is necessary, for the unity of Being implies the multiplicity of spontaneities. Each single spontaneity, as such, is not necessitated. But it is limited; whence it follows that the sum of spontaneous acts taken together constitutes a system, in which, precisely by means of spontaneity, necessity asserts itself.

The varying of reality may be considered from a double point of view. We have, on the one hand, reality which successively assumes ever new forms; on the other hand, the subjects which, in order to externalise themselves better in reality, endeavour to know it, to conceive its forms.[1]

The forms of reality which cannot be resolved into Being, are essentially variable. And our knowing them is, in short, nothing but a way of guiding ourselves in the midst of reality, such as it is presented to us in fact. The concepts, at which we arrive in this way, obviously are not invariable, absolute, neither with regard to reality, nor with regard to the subject. They are results of our endeavours to adapt ourselves to the reality of fact, and means by which we improve our adaptation. The reality amid which we try to guide ourselves, is that which touches us most closely, and is chiefly, though fools do not reflect about it, a human reality : everyone, whether he reflects about the fact or not, has much more to do with his own fellow-creatures, than with rocks, with water, or with stars.

The knowledge so obtained is therefore essentially a constructed knowledge, a product of spontaneity—not of individual caprice, but of the systematisation of single spontaneities into the whole of human society and of human culture. It is therefore an historical formation, and cannot but develop historically : its being a knowledge consists in its being such a formation ; I say the truth, if what I say has its *ratio essendi* in preformed culture, and is a means to the further development of culture.

[1] It is useless to recall to mind, that the double point of view is a doubleness only of the point of view : the varying of reality is simply the unfolding of the subjects, each one as it best can among the rest ; the duplicity of the point of view corresponds to the distinction between concrete doing-thinking and that moment of it which is abstract thinking.

## 11.

OF A KNOWLEDGE WHICH IS AT THE SAME TIME THE BEING OF REALITY. INTRINSIC TRUTH AND HISTORICAL TRUTH

But when we reach Being, we are outside the field of secondary forms, variable on the part of reality and always somewhat artificial on the part of the subject; we are outside the field of knowledge of fact, of factual (and not seldom, fictitious) knowledge. Our knowledge, then, is no longer simply a means, by which we guide ourselves in the midst of reality; it is a knowing, which is at the same time a being one with reality—which is the being of reality.

And Being is the end at which we aim, only in a certain sense. It is such for reflection; but the reflective proceeding would not have been possible, if Being had not been always implicitly present in it from the outset. Outside Being nothing exists, not even the possibility of research—a possibility which is not however, as perhaps some imagine, the least of realities.

In Being, which is the unity of the manifold spontaneities and of their manifestations, reality and thought strictly coincide. Therefore, every thought, every attempt, not only to know, but to formulate an hypothesis, a doubt, even a negation, implies the idea of Being. Vice versa he who thinks Being, has knowledge, although he knows no particular being. He thinks, he knows, not an abstract unity, but the unity of things—that character of them, in which the reality of their being consists.

We distinguish in reality—

1. The mere form of unity, Being together with everything which is deduced from it: real form, as unity of multiplicity; and

2. Matter of fact, resulting from the unfolding of the single spontaneities, each of which unfolds itself under those conditions which are imposed on its unfolding by the unfolding of the rest.

By studying reality under the former aspect, we construct philosophy; by studying it under the latter, we construct science.

Science and philosophy are constructed by reason, which develops in constructing them. And in both we have to distinguish an intrinsic truth and an historical truth.

A doctrine (scientific or philosophic) is intrinsically true when it is the explication of that implicit element, of which it claims to be the explication; so, to produce an example of which we have already made use, the solution of a problem is intrinsically true, when under its explicit form it coincides with the solution implied by the enunciation of the problem.

A doctrine is historically true, when, and in so far as, it is valuable as a means for the further development of thought—and not only, when and in so far as it gives rise, as is always the case, to certain consequences. It is necessary that in the consequences thought should unfold itself more and more vigorously, make actual its own intrinsic potentiality, realise the life of which it is capable. Historical truth obviously implies intrinsic truth.

Historical truth is the same both for science and for philosophy. But as concerns intrinsic truth, there is an essential difference between the one study and the other.

The reality of fact studied by science is, although dominated by necessity, contingent; as such, it is infinitely varied, and indefinitely, unpredictably, variable. Each spontaneity, within the limits prescribed to it by its relations to the other spontaneities, is capricious; whence it follows, that an element of indetermination makes its way even in the relations between spontaneities (relations, on which the laws of variation depend).

Science therefore cannot be constructed strictly a priori; it cannot be exhausted, and is never definitive. It is founded essentially on experience; and its intrinsic truth is yet an historical truth; we mean that being intrinsically true consists, for science, in being a history of the reality of fact, which varies without end.[1]

But every varying, without excepting the varying of doctrines, implies the unity of Being, the necessity implicit in Being. Therefore, the intrinsic truth of philosophy cannot be resolved into historical truth.

No doubt, philosophy also develops in time; and any philosophical opinion, whether systematic or not, whether published in print or not, has an historical value, positive or negative: it helps or hinders the effort of man towards an ever clearer consciousness of himself. But these are considerations of relatively secondary importance.

Philosophy in substance is nothing but the doctrine of Being; everything else is a cumbrous accessory, which has to be removed, and which is being gradually removed. And a doctrine of Being is either true or not true; if it is true, and in so far as it is true, it is true definitively; its intrinsic truth cannot be resolved into historical truth: it is a condition of history, and therefore outside, and above, history.

The historical construction of philosophy consists in the successive explication of an implicit factor, in which there is no succession—which is always, necessarily, the same.

[1] "Nature," as Leopardi remarks not less profoundly than poetically, "proceeds by such a long way that she seems to stand still" (*La Ginestra*). Hence the illusion, which has lasted so long, but from which we are beginning to free ourselves, that science (of nature, or of reality of fact) may be or may become definitive.

## 12.

### EXISTENCE AS A SUBJECTIVE-OBJECTIVE UNITY.

We have said that reality and thought coincide in Being. They coincide even in the subject; for the existence of the subject is simply its thinking, or its thinking itself. Naturally, we must not confuse together thought with explicit thought. Even the thought of man is always, for the most part, implicit; even a small boy is, implicitly, convinced of this, when he says, not without reason, that he knows his lesson, although he does not think the whole of it explicitly. The existence of the subject consists in its being present to itself, although such a presence, in a non-developed subject, is sub-conscious; an element, the reality of which could be resolved into its appearing to another, would be no subject. In this sense, we can and must say that the essential constituent of the subject is self-consciousness.[1]

The subject, in order to know itself, that is to say in order to exist, must know itself as a Being, *i.e.* as a determination of Being, that is to say, as one in particular of many subjects which imply each other, connected in the unity of Being. The subject has consciousness of itself, only in so far as it is conscious of something else; it has consciousness of something else, only in so far as it is conscious of itself; the other and the self constitute a unity—the unity of Being.

Therefore, Being is not only the unity of the totality; it is also the unity of each subject—that, which makes a subject of every subject. A subject is such in so far as it implies the rest, or in so far as it implies Being.

We are led once more to recognise the perfect coincidence

---

[1] Perhaps, the term "self-subconsciousness," would not be out of place for undeveloped subjects. But it is not well to invent barbarous words, when there is no absolute need.

of the two doctrines which we have above distinguished by the respective names subjectivistic and realistic. The content is the same, numerically one and the same, for both; the difference is in the way in which the content is considered, it consists in expression more than in anything else.

The subjects, although they are many, or rather, because they are many, constitute a unity—the unity of Being. Each subject exists, and is all that it is, in so far as it is an element of unity, in so far as it is a determination of Being. Consequently, all that a subject may say, all that may be said of a subject, or of any number of subjects, of their manifestations and of the interference of their manifestations—all this has its ultimate foundation in the unity, or universality, or necessity of Being.[1] The realistic doctrine proves to be incontestable.

Vice versa, Being is a thought of the subject; it exists in so far as it is thought by the subject. And it is not one of the many thoughts which a subject may form or not, *ad libitum;* it is an essential thought, constitutive of the subject, without which the subject would not exist—a thought, therefore, which the subject finds in himself, as he finds his own self in himself. The subject recognises that the other subjects are implied by him, for he knows that the other subjects are determinations of the Being thought by him. The Being thought by the subject is therefore the whole of Being. In other words, the unity of reality is the subject, and nothing but the subject. But whence does the subject infer that the content does not belong as exclusively to him, as the consciousness of which it is the content does, if not precisely from such content, in so far as it is the content of his particular consciousness,

---

[1] That such a necessity does not exclude, but on the contrary implies, the spontaneities of the subjects, is a point, on which it is no use to insist any further.

in so far as it is constitutive of himself ? The necessity, therefore, which the subject recognises in things, has its root in the subject himself : it is the necessity of his own thought.[1] The subjectivistic doctrine also proves to be incontestable.

The coincidence of the two doctrines, the strict unity of the content proves to be no less incontestable. Universal Being is not outside the subject; it is a constituent of the subject. The unity of reality, the root of necessity, is therefore the subject; but not every subject on his own account, not the subject in that which belongs exclusively to him—in his spontaneous and conscious being—; the unity of reality is the subject in that which he has in common with others, it is the content of his particular consciousness. All are in each; and therefore the existence of each is a being in every other; the proposition that each is the unity of the whole, and the proposition that each is subject to the unity of the whole, while they seem to contradict each other, are simply two different ways of expressing the same thing.

---

[1] The possibility of error can be resolved into the possibility, inseparable from spontaneity, of forming thoughts which exclude each other; each of which is contained separately in the unity of the subject, but which cannot be included together in the unity of the subject, cannot be resolved into a thought. On this point, we think it needless to insist.

# CHAPTER VI

# UNITY AND MULTIPLICITY

## 1.

### DEFINITION OF THE THEME.

THE universe is a system.

By this formula, which we shall call the *fundamental formula*,[1] we assert that the universe is at once one and manifold. Or rather, that it would not be one, if it were not manifold; nor manifold, if it were not one.

When applied to the objects of common (vulgar or scientific) cognition, unity and multiplicity exclude each other : many things are not one thing ; one thing is not many things. By our formula, we maintain that, when applied to the universe, unity and multiplicity not only do not exclude each other, but condition and imply each other; so that the two characters, apparently irreconcilable, are inseparable and coessential.

[1] "Your" formula—it will be objected—is intuitive and well known ; it expresses a truth of common sense. There is no person of ordinary cultivation, who has no concept of a system and who is not convinced that the universe is a system. Certainly, (we answer,) our philosophy simply makes evident something which everyone thinks—something which must be thought, for not to think this "thing" would be to exclude every thought. Philosophy, we believe, has nothing else to do. But this, which it has to do, is not so easy, as some imagine. We all know in some way the supreme truth ; otherwise no one would be able to discover it. But the cognition, which we all have of it, (the vulgar, non-philosophic cognition,) is an involved cognition, which we have to make clear and explicit to ourselves if we wish to possess it firmly. He who thinks that simple common sense is sufficient to justify philosophical assertions or negations (no one can really dispense with such assertions or negations), wishes for the end without the means. To put common sense in the place of philosophy is to construct a philosophy in opposition to common sense.

## Unity and Multiplicity

All this is soon said, but not equally soon understood. He who is not satisfied by an empty formula, will ask us to determine with clearness and with precision the meaning of that which we have declared to be fundamental.

The meaning of the formula, we say, consists in its being the summary and condition of every other meaning.

That there are significant formulas no one will deny. But no formula remains significant, when it is considered altogether separately. The meaning of a proposition tacitly implies the meanings of the terms; and the meaning of every term implies the meanings of other terms, of other propositions.

Single intelligible assertions and negations imply each other—all of them, though not all in the same way. And they are intelligible in so far as they imply each other. They all imply one and the same condition. And the formula which we have called fundamental, has a meaning, a value, in so far as it makes that condition explicit. This is what we maintain, and what we intend to explain.

It is not enough to explain a formula (it will be objected); it is further necessary to show that the formula is true.

A particular proposition (one having a limited value) may be significant, and nevertheless not true. I say, for instance, this ring is of gold. I may be mistaken, although I know what I am saying. For, between the concept which I apply, and the being to which I apply it, there is a difference; the difference may be such, as to exclude the possibility of applying the first to the second.

But in a proposition which is really universal, meaning and truth coincide. For, the distinction between thought and being, true and significant with regard to everything else, is no longer significant or true with regard to the universal. If the distinction between thought and being is abolished, the distinction between meaning and truth also vanishes.

The meaning of the fundamental formula must consist in its being the condition of every meaning. The formula, granted that it has such a meaning, is also, for that same reason, indispensable, or absolutely true.

## 2.

### EXPLANATIONS.

A philosophic conception of the universe is, in so far as it is philosophic, of an extreme simplicity.

For philosophy is not concerned with particulars, which are infinite and infinitely variable; but it inquires into the one condition of the infinite particulars, the invariable condition of infinite varying. It does not make a collection of objective cognitions; but it wishes to understand the possibility of objective cognition. If there is a knowledge, if knowledge is not irremediably disconnected and chaotic, the indispensable presupposition, or condition of all knowledge, cannot be but one alone.

Hence also, the philosophic conception of the universe, that is to say, the philosophic essence of a conception of the universe, can be justified in one way only, a way which is intrinsically simple. For its justification, as we have just lately remarked, must coincide with the statement of it: the former, as well as the latter, must be one only and simple.

In the preceding pages our conception of the universe has been already stated and at the same time justified. From a strictly logical point of view, it would therefore be useless to add anything else. Indeed, each of the preceding chapters contains all that is essential, together with a good deal which is superfluous. So that, in what we are going to add, we cannot but repeat ourselves.

And, instead of writing over again, we ought to think of making a brief summary of what we have written so far.

*From a strictly logical point of view*, this is true. But to satisfy the requirements of logic only, is not enough, does not avail.

I say : this book is worth a crown. A small boy will think that the real measure of the worth is one of those pieces of silver, which are called crowns. He will understand better when he knows that the crown can be replaced by five shillings, or sixty pence, etc.

The logic of a doctrine can be resolved, in the mind of him who wishes to learn or understand the doctrine, into the law, or intrinsic order, of certain psychical processes. He who wishes to arrive at a form, and realise it in himself, must assimilate to himself the matter, of which it is the form.

And the task is not easy. He who writes, speaks about certain things. He who reads, understands as well as he can, according to his own special preparation, or his own want of preparation ; according to his own capacity, and according to his wish to study, to reflect ; according to his own preconceptions, which are not seldom altogether foreign to the argument, but not less efficacious for that reason ; and he takes it into his head, that the other has spoken to him of something entirely different.

The logical connection of thought, sufficient in geometry where no material misunderstanding is possible, for the things treated by geometry can be reduced to a few simple very common abstractions, is insufficient in philosophy, where one of the most serious difficulties, if not the chief difficulty altogether, consists in the facility of misunderstandings.

I must take care that my words be understood in the sense in which I use them. To this end, I must present the questions under various aspects; so that the reader may, if only he likes, become familiar with my way of expressing myself. The variety, of course, has nothing essential in itself, for the questions and solutions are those given, nor could they be different. In substance it is only the expression which is varied. The varying of expression makes it possible for the reader to overcome the personal element inseparable from expression.

### 3.

#### CONCEPT OF A SYSTEM.

We all know limited, particular systems. And it might seem that we arrive at the conception of the universe as a system, by extending to the whole universe a conception which was suggested to us by the observation of some parts of the universe. Let us see, whether by explaining that character by which we say that a definite portion of the universe constitutes a system, we shall succeed in understanding with clearness what "system" means, when it is predicated of the universe.

Each of those manifold bodies, which we call the planets and the sun, has an individuality of its own. What is the reason, why they are said to form together a system, not a simple accidental aggregate? The planets and the sun are, relatively, very close to each other, and very remote from every other body; their aggregate is spatially well circumscribed, it might however be a simple aggregate. The true reason, why the aggregate is recognised by us as a system, is that the planets and the sun gravitate all towards each other, and only towards each other. So it seems at first sight.

But, in the first place, it is not strictly true that the planets and the sun gravitate only towards each other.

The gravitational actions, while they are within the system such as they are supposed to be, will also take place between the bodies of the system and the stars. That such external actions are so slight as to escape our measurements, as not to influence the configuration of the system, we are ready to admit; but these external actions are not for that reason less real. Whence it follows, that the solar system does not subsist by itself; that it has relations to something else, which we can neglect up to a certain point, but which are essential to it; that it can be conceived only as a portion of a vaster system.

Further, two bodies which gravitate towards each other, are, although visibly distant and although foreign to each other with regard to other characters, inseparably connected with each other as concerns gravitation. Each of them occupies dynamically the same space as the other, so that the two might be said to be one body; and nevertheless, in that same space, each constitutes a distinct dynamical centre. The two bodies are, as concerns their gravitations, inseparable and separate; each implies the other in so far as it is opposed to the other, and is opposed to the other in so far as it implies the other. They are neither two, nor one, and they are at the same time both one and two; briefly, their mutual gravitation has the system as its condition. The concept which we hoped to illustrate by means of a familiar example is presupposed by the very example by means of which we hoped to make it clear.

And each of those particular wholes which are commonly considered as systems, gives rise to the same difficulties. A bundle of sticks may be called in some way a system. What is it, which makes it a system? Obviously, the withe by which the sticks are bound together. But the withe would not connect the sticks together, would not make a system of them, unless its parts were joined to each other with some firmness; or, in other words, unless the withe were itself already a system.

Therefore, a particular system always leads us back to another, then to another, etc. In conclusion, it is impossible to understand a particular system without considering it as a part of the universe, and without considering the universe as a system.

### 4.

#### SYSTEM OF COGNITIONS.

The problem of understanding the universe, that is to say of understanding how the universe constitutes a system, how unity and multiplicity are associated in it and imply each other in it, may seem to surpass the powers of the human intellect.

To begin with, we have (each man has) certain cognitions. And nothing prevents us from attempting to reduce our cognitions—considered simply as cognitions which we possess—to a system.

I am speaking of "cognitions," that is to say, of opinions which have a value, of true opinions, not of erroneous or problematic opinions. In what way we succeed in distinguishing the opinions which certainly have a value, from those of which it is not certain whether they have it or not, and from those which have no value, is a question which it would be useless to discuss. There are certain sciences, however incomplete; therefore the distinction of which we were speaking, is made, in whatever manner it may have been made. And it existed long before the construction of the single sciences: the man, who was in a state of total ignorance, would not be able to construct a science, could not subject his own opinions to a skepsis; indeed, he would have no opinions at all.

Only after constructing the system of cognitions, shall

we know *what* precisely is the value of those cognitions of which we know that they have *a* value. But before constructing it, or even before ascertaining the possibility of constructing it, we know that this and that and the other opinion have each a value, are cognitions, are positively certain. What is merely a positive certainty, is yet no philosophy; but in so far as it is positively certain, it is independent of the explicit cognition of philosophy.

The cognitions which we possess, whatever their contents may be, are all cognitions which we have concerning some portions or elements of the universe. And the universe of which we are speaking, is that concerning parts or elements of which we have certain cognitions.[1]

If, therefore, we succeed in reducing our cognitions to a system, the system so constructed will be the cognition of that system which is the universe. (The object is inseparable from the subject; reality and cognition are fundamentally identical.)

Cognitions, to form a system, must be joined all together by means of explicitly known relations. They must be joined all together, that is to say, it is necessary that each of them, directly or indirectly, should become related to every other.

Let us imagine two propositions, that is as much as to say, two opinions, inconsistent with each other. They will not both be true; that is to say, both will not be cognitions. Inconsistency is a relation which can exist between two propositions, or between two opinions, but not between two cognitions; and which therefore we must set aside.

Between two cognitions of mine there is always a relation, in so far as both belong to me. Two propositions, however,

[1] Can one who speaks of a reality, which he calls unknowable, know what he is saying? If so, the reality of which he is speaking, is known to him in as much as he speaks of it; his discourse cannot refer in any way either to the unknowable, or to the unknown.

of which I recognise the inconsistency, belong also to me. That relation between two cognitions, which is constituted by their being included in one and the same unity of consciousness, does not seem therefore sufficient to join them in the unity of a system.

In an attempt to investigate whether all our cognitions (note that I say "all") can be joined together into a system, it is not requisite that those cognitions should be all taken into consideration, one by one. In fact, we already know, before the attempt is made, many relations between cognitions; indeed it is known that many of these relations are essential constituents of the cognitions between which they are established. I know something of geometry, and something of Greek grammar. My cognitions of geometry constitute, and they would not exist unless they constituted, a system, though partial and limited; so also do my cognitions of Greek grammar. It would be useless, or worse, to propose to build up again these or other partial systems, which are already built. But what relation is there between geometry and Greek grammar? Here is a problem not yet solved.

It is however in any case a particular problem, of which we shall naturally not treat: we have produced an example only for the purpose of briefly pointing out, that our object must be that of making manifest those relations which are not yet known explicitly. Among these, we shall treat those alone which have a character of universality.

The attempt, in order to be conclusive (in order that from its success or failure one may infer the possibility or impossibility of systematising cognitions), must not be limited to elaborating afresh explicit cognitions, but must go so far as to make their implications evident.

We have cognitions already arranged into partial systems. Not one of these partial systems is altogether without relations to others; the supposition that partial systems can be reduced to the unity of one single system is not without foundation. But at present it is a simple supposition. It is not clear in what way all the partial systems are interconnected; indeed, it is not fully certain whether they are so connected. In order that they may be connected, it is necessary that each one should imply, besides the explicit relations through which we know it as a partial system, further relations which are implicit also in every other.

The possibility or impossibility of solving the problem which we have proposed to ourselves depends on the existence or non-existence of universal relations.[1] We must therefore pause a little to consider the relations with which we are acquainted.

5.

RELATIONS—CAUSAL AND RATIONAL; DISTINCTION.

Relations are distinguished as causal and rational. So, in the conscious life of the subject we distinguish practical doing and theoretical thinking. And in external reality we distinguish matter of fact and logical form. To be sure, it is not possible to separate causality and ration-

[1] A really universal relation joins at the same time all cognitions together, and all (known and knowable) things together, and the things with the cognitions. It is, at the same time, an indispensable constituent both of thought and reality. We have to remember a former remark: in the field of the universal, reality and thought, between which it is possible and necessary to distinguish with regard to other fields, are no longer distinguishable. Supposing that those facts (we are speaking of real facts), the laws of which are summed up in Greek grammar, and those facts, the laws of which are summed up in geometry, had no mutual relations, there would also be no mutual relations between those cognitions, which we call Greek grammar and geometry respectively. Vice versa, if all relation between the one and the other of those two systems of cognitions had to be excluded, it would be necessary to infer that there are no relations between the facts of the two corresponding orders. To build up again the system of the universe (to understand the universe as a system) and to build up the system of our cognitions are two different expressions for one and the same thing.

ality, as if they were two independent realities; nevertheless it is possible to distinguish them; indeed, it is impossible not to distinguish them.

Let us consider in particular one of the processes of which subjective life is the result. It is called a thinking, or a doing, according to the prevalence in it of rational relations, or of causal relations; or, to speak more properly, according as it has the object of making certain rational relations evident, or of realising certain causal relations. (Thus, we may also say—according as the attention which is directed to the process in order to characterise it and estimate it considers its logical, or its causal connections.)

For instance, Peter solves a problem in geometry; Paul climbs a mountain. Each develops a particular process very distinct from that of the other. And, no doubt, each of the two processes is intrinsically connected by rational relations and by causal relations. But the end, to which the first is directed, is only logical; the end, to which the second is directed, is only practical.

Peter cannot solve his problem without a practical doing—without accomplishing actions, which will be the real causes of real effects. But the practical or causal factors might vary infinitely, while the logical connection of the process remains the same (I mean, the fundamental or essential relation, between the enunciation and the solution); therefore, although they have a great importance for Peter in so far as he is seeking a solution, they become altogether irrelevant to any one who wishes simply to know the solution. The process is capable of giving a solution only by means of its logical connections; these could not stand by themselves alone, but they are the only ones of importance; and the process is considered (obviously, to consider it so is to abstract) as a process of pure thought.

Paul, in order to accomplish his intended ascent, must

act in conformity with certain (physical, physiological) laws. For he is indeed free to accomplish certain movements or certain others; but the further practical consequences of an accomplished movement are then necessarily determined by the laws of equilibration and motion. We must remember that a law, in so far as it is necessary, in so far as it determines the course of events, is always a logical law. In the process of ascent we have therefore to recognise that logic fulfils an indispensable function. But, on the other hand, it is clear that the explicit cognition of those laws, to which in any case Paul's activity must adapt itself, is not essential at all; that the place of cognition can be taken by habit, the foundations of which are altogether subconscious; and that, if habit fails, even the most exact cognition is of no use. Therefore the process of climbing is considered (although it is true that to consider it so is again an abstraction) as a merely practical process.

The same is to be said of so-called external reality. In it causal and rational relations imply and condition each other: the ball presses on the cushion because it is placed upon the cushion; the book, which was before on the shelf, is now on the writing-desk because I have changed its place.

Nevertheless (or rather, just on account of this) the distinction between the two classes of relations is manifestly evident. Geometry (I am not speaking of the process, by which a subject learns or constructs geometry,) knows nothing of causal relations. And therefore it is outside time: in geometry, we often speak of the movement of a figure; but to say that a figure moves thus or thus, is the same as to say that in space there are all those figures, each of which is improperly denoted as a position assumed by the single moving figure. On the contrary, a physics in which abstraction were to be made from causal relations, is absolutely impossible.

Paul is born after Peter, Peter after John; therefore Paul is born after John. The argument is rationally connected; its meaning and its value are outside time, although its object consists of temporal relations.

### 6.

#### INDISPENSABLENESS OF CAUSAL RELATIONS; IMPOSSIBILITY OF REDUCING CAUSALITY TO EXTRA-TEMPORAL NECESSITY.

If facts, connected by causal relations (relations other than purely logical), did not happen, even our own thought would not exist. We have seen (just lately, and on other occasions) that our thinking can be resolved into a multiplicity of facts, connected with each other by causal as well as by logical relations. That which makes this doing of ours into a thinking, that which enables us to consider subjective thinking as our cognition of a thought independent of us, is the possibility of abstracting from it (of considering apart) the purely rational relations, of making the law of it thoroughly explicit; thought is this law, or form, if we prefer to call it so; form, in so far as we know it and in consequence of the way in which we know it, cannot subsist without some kind of matter (we do not say, without this or that matter in particular).

But let us grant what absolutely cannot be granted: let us suppose that it were possible to think independently of every fact and of every causal connection.[1]

Well, if the hypothesis mentioned were true, we should

---

[1] It is obvious that causal connection implies some kind of fact. It is not less true that fact implies causal connection. We do not mean that every fact must be merely an effect. But elements, which were joined only by rational relations, ought to be invariable, for pure rational relations are outside time, independent of time. A fact which is not absolutely outside all relation implies of necessity other than rational relations, that is to say, causal relations; how it implies them is another question, on which we have not to enter at present.

have no concept of reality. We should distinguish neither subjectively between our practical doing and our theoretical thinking; nor objectively between the thing and our cognition of the thing, between a datum of fact and the rational order to which the datum belongs. We should not distinguish ourselves from the universe, that is to say, we should not be self-conscious,—*i.e.* we should not exist. There would therefore also be no thinking (which we distinguish from thought, that is to say, from the thing thought); there would be nothing but thought—a purely logical thought. It would be something like geometry in itself; that is to say, not like the cognition of geometry (for cognition implies the subject and his doing), but like that geometry which we are discovering painfully little by little, of which nobody ever knows more than a very small portion—a geometry without anybody who knows it, a finished geometry (complete, entirely constructed), without possibility of development.

It is useless to inquire subtly, whether these consequences of the hypothesis mentioned are admissible, and whether they have a meaning. We make certain distinctions, which we could not make if we were reduced only to logical relations; therefore, not everything is logical relation. And not only do we make these distinctions: we make them necessarily. That pure thought shut up in itself, which does not even require the process of thinking, is at bottom nothing but the abstraction of the rationality essential to actual thinking—it is a result at which we arrive by our actual thinking, and we could not speak of it, if it were not such a result; it implies those very distinctions which it seems to exclude; in fact, to have any concept and to distinguish it from ourselves, who have that concept, are one and the same thing.

We are thus obliged to admit causal relations, that is to say relations other than logical, implying elements other than concepts (elements of pure thought), viz. elements of fact. The distinction between what is logical or rational, and what is a-logical or causal, has meaning in so far as it is implied by every other and is essential to every other.

## 7.

### CAUSALITY AND SUCCESSION.

—I hear the sound of a trumpet, and then I see the sun rising ; I immerse a thermometer in warm water, and then I see the quicksilver rising in the thermometric tube. I exclude in the first case, I assert in the second, a causal relation between the antecedent and the consequent. However, observation in both cases shows to me nothing but the succession of two facts. Certainly I can multiply my observations; and then I shall recognise that the succession, constant in the second case, is not constant in the first. But a relation remains the same, whatever the number of times that it has been remarked ; each of the shillings of which a milliard is composed, is a shilling, neither more nor less than this single one. The number of observations, agreeing or disagreeing, may indeed give rise in me to the formation of various expectations. And that such various expectations have in fact a practical importance, is not to be denied. But it remains to know on what such practical importance is founded. Further, the relation between two facts remains the same, whether I have formed a practically useful expectation concerning it or not. There is no assignable standard by means of which it would be possible to distinguish causal relations from other relations.—

The argument quoted above has only one defect: it touches the question, instead of penetrating into it. It is usual to say that certain facts are, and certain others are not, causally connected together. The argument quoted shows

## Unity and Multiplicity 149

evidently that such a distinction lacks a strict justification, and even a precise meaning. The complex H of the relations between two facts A and B, and the complex K of the relations between two facts C and D, however different they may be, can never be said with reason to be specifically different, so that, for instance, K would imply causality and H would exclude it. If we could make certain that some facts are not causally connected, we could not maintain that other facts are causally connected; vice versa, granting that two facts (even two only) appear to be certainly connected causally with each other, it will be necessary to say that all facts are causally connected with each other, although not all in the same way. Such is the incontestable logical consequence of the reasoning quoted. Whence, however, it is not to be concluded that the complex of relations between facts, and the complex of relations between non-factual elements (for instance, between concepts; in general, between formal elements), are not specifically different from each other.

We assert that causality is absolutely beyond question. We assert, that is, that certain relations (called causal) are specifically distinguished from certain others (called non-causal) and are distinguished from them, in so far as the former possess certain characters (temporality, intrinsic variability) which do not belong to the latter; between formal (non-factual) elements there subsist only relations of the second kind; the first kind of relations, on the other hand, can only arise between material (factual) elements. And the specific difference between the former and the latter is therefore of the same order as the difference between matter and form. The distinction which we make has nothing to do with the common, purely empirical or habitual distinction, between facts which are believed, and facts which are not believed, to be causally connected with each other: therefore, a criti-

cism which exposes the philosophic worthlessness of the
common distinction, leaves the value of our own intact.[1]

8.

RELATIONS AND THEIR TERMS; ACCIDENTAL AND
NECESSARY RELATIONS.

Every relation implies certain terms, that is to say
elements, whatever they may be, other than the relation
considered, and having that relation to each other. In
fact, if something existed or were thought independently
of any other element, it would exist or would be thought
as an absolute, not as a relation. The terms of a relation
are at least two.[2]

---

[1] We have stated (briefly, but exactly) and discussed Hume's criticism of
the concept of cause. Hume is not wrong from his own point of view; but
his point of view is not sufficiently high. The doctrine which we oppose to
it (already formulated in the *Great Problems*, and also above in the present
volume), is in substance that which we all imply continually; we have
done nothing but try, perhaps not altogether in vain, to make it explicit.
Detached phrases, or even fragments of doctrine, which are indications of a
more or less vague intuition of the same doctrine, and from which, if they
were integrated and developed logically, it would be possible to infer the true
doctrine, are not wanting. For instance, A. COURNOT (*Ench. d. idées fondamentales*, etc., Paris, 1911; reprint of a much older publication) admits an
"intervalle qui sépare . . . la théorie géométrique de la combinaison des
mouvements d'avec la théorie de la combinaison des forces" (p. 103); he remarks that "sans le sentiment de l'effort exercé nous n'aurions jamais l'idée
de corps" (p. 193); with regard to the concept of force, and to Hume's
criticism of the concept of cause, he notes that "les catégories fondamentales
s'enchaînent, sans pourtant s'identifier" (p. 101), and that "à mesure que l'on
s'élève aux étages supérieurs du système de nos connaissances" (not only so, but
also, as we should say, as we go gradually deeper), "l'importance de l'élément
historique grandit" (p. 87). And history means a succession of facts, which
is not a merely rational system: a conception, on which the writer insists.
This is not all, nor even much; but it is something.

[2] A few words on the identity of an element with itself. (Identity and
equality are not to be confused; for the latter implies always a couple of elements, distinguishable on account of some characters, while in identity the element must be numerically one alone. It is impossible to reduce identity to
equality; on the contrary, equality cannot be conceived without identity.)
In A=A, the A's are two. They are two as signs, and we are speaking of
meanings. This is true; but it is also true that we always think by means
of signs. Just so: identity implies the signs, and its object is that of pre-
venting the multiplicity of signs from concealing the unity of meaning.
As we have two A's, each of which has a meaning, the meanings (or objects)
will seem two; they will be estimated as two, unless we expressly assert their

## Unity and Multiplicity 151

The terms of a relation may be again relations. For instance, a distance of four miles is the half of a distance of eight miles. Here a relation between two distances is formulated; now a distance is a relation.

But it seems impossible to admit that in every relation the terms can be resolved into relations. Since every relation implies certain terms, it is manifest, that if the terms of every relation were again relations, the explicit formula of every relation would imply a process to infinity. This apparently must be excluded a priori: the impos-

unity by writing $A = A$. An element, numerically one, in order that it may be said to be always identical with itself, must be invariable. Well, if the single invariable A were also the single invariable object of thinking, we should not think of the alleged identity of A with itself. (Note how in this argument, in which we try to dispense with signs, we are in reality making continual use of signs.) Nor can we say that, by thinking, we make explicit something which in the thought of A was before only implicit; in fact, by $A = A$ we simply assert the uniqueness and invariability of A (as object, as meaning)—characters which, according to our hypothesis, we already knew before. I think one single and invariable element. (Or, if we prefer it, I think it as single and invariable; here it matters little, whether those characters belong to the element in itself, or are ascribed to it by the thought which considers it.) But my thinking this single invariable element breaks up necessarily into a variable multiplicity of cogitative acts. To think, either means nothing, or means to accomplish a process. The content of thought is always, at least in part, variable. Let us suppose that I think A constantly; in any case the A, which I think constantly, is thought by me now together with B, now with C, etc.; this is a thinking or considering A several times. The multiplicity of the acts, by which A is thought, cannot be excluded even in the case that to think A were an indispensable condition of thinking, and that therefore A were thought always necessarily; a fortiori it cannot be excluded in any other case. I consider A a first time, then a second time; and I have present to my mind both considerations. (I have them present to my mind, either both as remembered, or one as remembered and the other as actual, or both as actual; if both are actual, it will be necessary that the two should be distinguished on account of some other character. It is useless to stop and notice how all this necessarily implies the use of certain signs.) In the reality of the cogitative process, the act and the object of consideration obviously constitute one unity. As I have made two considerations about A, which are both present to my mind, I have in my thought two of these unities. By comparing them together, I remark in them this fundamental character: although the acts are two, different from each other, the object is numerically one alone. And I express this uniqueness of the object by the formula $A = A$. It seems to me that I have shown clearly, even too clearly, that identity expresses the permanence of a content in a thought which varies, the uniqueness of meaning in many signs, which might even have different meanings. Identity necessarily implies the variable multiplicity of thought; it cannot be called a relation of the single permanent A to itself.

sibility of making any relation entirely explicit would imply the impossibility of thinking with clearness in any case. The same result may be obtained a posteriori; and the example just adduced may suffice. We have a relation between distances, which are relations—but relations between points, and points are not relations.

It seems therefore that relations imply, in the end, certain elements, whatever they may be, and which in any case cannot be reduced to relations.

Relations are either accidental or necessary. For instance, the inkstand is on the manuscript; this is an accidental relation. The square A, in which the side is equal to the diagonal of the square B, has an area twice as large as the area of B: this is a necessary relation. If a relation is necessary, its terms are reciprocally coessential, they imply each other. In other words, those ultimate elements (not reducible to relations) which are presupposed by the relation considered, are such that none can exist unless all the others exist. For instance, in a polygon the relation existing between the number of sides and the number of diagonals is necessary. Therefore it is impossible to vary one of the two numbers without varying the other. Also adding 1 to the number of sides of a quadrilateral, the number of diagonals increases by 3. The reciprocal implication of elements which are bound together by a necessary relation, is manifest.

But not every one of the elements which imply each other, has its own separate, independent existence. Although they are many, or rather because they are many, they constitute together one single element, one only thing.

This conclusion gives rise to difficulties, which we shall remove by degrees. For the present let us be contented with a very simple remark. "Thing" is a word, which may be understood in different meanings; and the chaos,

## Unity and Multiplicity

which arises from confusing these meanings together, constitutes no objection to any doctrine.

On a sheet of paper is marked in pencil a pentagon, with its five diagonals. I erase one side of the pentagon: the other sides and the diagonals remain. This means, that the particles of pencil adherent to the sheet and forming the marked lines do not imply each other. They do not constitute one single thing, but several distinct things, at least with regard to the spatial disposition, of which we are speaking. What we have called one single thing, is the polygon as geometrical figure.

Let us suppose five points in the same plane, of which not more than two are on the same straight line. These five points determine ten straight lines, five of which delimit a portion of the plane, and are the sides of the pentagon; the other five are the diagonals. If of the five points we leave out one, the sides are reduced to four, and the diagonals to two. The straight lines which join certain points, do not therefore exist (as geometrical straight lines, though they can exist as marked, corporeal straight lines) independently of each other. Each one is distinguished from every other; so that each of them may be said to be one thing. But, on the other hand, it cannot be denied that not one of these various things is separable from the others; each is a thing, in so far as the complex of them again constitutes ONE thing, just as much one as each of those of which it is the result.

The elements of a polygon (without excluding the vertices, for each straight line passing through a point is not less essential to that point, than the points through which a straight line passes are essential to it) exist only as constituents of that unity which is the polgyon. (Analogously, the polygon exists only as a constituent of that unity which is the plane, etc. It is not necessary for the present to go deeper into the question.)

## 9.

**UNITY AND MULTIPLICITY AS RECONCILED BY THE NECESSITY OF RELATIONS. DIFFICULTIES WHICH ARISE FROM ACCIDENTAL RELATIONS.**

It is now clear that the necessity of relations completely solves the problem of reconciling unity and multiplicity—of making us understand how unity and multiplicity imply each other, so that the one is impossible without the other, exists only in the other. Since relations exist, their terms also exist; and there are many (at least two). On the other hand, each term is essential to every other; each exists, but only together with the other; the complex of them is no aggregate, but a true unity. We find before us several things which constitute a single thing, and none of which would exist, if all did not together constitute this single thing; while the latter would not exist, and therefore would not be one, if it did not result from those many.

The unity of multiplicity, the unity in multiplicity, which seemed an incoherent jumble of words, appears to be a concept as clear and exact as could be desired; for it is impossible to surpass the evidence of rational necessity. It is also manifest that this concept—the concept of a system—is fundamental with regard to every other: with the suppression of the unity which is disclosed to us in rational necessity, which is constituted and implied by it, all coherence and therefore all clearness of thought would vanish—the possibility of thought would vanish.

But the problem is solved only with regard to elements connected solely by necessary relations; in other words, it is solved only with regard to abstractions. And we must solve it with regard to reality.

The relations with which we are acquainted in the field of actual life, or experience, or doing-thinking (that think-

## Unity and Multiplicity

ing which is at the same time a doing), or briefly of reality, are not all exclusively necessary. There are also accidental relations. We have to take into account, not only rationality, but also causality.

Necessity and accidentality, rationality and causality, are mutually irreducible concepts. Now, there are no cognitions concerning reality, in which these concepts are not to be found associated with and implying each other. Mutual irreducibility, and mutual implication, seem to exclude each other. If they really excluded each other, the hope of conceiving the universe as a system, of understanding anything, would be vain. But it is not yet clear how they are associated and mutually imply each other. Let us inquire.

And, in the first place, let us notice that causality and accidentality imply each other necessarily.

A book is now on the shelf, now on the writing-desk; it is not at all essential to it to be in one place rather than in the other. We have here a manifest accidentality, which, no doubt, can be referred to causality: the book may be indifferently in various places, for I can transfer it from one place to another. Vice versa, to say that the book is transferable from one place to another, is to say that none of the places whither it can be transferred, is essential to it.

Such reflections are fundamental as well as simple. No one, however prejudiced in favour of a contrary doctrine, can consider the fact as other than accidental; there is no one, who fails to distinguish between that which is as a fact, and that which is necessarily—who does not refer the datum of fact to certain causes, while he refers to certain reasons, known or unknown, that which not only is, or is in a certain way, but which could not but be, or could not be differently.

To suppress accidentality and causality means to declare

illusive, not a doctrine, but that first subconscious and spontaneous organisation of experience, which serves as foundation to every doctrine.

### 10.

#### OF PHYSICAL DETERMINISM.  IMPOSSIBILITY OF EXCLUDING A CERTAIN INDETERMINISM.

So-called physical determinism proves nothing to the contrary. An astronomer calculates an eclipse at an immense distance of time ; and observation agrees with the results of calculation. The movement of the heavenly bodies is therefore much less capricious than the flight of swallows ; and yet, it might be partially indeterminate ; indeed, a certain indetermination might be essential to it.

A crowd squeezes itself slowly through a long and narrow corridor. Each member of the crowd wishes to go forward ; he goes forward as best he can. The numbers who are pressing on him, deprive him of almost all freedom of movement, and oblige him to make certain movements which he would not make on his own account. In the movement of each person we have to distinguish two factors : the motor activity belonging in particular to that single person, and the resultant of the motor activities of the other members of the crowd.

The movement of the crowd therefore is at once indeterminate (accidental) under one aspect, and determinate under another. It is indeterminate, in so far as it is to be referred to the motor activities of its single members. It is determinate, in so far as the respective activities of the single members, who are in contact with each other in a relatively small space, are mutually conditioned and limited ; the determination depends entirely on the circumstances, in which each activity, intrinsically indeterminate, can manifest itself.

The indetermination of movement, for each member as well as for the whole crowd, is reduced to a minimum by the circumstances, by the fact that each member is in the crowd. So that the crowd moves on, all together, almost as a viscid liquid. Its movement, to anybody who observes it at a sufficient distance, will appear as rigorously determined, as any purely physical fact. And yet it will not be denied that such a movement implies elements of indetermination; it will not be denied that the elements of indetermination are essential to the movement; for, if every man were converted into a statue, the crowd would stop.

In physics exactness of measurements is never absolute. The agreement between the results of calculation and the data of observation, however great it may be, is never (unless perhaps accidentally on rare occasions) a punctual coincidence; hence it is not permissible to infer from it, in any case, that among the facts there are none which are indeterminate. The determinism which is proved by physics, and without which physics would not exist, is an approximate determinism; to infer absolute determinism from it is a fallacy.

Such an inference would leave the field of physics for the construction of a fantastical metaphysics. Let us suppose a law recognised to be valid now in our whole sidereal system. Are we certain that it has been and will be always valid, notwithstanding any past or future transformation of the system—that it is valid now in any other sidereal system, however different from our own? Evidently not. Physics is an inductive science, founded on experience. And experience is limited in time and in space, and is conditioned. Whence it follows, that concerning the prerequisites of variation, or its essential conditions, physics says nothing and can say nothing.

Is every fact (and every element of each fact) determined ? Yes, or no. A physicist, who neither wishes to go wrong, nor to leave his own field, can see in the two heads of this alternative simply two hypotheses, both foreign to his branch of learning, and between which consequently he neither is able nor has any reason to choose.

But physics is one thing, and epistemology another. Epistemology shows that every fact implies, and necessarily implies, an indeterminate element, by showing that this is a condition *sine qua non*, in order that facts may happen—in order that variation may be possible.[1] Physics which considers facts as given,[2] and does not inquire into their possibility, has nothing to say against a conclusion which, moreover, is not opposed to and does not concern it.

## 11.

### CONNECTION BETWEEN DETERMINISM AND INDETERMINISM.

The course of events [*l' accadere*], while it is certainly not wholly determinate, cannot be wholly indeterminate either.

Facts which would be inconsistent with rational necessity do not occur, and are not possible. For instance, a fact is impossible, the occurrence of which would be the abolition of a fact which had already occurred—would make it false that this fact had occurred.

Obviously, here there is no mystery. A stone has fallen; to suppose that, in consequence of any other fact, it may not be true that the stone has fallen, is nonsense. But, not less obviously, the impossibility that facts should be inconsistent with rational necessity, constitutes a character

---

[1] Compare the preceding chapter, *Reality*, § XI.
[2] We shall not take into account that it considers only extended facts, whereas facts are not all extended.

## Unity and Multiplicity 159

of the universe which we cannot disregard, if we wish to form a valid conception of the universe.

We have seen, that rational necessity implies the unity of the elements which are joined by it. Certainly, the elements are many; for, unless there were more than one element, neither would there be interconnected elements. But the elements are essential all to each and each to all, so that none is separable from the others—none exists outside the system of all. What we were just now remarking with regard to a rational necessity, to which it is impossible that any fact should be contrary, proves that unity does not belong only to the rational forms which we can abstract from the universe, but belongs to the universe as a tissue of facts, to the real universe—it involves, not only the form, but also the matter.

Temporality, which is essential to the course of events, implies a necessity; for instance, two beginnings are either contemporaneous or successive. The necessity implied by temporality is not purely rational; for, pure rationality not only does not imply, but excludes, temporality. Nevertheless, it is rational necessity; for, a non-rational necessity is simply a word without meaning. It is therefore a rationality implied by matter of fact, not by mere form.

The same is to be said of spatial necessity. (What we shall say about space, may also serve to throw further light upon what has been said about time.) The laws of geometry are applicable only to spatial facts. Supposing for a moment that spatial facts did not happen, there would be no space, and there would be no geometry; geometrical necessity would have vanished. That geometrical necessity is rational, cannot be doubted; but it is not purely rational. It is a rational necessity which requires as its condition not any and every kind of matter (as is the case with the necessity implied by temporal succession), but a certain definite matter.

From all this it follows, that the course of events is subject both to pure rational necessity (logical necessity, or necessity of pure form) and to a mixed rational necessity which concerns the course of events as such, matter as matter. In so far as it is in such manner subject to necessity, and in particular to the second kind of necessity, the course of events cannot be resolved into a disconnected series of facts: it is necessarily connected in itself. In other words, facts have first of all logical (formal) consequences,[1] and are, moreover, necessarily connected with each other as facts; that is to say, they determine each other causally.

The merely logical, the temporal, the spatial relations, which we have just now mentioned, do not wholly determine facts. And, indeed, no science of facts can be constructed by taking into account those relations only. They mark certain limits, which no fact, in any case, can surpass; but, within those limits, they leave the fact in complete indetermination. (For instance, a body having an external form contrary to the laws of geometry is impossible; yet the possible forms of a body remain infinite.) Those relations are, though not all in the same way, abstract; they are true of certain concepts, which are essential to facts or to certain classes of facts, but they have nothing to do with the fact in that which constitutes it as a real, material, concrete fact.

In a fact, in every fact, there cannot but be an element *ex-lege*, absolutely *a*-logical (not *il*-logical); for in case there were not, (and by now we have repeated it too often,) there would be no course of events; reality would be resolved into abstract thought. But facts, though each of them

---

[1] On the logical (purely logical) consequences of facts, we have said something which to us seems sufficient, in the *Great Problems*.

## Unity and Multiplicity

includes an indeterminate element, cannot be connected only by the relations which we have mentioned; for, in that case, they would not even be connected by these relations. Let us give the proof of this.

Let us consider the facts A, B, C, . . . and let us suppose each of them to be wholly indeterminate, and therefore independent of the others. This means that, for instance, the fact A might either happen as it has done, or happen in some very different way, or even not happen at all, and that it would be indifferent relatively to each of the facts B, C, . . . which of these three hypotheses had been realised. (And we may note that the second of the three includes an infinity of cases.) Such a congeries cannot be subject to any kind of laws. Obviously, a congeries, to which no kind of laws were applicable, would not even be a congeries : it cannot exist. The consequence obtained is absurd ; but it is regularly drawn from the hypothesis that absolutely indeterminate facts are possible : this hypothesis is therefore absurd, as we wished to show.

Facts, precisely because they are subject to rational laws which, within certain very large limits, leave them indeterminate, must, while they remain on the one hand singly indeterminate, mutually determine each other on the other. The partial (note that I say only partial) mutual determination of facts constitutes their causal connection.

### 12.

#### OUR INTERPRETATION OF THE COURSE OF EVENTS.

Many facts happen. There is, in every fact, something essentially indeterminate, and something necessarily determinate. Rational relations and casual relations arise between facts. Such is, briefly, the result of the inquiry made in the present chapter—a result, which can be called neither new nor singular: everybody knows these things. But in these things which everybody knows, we can and must recognise, now, the ultimate foundations of all cognitions: such is our novelty (a very relative novelty, we are ready to admit, and that with pleasure). In order to construct the system of cognitions, we shall have only to reduce to a system the few, simple, most obvious fundamental cognitions.

To this end we shall assume: (1) that there are certain primitive (original) unities; (2) that everything which belongs, for any reason, to reality, belongs in all cases to some of the primitive unities, or to each of them; (3) that each primitive unity is a principle of spontaneity, or of indeterminate variation; (4) that each primitive unity is essential to each of the others, *i.e.* that primitive unities, though irreducible to each other, are elements of one and the same reality—are (we may say) solidary.[1] (Obviously, the concept of primitive unity, and that of solidarity of primitive unities, require further more precise determination; but it is already possible to draw some consequences from them.)

Since primitive unities have solidarity, to any variation in one of them there will necessarily correspond a variation

[1] We are stating our doctrine in its main lines, and showing that this doctrine is true, that is to say, that it is the only one admitting the required systematisation. Such a proceeding (analogous to that which in geometry is called synthetical—to that of Euclid who first enunciates and then demonstrates the theorem) is not without inconveniences. To a reader, the doctrine at first makes the impression of being an hypothesis; and the impression once received, is never wholly eradicated. A constructive method (analogous to that which in geometry is called analytic) would have been more suitable: by making clear the assumptions and consequences of common cognitions, it would have been possible to lead the reader step by step to discover by himself the way of systematising common cognitions, to construct the doctrine by himself piecemeal The reader who has followed us will recognise that we have made use of this method all along; indeed that in general we have made use of it chiefly. But to make use of this method alone would take us too long. The suspicion that we are trying to prove a fantastically constructed doctrine by means of captious arguments, will not even cross the

in every other. This can be expressed by saying that the spontaneous varying of a primitive unity is the cause of that effect, which is the corresponding determinate variation of each other primitive unity. The causal necessity just mentioned is a rational necessity, for its foundation is the solidarity of primitive unities, the fact that they are elements of one and the same reality. It is called causal, to distinguish it from pure rational necessity, in so far as it has as its essential condition the spontaneous varying of primitive unities. A spontaneous variation is a variation which not only is no effect of another variation, but cannot even be deduced in a purely rational way from anything else.

Every primitive unity is a unity; and therefore all the elements constituting it, and for the present all its variations, will be solidary. That is to say, rationally necessary relations will arise between the variations, and in general between the elements of every primitive unity,—relations which, in so far as the elements are variations, acquire (for the reason just mentioned) the character of causal relations. Hence, not only do the spontaneities of different unities interfere with each other; but also the variations, spontaneous as well as determinate, of each unity interfere with each other. Whence it follows, that no fact occurs in which there are not at once, as reciprocally

---

mind of a sincere reader. On the other hand, the proceeding to which we now adhere, has also its own advantage, and a remarkable one: it allows us to form clearly and exactly that general concept, without which my doctrine cannot be grasped, even if fragments of it may be grasped. And, after all, I wish to admit that my book has defects of exposition, even of a serious kind. But it is also true that no one has ever succeeded, or can succeed, in expounding a doctrine in such a way that a badly prejudiced reader will not misinterpret it. In every exposition, together with the essential elements there are always, inevitably, mixed personal, transitory elements. A reader who reads in order to gain profit, will receive profit: in the conception which I present of the universe there is something which further inquiry will have to take into account and will be able to single out. I may be satisfied; and even the reader may be satisfied. About putting the dot on every i, I care only to a certain degree. In any case, it would be useless labour.

co-essential, an indeterminate and a determinate factor. Spontaneity is intrinsically indeterminate. But the primitive unities are many; the variations of each primitive unity are also many. Whence a determinism which results from the connected multiplicity of the indeterminate factors.[1]

We seemed to have before us a double dualism: the dualism causality-rationality, and the dualism indeterminism-determinism. From the considerations just mentioned it appears that those dualisms (each, and both of them), without vanishing, are reconciled, and indeed mutually imply each other.

The universe is one: here is the reason why nothing can be in it, nothing can occur in it, in opposition to rational necessity. But in what sense is the universe one? It is one in so far as it is manifold—in so far as it is the system of many solidary spontaneous unities.[2]

Variation[3] takes place, for each primitive unity is spontaneous. But real variation is no simple succession, it is an interference of facts. Well, those absolute beginnings which are essential to variation, and which are made possible by the (indeterminate) spontaneities of primitive unities, interfere with one another because each primitive unity is a unity, and because all primitive unities are solidary. The very unity, which rational necessity obliges us not to disregard, gives us also the reason of causal necessity. Indeed, we must recognise it to be essential to spontaneity itself. In fact, a primitive unity is modified only in so far as it modifies the others at the same time; spontaneity implies the resistances opposed to it by other

---

[1] Compare above the chapter *Reality*, §§ 11, p. 82, and 12, pp. 83–4.

[2] Not only does each of the spontaneous unities exist; but these unities are essentially solidary; and in consequence of their solidarity they are elements of a system, of the universe. We have already observed that we shall have to take up again the concepts of primitive or spontaneous unity and of solidarity.

[3] [accadere.]

# Unity and Multiplicity

spontaneities, it implies the stimulations (not to be confused with determinations) coming to it from other spontaneities.

Pure rationality and variation, which cannot be reduced to pure rationality and is nevertheless subject to rational laws, no longer appear to us as heterogeneous elements, concerning which we could not understand how they co-exist, though we had to recognise that they do co-exist: their irreducibility can be resolved into that of matter and form. Form is not matter, but it is the form of matter —it is unity, without which there would be none of those elements of which matter as matter is the aggregate. Thus, reciprocally, without matter there would be no form, for the latter is nothing but the form of matter. The same, with a few easy changes, may be said with regard to the dualism between determination and indetermination.

A multiplicity of spontaneous primitive unities, solidary with one another and therefore elements of one single unity: in this way, and in this way alone, the universe is conceived as a system.

### 13.

MAINTENANCE OF IT AGAINST COMMON PRECONCEPTIONS.

A very serious, and for many an insuperable, obstacle which makes it difficult to convince oneself that the concept indicated (not yet sufficiently developed) is the true one and the only true one, and even hinders a clear comprehension of it, is constituted by the habits of common thought.

Common thought is essentially directed towards practice. Practice derives its specific characters from causal relations; consequently these assume a predominant importance in common thought. The least cultivated man has also a knowledge of rational relations, and profits by them; but he scarcely cares about them except in so far as they help him to unwind the tangled skein of causal relations. Those rational relations with which he is acquainted and by which he profits seem to him something too natural, too ready to hand (and so they really are, but not in the sense of the vulgar), to be dwelt upon; whereas causal relations, which mean struggle, pleasure or pain, safety or ruin, attract the attention even of the lazy and the incurious. A hungry infant seeks the mother's breast; he does not seek the air, of which he has even more need than of milk. It is useless to observe that the vulgar do not know all causal relations, and that, among the relatively few with which they are a little acquainted, they take expressly into account only those which have a manifest and immediate practical efficiency, or which seem to have it.

Whence it follows, that "things" are conceived, on the whole, as having no essential relations, and that "causes" are conceived, still on the whole, as accidental acts of violence. These two concepts are closely correlative, and the one explains the other. A stone may be deformed, or modified in any way, both through the agency of man and through that of natural agents; but, unless some one of these causes, which break in upon it directly violently, intervenes, it remains such as it is, however the bodies among which it is placed may vary. Even mere translation is a violence, for if it is effected by man, it costs a certain labour; but it is a violence *sui generis*, which produces no modification in the stone in itself. In conclusion, every body is something standing by itself, independently of the others; and the same may be almost said of souls, in so far as the vulgar have some sort of concept of the soul. Therefore, the cause which modifies a thing cannot be anything essential to the thing; and, reciprocally, since modifying causes are not essential to things, it is impossible that the latter should not seem, by themselves, independent of each other.

I will not say that the vulgar think explicitly, with full consciousness, in the way indicated; the vulgar construct no metaphysics; their thought, in so far as it is explicit, is fragmentary: it constitutes a complex of concepts, not a concept of a complex. We cannot even say that the vulgar are in error: causality implies accidentality, and in this sense a real violence; reality implies an irreducible multiplicity; the things which the vulgar imagine (without further definition) to be separate, are in fact distinct. It is certainly true that besides multiplicity, and consequent accidentality, there exists also rationality, implying unity; but the vulgar are very far from denying rationality, of which indeed they recognise the supreme value; (the vulgar do not theorise about reason, but they make a use of it, which presupposes its infallibility and universality).

The vulgar construct no metaphysics, and therefore do not even construct a false metaphysics. Not only so, but in order to construct metaphysics we have simply to penetrate deeper into the thought of the vulgar, so as to introduce into it the order which it lacks, making explicit that which it implicitly contains, and bring clearly into view its implications. He who proceeds in any other way, is almost inevitably led to draw from common thought a false and absurd metaphysics: a pluralistic metaphysics.[1]

[1] He who has read so far with some diligence, knows that I am no monist, if the word is taken in its commonest meaning. Indeed, it might be maintained, not without good reasons, that my doctrine is precisely a pluralistic doctrine. I am not fond of labels, which in general falsify concepts by making distinctions of which the real nature is an inexact complexity, look as though they were simple and precise. I am not fond of them, and do not wish to make use of them. He who wishes to know my doctrine should study it; I have tried to satisfy his wish, however hypothetical, with a book: I could not substitute a word for the book. But for once a word is necessary in order to avoid wearisome, or worse than wearisome, periphrases. There is a metaphysics (professed with more or less clearness of thought, developed with more or less coherence), the sum of which can be resolved into the admission of a certain number of ultimate realities, independent of

## 14.

### PHILOSOPHIC DOCTRINES FOUNDED ON THESE PRECONCEPTIONS.

Pluralism is just the metaphysics of primitive philosophers; that is to say, of all those who, not satisfied with common thought, wish to go beyond it, and try to do so carrying with them the habits of common thought.[1] The primitive philosopher has not even the slightest suspicion of the possibility that the most common and most assured cognitions imply certain suppositions (such a suspicion arises only after the insufficiency of primitive

each other, having no mutual essential and constitutive relations. To this metaphysics, which I have to mention, for the rejection of it is the best means I know to make my doctrine fully clear, I give the name of pluralism. Of course, I divest this name of any other meaning. If any one has anything to say to the contrary, let him say it: I shall not answer him, for I do not wish to quarrel about words. It remains understood that in opposing pluralism I oppose the doctrine which I have mentioned, and which alone I denote by that name, not any other. And by opposing that doctrine as absurd, I simply intend to make the cognition of truth easier, not to maintain the monism of Spinoza, or of Hegel, or of Haeckel, or of anyone else. Nor am I under any illusions: I know that my words, although sufficiently clear, will not take from him who seeks it the chance of entangling himself, or of trying to entangle himself, in misunderstandings. I have said what I had to say; for the rest, every one may do what he likes, or what he thinks best.

[1] A primitive philosophy is at present as justifiable as a primitive astronomy would be. However, the world is full of primitive philosophers, even or chiefly at the present time. They do not generally assume the name of philosophers; indeed they affect to despise philosophy: they are physiologists, physicists, economists, scholars, sometimes not without merit in their own speciality, or so-called persons of culture, who pretend to know, to teach that which they have never studied. Of course, an opinion preserves its philosophical character, and may be a most vulgar philosophical error, even if he who adheres to it pretends (thus making another mistake) to found it on non-philosophical arguments. For instance, materialism (the name is no longer fashionable, but the blunder, under the name of energetism, is more fashionable than ever), total or partial agnosticism (such as the conviction that consciousness is an inscrutable mystery), scepticism, are philosophical follies. And there are some good people who, while they adhere with enviable assurance to one or other of these opinions, or even to all of them together, declare that they do not meddle with philosophy, and that philosophy is a loss of time. Apelles did not tolerate that the "sutor" should speak about anything else than the "crepida." If he had chanced to live in our own days! . . . It is needless to observe that primitiveness is not the same thing as antiquity; not a few of the moderns are infinitely more primitive than Parmenides.

philosophy has become manifest); he starts from common thought (in which respect he is not wrong : it is necessary to begin there), but he reasons, (and here is the mistake,) as if common thought could be reduced only to its most apparent and most massive parts. Therefore, though besides extending our cognitions he succeeds in arranging them into partial systems, he does not reach the unity of the system.

By a more extended and more delicate experience and by a more ordered, methodical reflection, both intentionally directed towards a cognitive end, one soon comes to recognise with clearness the necessity essential to causation : the primitive philosopher is, at least with regard to the external world, a determinist. Now, necessity implies rationality ; it implies between the things, whose variations mutually determine each other, certain essential relations, constitutive of each of them ; it implies the exclusion of pluralism. (Indeed, we have seen that strict determinism implies the absolute negation of any multiplicity and therefore also of any succession, or, in short, destroys itself.)

But the primitive philosopher is not aware of this consequence of determinism. He still admits, like the vulgar, that things have no essential (rational) relations to each other ; and in order to reconcile this naïve conviction in some way with determinism he has recourse to the concept of forces acting on things and subject to necessary laws. Forces are, at first, still conceived as things distinguished from those on which they act ; in the same way as the horse is a thing distinct from the cart which it draws. Then it comes to be understood that the concepts of thing and of force must in some way penetrate each other ; in trying to make them penetrate (we shall not enter into the particulars of the attempts) a more or less thorough modification of both concepts takes place in the end.

Poor remedies! There is in the concept of force but one element having any real importance, and the element is this—that forces act according to necessary laws. But we are still at the same point. By saying that forces act according to necessary laws we mean that variations occur according to necessary laws. If this is true, as it is certainly true (provided that we do not exaggerate by believing every variation to be necessary, for then variations would be excluded), it is impossible that realities, whatever they may be, whose variations appear to be necessarily connected, should have singly their own separate existence—that they should not be co-essential to each other, or not mutually imply each other.

The primitive philosopher knows (everybody knows) that there are particular systems: a stone, a machine, the Earth, an animal, a man even from the psychical point of view, etc. But he thinks, or he speaks as if he thought that a particular system exists in so far as its parts are joined together (exclusively, or at least chiefly,) by certain causal connections. So, to avail ourselves of an example of which we have already made use, the solar system owes its existence as a distinct system to the fact that its parts all gravitate towards each other, and (approximately, but with a very great approximation,) only towards each other. The universe is a system. According to primitive philosophy, this proposition would mean that intense or feeble exchanges of force, either always take place, or at least may occur, between any two parts of the universe.

### 15.

#### EXAMINATION OF THEM.

Primitive philosophy is radically absurd. We do not mean that it does not contain some particular truths;

## Unity and Multiplicity

but these same particular truths presuppose a universal truth which the doctrine denies. That a particular system owes its being such a system precisely to the causal connections which join the parts together, and to the fact that these parts are not connected, or only feebly connected, with external elements, so that all externally appear to be subject to that unity which is the system, is true. But it is not the ultimate truth.

Two things, it does not matter what they are called nor how they are otherwise characterised or conceived, each of which has its own separate and independent existence, so that they are not essential to each other, and that there is no contradiction in the hypothesis that the one could be destroyed without the other being necessarily modified in consequence, cannot in any case become causally related : it is impossible that any varying of the one should imply a varying of the other. In order that the varying of the one should influence, or should be capable of influencing, the varying of the other, it is required that between the two there should be a rational, necessary relation, as an indispensable constituent of both. No things exist in the universe, which are not capable of becoming causally connected with each other, even if at present they have no causal connection ; therefore no things exist in the universe, which have no essential relations to each other ; or in other words, all things constitute together one single thing, and are neither possible nor conceivable except as constituting this thing, which is the universe.

This consequence appears evident a fortiori when we consider the fact of cognition.

Primitive philosophy is not aware of any difficulty in giving a causal interpretation of cognition. *Nihil est in intellectu, quod prius non fuerit in sensu.* And that sensations are the effects of certain causes acting on us, is manifest. It is admitted that as to the way in which cognition arises from sensation, everything is not clear. But it has to be recognised (and no question is prejudged by recognising this), that our cognitions are states of our own consciousness, and therefore causally connected with other variations.

Just so. But between an effect and a cognition there is a difference, for not every effect is a cognition : the rising of the quicksilver in the thermometric tube is the effect of an increase of temperature, but it is, with regard to the quicksilver, an increase of volume, not a cognition. My cognition, it is said, is an effect. I recognise the effect, and I recognise it as essential to the cognition. But I do not see the possibility of reducing the cognition to the effect only. I know, for instance, (that is to say, the primitive philosopher knows, or imagines that he knows,) that cognition is an effect. I ask whether this knowledge of mine is simply the effect determined in me by the reading of a book. That the reading produces an effect in me, is out of question. This effect is a modification of my consciousness, and, as such, I shall admit (not because there is nothing to the contrary, but in order to avoid new questions,) that it is known to me. But this effect, this mode of my being, is a particular fact in me, different from that other particular fact in me which is the being warm, but not less particular.[1] Now, as long as I limit myself to being conscious of this particular fact in me, which is the effect determined in me by my reading, I do not yet know anything either of cognition in general, or of effect in general : I am still very far from knowing, that cognition is an effect.

The fact of cognition implies, first of all, like any other

[1] Even seeing blue is a fact no less particular than being warm, though specifically different; the specific difference of two facts has no importance with regard to their particular being.

fact, rational relations which give rise to it : it would not be possible, unless certain elements were already essentially related to each other. Further, the fact of cognition is a fact of the subject ; it is not simply a state of the subject, but a state in which the subject is conscious of certain relations, rational or causal (and the latter always imply rational relations), between those other elements which just for this reason are said to be known. Therefore, even before the fact of cognition, the relations, the explicit consciousness of which constitutes cognition, are already a constitutive element of the subject. The causes which produce cognition presuppose, for a double reason, certain essential relations between the subject and the totality of things knowable by the subject, that is to say between the subject and the universe. Causes, among which we must not forget the spontaneity of the subject and other spontaneities (for, without spontaneity there would be no causes, there would be no varying), perform the important function of making certain relations explicit ; but, although it is true that we must ascribe such a function to causes, it is not less true that we cannot possibly see in cognition only the effect of the causes co-operating in the production of it ; here also, and here chiefly, causality necessarily implies rationality, which is its essential foundation.

### 16.

#### CONTINUATION OF OUR OWN INTERPRETATION (COMPARE § 12).

The *unity* of all the elements, of whatever kind, which constitute the universe, cannot be doubted in any way. Although it does not seem to be, and is not, explicitly known to the vulgar, it is the most certain of all cognitions ;

for, if this is denied, every other cognition becomes impossible.

Of course, we speak of unity in the sense which we have defined, and which, without inquiring in what measure it may be said to be our own or defined by us, certainly is not to be confused with any other. We do not say that there is only one substance, nor that distinguishable things can be distinguished only in appearance. Distinct things are connected, each with each, by rational relations which are all constituents of each of them : for none can exist, or be thought, except by an abstraction, outside such a system of relations. Since one thing exists only in so far as others exist—since therefore each thing is an essential constituent of every other, we can and must say that all things together constitute one thing : the universe.

But the universe, in its turn, exists only in so far as the single things which are distinguished in it exist. And this for the same reasons for which every single thing exists only as a constituent of the universe. When we say that A and B are essentially related to each other, we make two assertions at once : (1) that both A and B exist only as elements of the group AB, of a higher unity ; (2) that this higher unity is the unity of a group, and precisely of the group AB. Suppress A and B and you will have suppressed the relation, and consequently even the unity in question ; vice versa, suppress the unity, and you will have suppressed the mutual relation, which, according to the hypothesis, is essential, and without which consequently neither A nor B is any longer possible.

According to our doctrine, the many are not less essential to the One than the One to the many.

No doubt, among the many, that is to say the distinct elements, not a few are transitory and (as we must not forget) always, at least in part, accidental. And therefore they cannot be essential to the One ; how can it be maintained that the two lines written by me just now, which I have written because I wished to do so (not capriciously, though the fact of having written them is not possible independently of my spontaneity,) and shall perhaps blot out a few minutes hence, are essential to the universe ?

The objection seems of a certain importance. But the answer is, in the first place, that the distinct elements are not all accidental or transitory. The primitive unities, of which we have spoken and to which we shall come back, are permanent with regard to their form, though not with regard to their content. Among the distinct elements there are consequently some about the essentiality of which no doubt can arise.

The transitory distinct elements are the variations of primitive unities. These variations are accidental precisely in so far as they can be referred to the spontaneity of such unities, which are (we say) essentially spontaneous. Now, if the universe is in its essence the higher unity (the system) of spontaneous unities, it will consequently be essential to it to include accidental elements ; none of the single accidental elements is essential, but nevertheless it is essential that there should be accidental elements. While they are accidental from one point of view, viz. in so far as they can be referred to the single spontaneities, variations are from another point of view determined, viz. in so far as the single spontaneities interfere with one another. And the mutual interference of the single spontaneities is conditioned, as we said, by the reciprocal essential relations of primitive unities, and by the fact that each of them is an essential constituent of the universe.[1]

[1] " Indubium est res externas . . . exhiberi sensibus nostris ut plures substantias, quarum unaquaeque seorsum ab aliis complete in se subsistat. Singulae enim . . . suis videntur propriis terminis claudi, ac proinde exsistentiam habere a ceterarum exsistentia separatam. Et rursus singulae, ad modum principiorum completorum, agere et pati videntur. Quare quisquis . . . affirmare cogitur existere plura entia in se subsistentia " (P. St. De Backer, s.j., *Instit.*

## 17.

### THE UNIVERSE AS THE UNITY OF A MULTIPLICITY. THE SUBJECT AS THE UNITY OF THE UNIVERSE.

Thus the universe is the unity of a multiplicity. That is to say, each single element exists, in so far as the others exist also, and the unity of all exists; the unity exists in so far as the single elements which constitute it exist, some invariable, others variable, and even accidentally variable.[1]

That single elements exist, we know in so far as we have single, distinct cognitions; that the unity of all exists, and that the unity and the single elements mutually imply one another, we know in so far as we recognise, between all the single actual or possible cognitions, certain rational relations, essential to each, or in so far as we recognise

*Metaph. spec.*, Vol. IV, p. 170; Paris, 1908). We have observed that it is characteristic of primitive philosophy (of that philosophy which considers itself to be founded on common sense, because it unreflectively ascribes a metaphysical value to propositions which in common thought have only a practical value) to ascribe to each thing a separate existence, except in so far as the one acts on the other accidentally. The doctrine summed up in the passage quoted (I have taken the quotation on purpose from an otherwise excellent treatise for the use of schools) will appear evident to anyone who does not reflect that causal relations between things ("agere et pati") are neither conceivable nor possible, if the things in question are "entia in se subsistentia." An absolute can neither act upon, nor suffer from, another absolute. I am well aware that the author does not wish to consider single things as so many absolutes. But the question is not what he wishes, but what is necessarily implied by his assertions. We agree that things have to be distinguished; the inquiry concerns the importance of the distinction. The distinction either excludes or does not exclude the possibility that things are essentially related to one another. Only under the first hypothesis we may say that each thing has "exsistentiam a ceterarum exsistentia separatam"; but then each thing is an absolute, and mutual, causal relations are impossible. Under the second hypothesis causal actions are possible; but each thing becomes a constituent of every other; and, in spite of the distinction, the higher unity of things is no longer deniable. The other arguments which the author alleges against monism in general, or against certain forms of monism, do not touch the doctrine set forth by me. The question here discussed has an obvious connection with that concerning the value of pantheism, which will be briefly treated further on.

[1] We have seen that variations, and the accidentality of certain variations, are also essential to the universe; and, as they are presupposed by unity, so they presuppose unity.

that the single cognitions all imply one and the same necessity, which connects them all together.

The unity is therefore unity of relations, formal unity. On the other hand, we cannot be satisfied with recognising necessity as a simple fact. It is a fact that, if I have pronounced a contradictory proposition, I have said nothing (nothing having a value, a meaning); but it is a fact which must imply a necessity, or else it would be, what it is not, a fact like any other, for instance seeing blue, feeling warm. We must be able to give an account to ourselves of the rational necessity, which becomes fragmentarily manifest to us in every deduction. The reason of reasons, the necessity on which the indispensableness of those single relations which exhibit such a character is founded, can be only the unity of the universe. But, as we have just said, the unity of the universe is a unity of relations—the universe is one in so far as the single elements of it are connected by relations having the character of necessity.

Indeed in substance we found the necessity of reasons on unity, and unity on the necessity of reasons. We seem almost to be turning in a vicious circle. This appearance should not disturb us: the two " things," each of which can be resolved into the other, constitute but one, which appears to us differently according as we consider it under one aspect or under another. Anyhow, some further explanation seems desirable.

The unity of the universe can be only a unity of consciousness.

The only unity which can be reconciled with a coextensive multiplicity, the only one which at the same time implies and is implied by multiplicity, is the unity of consciousness. The extremely varied facts of which I become in any way aware, are all without exception facts of which I am aware; they are all constituents of one and the same unity of consciousness. Reciprocally, this unity exists merely as the single form of that manifold content; consciousness would disappear with the disappearance of its content.

That the unity of consciousness can be reconciled with multiplicity, is quite obvious; nor is it less obvious that such unity is the only one reconcilable with multiplicity. For instance, space is a unity which implies a multiplicity (of figures). But " continuous extension can exist only in a simple principle, as the termination of its act. . . . The reason of the continuum does not consist . . . in the single parts, but in a principle which includes all the parts together, and this principle must be simple.[1] . . . It is impossible therefore to consider the continuum as an aggregate of parts, and nevertheless each part, which can be assigned in it by thought, is outside the other. . . . It is required therefore that the whole continuum should exist by one single act in the simple principle which is aware of it,"[2] viz. in the unity of consciousness. And it is easy to apply the same considerations to any other case.

It is useless to add that under the name consciousness we mean, not only consciousness properly so-called, clear and explicit consciousness; but also at the same time subconsciousness. Besides the objects of which I am explicitly conscious, there are those which I have forgotten, and which I may eventually remember, and those of which I have not yet become aware, but of which, under certain favourable circumstances, I might become aware. Beyond my actual awareness, there is that which I have forgotten, and that which I have not yet realised, and which perhaps will not be realised, but in any case is realisable.

[1] That is to say, in order to explain the continuum, the principle must be simple.
[2] A. ROSMINI, Sist. filosof., n. 131; compare N. Sagg., nn. 823–30; Antropol., nn. 94–7; Psicol., nn. 443–9, 573, 630, 1136–8.

## Unity and Multiplicity

It is indeed obvious that it is impossible for me either to know or to assume anything, outside the unity in question. This consequently is as essential to the universe, as the elements of which that unity is composed. The universe of which I know something, or about which I assume something, results from the components of that unity, which is therefore the unity of the universe.

And it is no less obvious that (rational) necessity is founded precisely on the same unity, when we consider this unity not only in its momentary actuality, but also in its possibility. I may even make blunders, but my blunders are not favourable to my development, rather they hinder it: the cognition of truth and the realisation of good are the attainment of the end, the development of the unity in conformity with itself, its life, its reality.[1]

### 18.

MULTIPLICITY OF SUBJECTS AND DIFFICULTIES ARISING FROM IT. ACCIDENTAL MANIFESTATIONS OF THE SUBJECT.

But the subjects are many. And if each is the unity of the universe, we shall have to conclude that the universe is indeed one with respect to each subject, but is not one intrinsically. Since necessity is founded on the unity of the subject, there ought to be a particular necessity for each subject; and for the universe considered intrinsically there will be no valid necessity. We have here two conceptions which are both absurd, and the first of which is refuted by the fact that all men recognise one and the same rational necessity; so true it is that they understand one another, at least so far as is requisite to misunderstand each other. Further, to maintain that any person is the unity of the universe, is the ultimate ground of the

[1] Compare above, *Thought*, § 2, compare § 1 towards the end.

necessity dominant in it, while that person may be perhaps a poor fool, and is in any case a man having his defects, his extravagances, his unreasonable peculiarities, and is a variable tissue of elements for the most part accidental and irrelevant, seems a paradox. Let us make a reply.

And first of all, when we say that every man—indeed, every subject, even if not developed—is the unity of the universe, we do not mean that the particular limited group of elements which each of us calls himself is the centre of gravity of the universe and has in the latter that importance which it has in the opinion and the feeling of the single individual. We mean that the elements of objective reality are in the end nothing but the elements of the possible experience of each subject.

Experience becomes organised, as it gives rise to certain distinctions, among which the most important is that between the subject in the strict sense and the external world. The group "subject" and the group "external world" are distinct formations in the field of experience— of one single experience, that is to say of a unity of consciousness, and they presuppose the unity of consciousness. Since this unity is that which becomes organised, it is certainly no result of an organisation, it is primitive; of this unity, and not of any particular form which it assumes, we say that it is the unity of the universe. The strictly subjective formation (simultaneous with the formation "external world") has the office of making the primitive consciousness clear and distinct. This primitive consciousness, in comparison with consciousness more properly so-called, is rather to be considered as subconsciousness.[1]

[1] It is useless that we should insist on the impossibility of admitting the supposition that there is only a clear and distinct consciousness; on the necessity of recognising degrees of consciousness, by which *e.g.* we pass from the actual vivid perception to the perception which may be remembered but is not actually remembered, without being able to assign a point marking a precise break, a specific difference, between the one degree and the other.

## Unity and Multiplicity

Clear and explicit consciousness is always the consciousness of a particular person and presupposes that person. Consciousness never becomes wholly clear and explicit; indeed, the portion of it which becomes clear and explicit, is always extremely small by comparison with that which remains or gradually falls back into subconsciousness. Clear and distinct consciousness, more or less extended, more or less clear and distinct, depends on the simultaneous formation of the two limited groups "subject" (in the strict sense) and "external world"; more exactly, it is constituted by this formation.

Now, the accidental occurrences and even the unreasonable peculiarities which are never wanting in a particular person (in a strictly subjective group), and on account of which we consider him (not without reason) as a poor fellow, even if he is a great man, are essential to him, and therefore to his clear and explicit consciousness; they are conditions of knowledge as well as of good action. Of course, a given accidental or unreasonable element is never essential; but if one is absent, there will be another; no one of the elements in question is essential, but it is essential that there should be some of these elements. And we do not say that these must always be in the same number, nor that they must always have the same importance. Not all men are, either intellectually or morally, of the same worth; and the worth of a man increases the less he has in him of the accidental and irrational. But there is no man who is wholly without something accidental and irrational. And according to us, the fact that there is no one without it, is just the reason why one and the same rational necessity applies to all men and to all things.

### 19.

ACCIDENTAL MANIFESTATIONS OF THE SUBJECT, AND NECESSITY.

The presence of an accidental or irrational something in man is due to his own spontaneity and to the other spontaneities, with which the former interferes. The unfolding of a spontaneity (in so far as it is, as it certainly is, referable in part to the spontaneity itself) is always accidental; therefore, where there is spontaneity, there must be accidentality. Accidentality in man arises from within, and is introduced from without: it has two sources. These however are absolutely inseparable; a spontaneity exists only in so far as it overcomes the resistance opposed to it by some other spontaneity: to do, either means to do something, or means nothing. Two distinct spontaneities[1] perhaps do not interfere in fact *hic et nunc;* but they may always interfere; whence it follows that all spontaneities are connected in the unity of a system. Thus the accidental element in man is to be referred, both to the particular spontaneity of that man and to all the others, although the influence of the others is not the same for all.

The spontaneity which the developed subject recognises as one of his own constituents cannot be produced by that organisation of a primitive unity, which results in the two formations of the subject and of his external world. A produced spontaneity is a contradiction, though a spontaneity included in a formation receives from that formation certain characters which otherwise it would not have had. A primitive unity is a unity of all spontaneities; for any element which happened to be outside it, would

---

[1] A spontaneity, precisely because it exists only in so far as it is opposed to another opposing it, is always distinct from every other.

be as good as non-existent with regard to the primitive unity and all its formations; but, among all the spontaneities which it includes, one occupies a central position in it. I mean, central in the primitive unity considered, so that all the others are, within the unity in question, subject to that special one. In the process by which the primitive unity is organised, that spontaneity which occupies a central position in it, and fulfils an absolutely indispensable function in effecting the organisation, assumes the character of a spontaneity peculiar to the subject and, in a developed subject, the character of a will.

From this it follows that to suppress accidental occurrences and irrationalities would be to suppress the process through which a primitive unity passes from subconsciousness to consciousness: it would be the suppression of cognition. Indeed, it would be the suppression of the primitive unity; for this, however deficient its organisation may be, is still a system of spontaneities, and in consequence necessarily implies accidentality. It would be the suppression of spontaneity, for spontaneity implies accidentality; and, on the other hand, a spontaneity which is not a centre of a primitive unity, is a contradiction. Finally, it would be the suppression of the universe, for the universe is really nothing but a unity of facts; it is quite clear that without facts, which imply accidentality and spontaneity, there would also be no unity of them. Manifestly, the conditions of existence and those of knowledge coincide.

By recognising this we do not justify in the least either errors or bad actions: processes which tend to destroy the primitive unity, and hinder its development. But the intrinsic orders of thought (theoretical) and of life (practical) can be obtained only by means of a continual manifestation of subjective energy, and on condition that subjective energy be favoured by circumstances;[1] they are never definitively obtained : he who falls asleep, dies. We may add that the harmony of the subject with himself and with his external world, whatever degree it may reach, is never the abolition of the accidental; indeed, it is never anything but the harmony of facts each of which necessarily implies something accidental. Without the accidental, the world would simply be a logical process; error and fact would have no place in it; indeed, it would not even be a logical process, for even the logical process is a process, and knowledge exists only in so far as it is developing.

Let us not then undervalue accidental manifestations, although it is true that among accidental manifestations there are also aberrations. Of no aberration can we say that it is essential; but that there should be aberrations is essential. *Necesse est ut eveniant scandala,* for it is essential that there should be accidental manifestations. Let us not undervalue the particular subject, although we are not concerned with his accidental manifestations, and are offended by his errors or his sins; without particular subjects neither the universe, nor cognition would exist.

We do not resolve rational necessity into the accidental manifestations of the subject, which are variable from one subject to another and in the same subject: we resolve it into the unity of each subject. But the unity of each subject is nothing but the unity of facts each of

---

[1] "On the way of our life
Without the rays of kind heaven
Every brave soul loses its way,
The heart trembles, the step is unsteady.

"To accomplish beautiful deeds
Art is useful, judgment helps;
But judgment and art are deceitful
When heaven is not friendly." (Metastasis.)

The construction of knowledge too is among the "beautiful deeds."

## Unity and Multiplicity

which implies accidentality, though it implies at the same time the law deriving from unity.

### 20.
#### RECIPROCAL IMPLICATION BETWEEN SPONTANEITIES.

Let us denote by A, B, C, ... the distinct spontaneities; by $S_A$, $S_B$, $S_C$, ... the corresponding likewise distinct unities. Each of these unities includes all the spontaneities, is the unity of all. But in each there is one, and only one, central spontaneity—that which, if the unity develops into a subject, is to become the will of that subject.

Let us define exactly in what the central position of a spontaneity consists.

One of the unities in question, for instance $S_A$, is a unity of all the spontaneities—a unity of consciousness, the existence of which consists in the existence of one single apprehension of all the spontaneities. Such an apprehension, when the unity is not developed, is entirely subconscious; but its subconscious character does not make it specifically different from that in which our explicit doing-thinking consists; our own doing-thinking can be resolved into facts which arise out of subconsciousness and fall again into it. The single apprehension constituting the unity is both theoretical and practical, for the two aspects are inseparable from it.

Now, in this apprehension the central spontaneity A is apprehended as activity, while the others are apprehended as resistances. Every unfolding of A is a doing; every unfolding of B, C, ... is a resistance—a resistance which no doubt is essential to doing, but is not the same thing as doing. This is the case with regard to practical consciousness; theoretically, the consciousness of A is the act of knowing, the consciousness of B, C, ... is the consciousness of the known—of something known, which no doubt is essential to the act of knowing, but is not the same thing as the act of knowing. The developed subject is conscious of his own doing, conscious of his own knowing,[1] and is, correlatively, conscious of the resistances which are opposed to his doing on the part of the objects which are presented to his knowing. The subconscious life of a primitive unity can be resolved into the same elements, with the omission of the explicit clearness of consciousness.

It is manifest in what the difference consists, which in $S_A$ sets the single element A in opposition to each of all the others B, C, . . . The relations of A to B and of A to C may be very unlike; it does not matter: whatever the relation of A to any other element may be, the two terms of the relation are irreducibly opposed to each other. This is the reason why we have said that A occupies a central position in $S_A$; and so we have explained in what the centrality of A consists.

We have just observed that the constitutive consciousness of $S_A$ is at once theoretical and practical. Before going further, it will not be inappropriate to insist a little further on this point, which is of fundamental importance.

If B, C, . . . did not all interfere with A, $S_A$ would not exist, indeed not even A would exist; for a spontaneity exists only in so far as it manifests itself, and its manifestation consists in overcoming resistances. It may seem that $S_A$ is a system constituted by the causal connections between its elements, precisely according to the concept which primitive philosophers form of a system. We know that such a concept is absurd: between elements which do not already for some other reason constitute the unity of a system, no causal connections are possible.

---

[1] I am speaking of direct consciousness, which constitutes doing as well as knowing, and not of reflection, which treats doing or knowing as if they were two things capable of being known.

Consequently, $S_A$ cannot be a simple assemblage of elements, each having a separate existence, and connected by the mere accidentality of causal connections so as to form a system. If it were so (it cannot be so, but let us disregard for a moment the absurdity of the hypothesis), $S_A$ could never become a rational unity, implying logical necessity. Now, the developed subject is certainly a rational unity, a unity of knowledge, and implies logical necessity. We are thus necessarily led to admit that $S_A$ is, originally, also a rational unity, a unity of theoretical consciousness.

But, vice versa, we cannot even admit that $S_A$ is originally a mere rational unity, or unity of theoretical consciousness. For if it were only this, it would include no principle[1] of variation—it would give rise to no variation; whereas the developed subject is certainly a unity of fact, a unity of practical consciousness.

We must therefore admit that both moments, the practical and the theoretical, are essential to, and are original characters of, $S_A$. They are indeed essential to each other. In fact causal connection implies rational unity. Vice versa, in this unity, if we speak of it in so far as we know it, we have to recognise the unity of a multiplicity, the law of a process of variation, the form of a matter of fact.

### 21.

#### THE COMMON ELEMENT AS CONDITION OF RECIPROCAL IMPLICATION—BEING.

Spontaneities imply each other: it is impossible to separate A from $S_A$, or in other words it is impossible to

[1] I say "principle," and not "beginning." Variation might have had no beginning; but to say that it has not even a principle is to declare it impossible. On this point we have already dwelt at length on another occasion, and we do not think it necessary to insist.

separate A from B, C, ... And so also the unities $S_A$, $S_B$, ... imply each other. Manifestly, that same B which is a non-central constitutent of $S_A$, is the central constituent of $S_B$; reciprocally, that same A which is the central constituent of $S_A$, is a non-central constituent of $S_B$, etc.

Since spontaneities and the corresponding unities imply each other, or, in short, since the existence of one is impossible, contradictory, without the existence of all the others, so that they would all vanish if even one were to vanish, we must conclude that all spontaneities and all corresponding unities exist as constituents of one and the same thing, of the universe. But here, and here chiefly, we must guard against equivocations of thought, or rather of language.

The mutual implication of two things presupposes that the same element is in its entirety an essential element of both.[1] Why do we say that the universe is one, that it exists as one? Why, in other words, do we say that all unities and all spontaneities constitute a system, and not merely an aggregate? Because unities and spontaneities

---

[1] I shall make my meaning clear by an example, which I have used on another occasion; but I cannot think of any other more suggestive. Peter and Paul are joint owners of the same house; and neither of the two possesses anything else. Let us neglect the possibility that one of the two should give up his own right. Then obviously the disappearance of the property of Peter implies the destruction of the house (or of the exchange value of it; for us it is all the same). But the destruction of the house implies the disappearance of the property of Paul also. Therefore, the property of Peter and that of Paul imply each other. And note, that the properties are actually *two:* the revenue obtained from the house is divided between Peter and Paul, each of whom spends his own portion on his own account. They are two; but with the disappearance of the one even the other necessarily disappears; their mutual implication consists in this. If we abstract from the numerically single element which as a whole (that is to say, in its integrity) is an essential constituent of the one thing as well as of the other, so that the disappearance of either of the two can take place only if the element itself disappears; it is impossible that the disappearance of either of the two things should have as a necessary consequence (*i.e.* as a logical consequence, since we must here abstract from causal relations) the disappearance of the other; the mutual implication of two things becomes impossible.

mutually imply one another. The universe therefore is a system, because all spontaneities include as a constituent of each, one and the same element which is as a whole in each of them.

This single and common element can be resolved into Being—into our concept of quite indeterminate Being. We do not say (note well) that all spontaneities include an element which is conceived by us as Being, so establishing a difference between the element in itself and our concept of that element; we say that the element in question *is* our concept of Being. The element and our concept of the element are *unum et idem*.

On this point a few words will perhaps not be out of place, although above we have already given exhaustive explanations.

This book occupies a definite place in the library: it is Case B, shelf III, No. 5. The concept which I form of its place, is constituted by the complex of signs 5, III, B; obviously, the place is something else, it cannot be reduced to such a complex of signs.

Well, to suppose that between the element common to all spontaneities and our concept of Being, there is merely a correspondence, more or less as in the alleged example, is nonsense: the element must coincide with the concept of Being. In fact, the element in question is common to all spontaneities and to all unities; now, that unity which is I is (like any other, after all) a unity of consciousness; the element must therefore be, in a more or less explicit form, within my consciousness; and within my consciousness there is nothing common to all that which it includes except my concept of Being.

In conclusion, the unity of the universe is nothing but the unity of Being. The universe is one, is a system, in so far as the concretes which constitute it are all determinations of the same concept of Being.

We say, of one and the same concept. The difficulties mentioned just lately, which prevent our seeing in concretes so many determinations of one and the same concrete, vanish if in place of one and the same concrete we put one and the same concept. So, for instance, one sheet of paper can have only one of the three forms of the triangle, equilateral, isosceles and scalene; but the concept of triangle admits, or rather requires, all three determinations at the same time.

## 22.

### CONCEPT AND REALITY.

Any doctrine concerning reality implies the presupposition that what is said in the doctrine about reality (a concept) coincides with some character of reality. To say, we must conceive reality as K, but it is not K, is absurd; in fact, if we know that reality is not K, not only it is not true that reality must be conceived as K; rather the truth is that it must not be conceived as K, and that indeed we do not conceive it as K. Agnosticism itself cannot escape this requirement. To say, we do not know reality, means not only that our thought does not penetrate reality, but that reality cannot be penetrated by our thought: its impenetrability is a character of it which coincides with our concept of that character.[1]

The doctrine which we have summed up completely satisfies the requirement just formulated. Being is not merely a concept, "an idea in my own head." It is a concept in the consciousness of everyone, and is at the same time a character of everything, the ultimate foundation of all reality. In this sense, reality and cognition strictly coincide.

---

[1] Therefore, we may remark incidentally, agnosticism is absurd; for the phrase used to express that doctrine can have a meaning only in so far as it is a cognition of reality.

Rational necessity which dominates the thought of the subject (of a definite subject), and applies to any content of subjective consciousness whatever, without excluding even the accidental manifestations which are indeed implied by it, has its foundation in the unity of subjective consciousness. But, while on the one hand this unity is the essential form of subjective thought, on the other hand it is the common character of all spontaneities and of all unities, that is to say of all subjects and of everything which may become an object for a subject. For the unity of subjective consciousness consists in Being, of which every thought of any subject and every subject and every thing are determinations. After this, the universal validity of necessity requires no further explanation.[1]

But Being exists only in its determinations. It is a unity, necessarily implied by multiplicity, but in its turn implying multiplicity. It is impossible to ascribe to Being (which, in so far as it is abstract, is outside time) a chronological precedence relatively to its determinations. But we cannot even ascribe to it a strictly logical precedence; although it is true that in a doctrine, *i.e.* in an abstract thought, it is inevitable to ascribe to Being a certain logical precedence. A relation which must be considered as a real correlation exists between Being and its determinations.

It is necessary that spontaneities should exist. For, if no spontaneities did exist, nothing would exist. Not even Being would exist. This in fact, although it cannot be called " merely " a concept, in the sense in which concept is commonly understood, is still a concept; it is the thought (more or less explicit) of a conscious spontaneity. And a conscious spontaneity thinks in so far as it acts;

---

[1] A necessity which were not universally valid would be a non-necessary necessity. But we had to show that the foundation ascribed by us to necessity was its true foundation.

which means, that it thinks in so far as it is one of the many spontaneities which interfere with one another—interfere with one another, that is, because they are all determinations of Being. As Being cannot but be, so also the many spontaneities cannot but be.

By the many spontaneities we can explain the many subjective consciousnesses. The distinction between the subjective consciousnesses, though each of them is in the end co-extensive with the universe, is to be explained by the difference between their centres ; A is central only in $S_A$, B only in $S_B$, etc. ; this is the reason why one is distinguished from another. But the content is one and the same for every subjective consciousness, and the element which unifies the content of each of them, is one and the same. In short, though the content without the thought of which it is the content, is nothing, it is also true that the thinking activity is nothing without the content. As determinations of Being, which exists only in such determinations, the single consciousnesses are distinguished as consciousnesses, while they agree as to their content; each of them is a varying on its own account, and at the same time, for the same reason, the varying of each takes place, that is to say, each one evolves or becomes involved according to the same universal laws.

We have shown and explained the necessary reciprocal implication of unity and multiplicity ; the problem which we had set before us, has been solved under the form in which we had proposed it.

## CHAPTER VII

# THE ABSOLUTE

### 1.

MEANING OF THE DOCTRINE EXPOUNDED. THE DOCTRINE OF PHENOMENA AND METAPHYSICS. OBJECTION AGAINST METAPHYSICS.

THE doctrine developed so far concerns phenomena, that is to say experience; nothing else. We have worked back to a general concept of the universe. But we have worked back to it with the single object of understanding common cognition, using no other means but that of making clear the implications of common cognition. That is to say, we have remained within the field of common cognition, or experience. The universe of which we have formed a concept, is the phenomenal universe—that which experience makes known to us, which itself can be resolved into experience.

And now the question arises, whether it is possible, or perhaps inevitable, to go beyond phenomena. The name metaphysics is commonly given to the science of something non-phenomenal, of something which serves as the foundation of phenomena.[1] Is such a science possible?

[1] We decline to define exactly, once for all, terms which are used with many meanings, and which it would be neither possible, nor perhaps convenient, to divest of their variety of meanings. We do not think, however, that our language can give rise to misunderstandings; for, whenever we use one of those terms, we are careful to state precisely the meaning which we then ascribe to it, if the meaning itself does not appear sufficiently clear from the context. To us this seems the best way. Others may think differently. But though a reader has the right not to be left in a state of uncertainty about what is said to him, he has no right to impose on the writer a particular way of eliminating uncertainty. The doctrine which I am setting forth may not be a metaphysics in the sense just explained: on the other hand, I

Metaphysics (understood as above) has never become a science; it has never reached a conclusion about which its followers could agree: it is a field of perpetual strife on which no lasting conquest is possible.[1]

If we give up the attempt to construct metaphysics as hopeless, ought we to resign ourselves to scepticism?

The impossibility of going beyond phenomena, and the difficulty of knowing certain phenomena, are two different things which must not be confused together. To think that the impossibility of going beyond phenomena has as its consequence the impossibility of arriving at cognitions having the character of certainty—at a real and proper " science " in the field of phenomena, is the same as to confuse those two things; in substance it is to suppose that the phenomenal and the non-phenomenal belong to one and the same sphere; it is to remain under the influence of metaphysical prejudice.

In fact there is a " science " of phenomena (there is mathematics, and there is physics); it is therefore possible. When we ask how it is possible, we recognise that the existence of the phenomenal as such, *i.e.* its appearing to the subject, is conditioned by certain subjective forms imposed on it: time, space, categories. As subjective, these forms are a priori, and therefore universal and necessary. The laws which they implicitly contain are therefore absolutely inevitable, and constitute that certainly known foundation without which we should have only problematic opinions concerning phenomena, (or rather, not even these would be possible; but we shall not insist on this point).

Particular phenomena are, evidently, particular phenomena; they cannot be deduced, but only experienced (for they are phenomena); though necessarily

---

see no reason why I should not call it metaphysics in a more indefinite sense; and I do not know what other name to give it. [1] KANT, *op. cit.*, I, 19.

subject to a form, they are not however implicit in the form. Therefore, that which to us seems cognition (of phenomena) is not always really cognition : in order not to err, man must observe, experiment, by a method the determination of which constitutes a remarkable part of the science of phenomena. But we can no longer doubt that such a science is possible, since we have recognised the rational foundation of it.

And the same reflection from which we have learnt that the science of phenomena is possible, shows that a science of the non-phenomenal, a science of the "thing in itself," is impossible. In fact, a science is possible in so far as man possesses certain universal forms, on which, and on which only, necessary a priori reasoning is founded. But these forms are forms of phenomena and only of phenomena. When we come to the thing in itself, we remain therefore not only without the help of experience (an experience of something other than phenomena is a *contradictio in adjecto*), but even without the instrument of reason, which in short is merely the system of those forms.

2.

PHILOSOPHIC AGNOSTICISM.

The doctrine[1] which we have just summarised, goes beyond scepticism while it completes it. It is not true that we have always to suspend our judgment, and doubt of everything; a science of phenomena is possible. But a science is possible only of the phenomena : scepticism, in so far as it denied the possibility of metaphysics, is found to be justified, though by reasons which are no doubt superior to those ever excogitated by sceptics, and which seem definitive, ultimate.[2]

[1] Of KANT.
[2] Indifference to metaphysical inquiries "is certainly no effect of levity, but of the mature judgment of modern times, which does not wish to be

To this doctrine we may give the name, introduced much later, agnosticism. As is known, men of science (and many whose culture is limited to a sprinkling of science) for the most part profess agnosticism.[1] We ask what the arguments on which agnosticism seems to be founded are worth.

Agnosticism and metaphysics agree in admitting, beyond phenomena, the thing in itself, which the latter pretends to know while the former denies that it can be known. By what reasons is the existence of the thing in itself proved?

There is no man who does not recognise certain limits

baffled any longer by a semblance of knowledge; and it is a summons to reason to undertake again the most serious of its duties, namely, the knowledge of itself, and to erect a tribunal which shall guarantee it in its just claims, but condemn (not arbitrarily, but according to its eternal and immutable laws) those which have no foundation" (KANT, *op. cit.*, I, Preface). For the sake of clearness, I have changed the punctuation in one place and anticipated a phrase, putting it in a parenthesis.

[1] And those among them who do not profess themselves agnostics, generally ascribe "metaphysical" value (the absence of the name does not matter, when there is the thing) to the "physical" conception of the universe. Here is an example. "It is indeed true that in conformity with modern positivistic and utilitarian tendencies, many . . . prefer to consider a theory chiefly as a convenient means of arranging . . . facts, or as a guide in the investigation of new phenomena. But while in the past too much faith was put in the powers of the human mind, and it was too readily believed that the supreme reason of things was on the point of being discovered, at present we perhaps fall into the other extreme" (A. RIGHI, *The Modern Theory of Physical Phenomena*, 2nd. ed., Bologna, 1904, pp. 3-4). Now, one may have the utmost confidence " in the powers of the human mind" and yet be firmly convinced that physics, or in general any objective science, is absolutely incapable of "discovering the supreme reason of things." It is not out of place to remark that many profess themselves agnostics, simply meaning that they are not occupied with philosophy; whereas really they take part in it, without knowing what they are talking about. Men who really do not care to form an opinion concerning philosophical problems cannot exist. On the other hand, why do they call the investigations of philosophers vain? Because they believe them to be vain, it would seem. But, since they have no knowledge of them (as appears from the way in which they speak about them), they would have no right to consider them vain, unless they considered themselves possessors of the "true key" necessary to open the doors which philosophers uselessly try to break down. In substance, their anti-philosophical invectives imply (without their knowing it: the unconsciousness of some people is amusingly marvellous) the assumption that philosophy studies the same questions as their science, or that their science studies the same questions as philosophy; they imply the opinion formulated by Righi, that "science" can make known to us "the supreme reason of things."

to his own cognition. But these limits, in the sense in which they are commonly spoken of, have nothing to do with the thing in itself. I do not know, that is to say I do not remember, how many times I have gone out of the house since I have possessed the light of reason, nor even during this year; and yet I know very well that I was going out, every time that I went out. I know that besides the phenomena about which I have a sufficiently definite information, many others or an infinity of others have happened or are happening; this is what I mean when I assert that my cognition has certain, and even very narrow, limits—that it is as nothing in comparison with (phenomenal) reality. But I have never become aware, nor do I think that others have become aware, of an intrinsically unknowable reality, which would put an absolute limit to my cognition.

To imagine that the existence of the unknowable is proved by the fact that no one knows everything, is childish. From this it does not follow that the unknowable is to be excluded without further consideration. But the unknowable is certainly neither something immediately known, nor the immediate act of knowing; therefore we shall be justified in asserting its existence only if it should appear to us necessarily implicit in the immediately known, or in the immediate act of knowing; if this should not appear, the unknowable will have to be excluded as a worthless, or rather meaningless, hypothesis.

It is necessary therefore to inquire whether the immediately known, or the immediate act of knowing, imply anything which is not a phenomenon; *i.e.* it is necessary to construct the theory of knowledge.[1] Let us

---

[1] That is to say, to plunge into the "mare magnum" of philosophy. The agnosticism of Kant (and to a minor degree though at a great distance that of Comte and of Spencer) without being justified is not altogether unfounded. The agnosticism of so many men of science, whose philosophic culture is wholly derived from some review into which they have dipped, is

suppose that the theory of knowledge compels us to admit something which is not phenomenal. This "something," since we have deduced it, *i.e.* since we have made it explicit by drawing it from common cognition in which it was implicit, has become consequently KNOWN, although it is known otherwise than phenomena and perhaps less definitely than some phenomena. Either we have no reasons for assuming the thing in itself, and we must exclude it; or we have reasons for assuming it, and it is not unknowable.

The method by which the problem of the thing in itself, or of metaphysics, has to be discussed—a method which is the only possible one, and the application of which cannot but lead to the solution of the problem—appears thus to be fully determined. The theory of knowledge which we have constructed, seems not to prove the necessity, and therefore to exclude the possibility of assuming the thing in itself. Let us see whether, by considering it more profoundly, we shall be led to a different result.

### 3.
RELATIVITY OF KNOWLEDGE. LEGITIMATE CONCLUSIONS. THE THING IN ITSELF.

Knowledge is relative. In other words, the object is known by the subject as object. It is known therefore in relation to the subject, for no object is possible except for a subject. From this it seems necessary to conclude that the thing in itself, the thing as thing and not as object, the thing in so far as it is outside that relation to the subject which makes it an object, is not knowable.

mere empty tattle. Philosophy treats questions, which are treated by no other branch of learning; and therefore it can be contested only by means of philosophy. This means that a pretended philosophy can be contested, but not philosophy. A defective philosophic doctrine is, in so far as defective, unphilosophical. Another doctrine, which corrects its mistakes, is simply a development of its philosophical portions.

If we assume the existence of a thing in itself, the consequence is inevitable. But (according to the very doctrine we are examining) we know only objects; hence an existence which is not the existence pure and simple of the object as such (its appearing to us), is not known: it is only presupposed. And presuppositions must not be admitted without proofs. The reasoning we have reproduced contains no proof; it is therefore, notwithstanding its apparent stringency, reasoning *in vacuo*.

To sum up, it is not to be inferred from the relativity of knowledge that knowledge has an insuperable limit; in order that the inference should be justified, some other argument must be associated with the relativity in question. The legitimate consequence of relativity (in so far as nothing else but relativity is considered) is entirely different from that which sceptics and agnostics have pretended to infer from it.

The consequence is this, that existence coincides with being an object. That is to say, things, independently of that relation to the subject which makes them objects, would not exist. That same relation to the subject, which is an essential constituent of cognitions, is also an essential constituent of things. Things do not exist except in relation to subjects; and therefore even subjects only exist in relation to one another and to things; the universe consists of, resolves itself into, a system of subjects and of phenomena which are phenomena of the subjects— essential constituents of the subjects.

Nothing can be opposed to all this—nothing can be put in place of it, unless the above-mentioned assumption can be proved. Let us now discuss the proofs of it.

I know that this is an orange; this is known to me as an orange. It does not even cross my mind to identify the orange which is known to me with the cognition which I have of it. I distinguish the orange as a known object from the orange in itself. It remains to know precisely what my distinction means.

I do not yet know the taste of the orange which I see, touch, etc.; but doubtless it has a taste; the cognition which I possess is imperfect, the thing has not the same imperfection. I became acquainted with the orange five minutes ago; but it already existed before: the tradesman who sold it to me, did not manufacture it for me then and there, he simply took it out of a box. And so on.

It is now manifest, in what sense I speak of the orange in itself—of the orange as a distinct thing, quite other than my cognition of that thing. By the expression "orange in itself" I denote a group of phenomena, connected by a relatively fixed law, and constituting a relatively closed unity—but a unity of phenomena which are not all actual phenomena of my own, and each of which might not be (at least so it seems to me) an actual phenomenon of my own. On the other hand my cognition of the orange (1) in any case contains only a portion of those phenomena, and a portion which would not exist by itself alone; (2) implies (besides certain phenomena which are my own, but which might not be my own, and which belong to the group which constitutes the orange in itself) certain phenomena exclusively my own, which do not belong to the orange in itself: my looking, my touching, my reflecting, etc.

I am therefore right, when I distinguish in the way of which I have spoken, and when I speak correlatively of an orange in itself. But this distinction of mine is simply a distinction in the field of phenomena; it is no distinction of the phenomenal from something which is not phenomenal. The orange in itself of which I am speaking, is said by me to be in itself, in order to distinguish it from that different group of phenomena which is my cognition; but it is equally a group of phenomena, each of which might also become included in my cognition. The "in itself" of which we are speaking here, is a phenomenal "in itself"; it has nothing to do with that "in itself," which is considered when the thing in itself is opposed to the phenomenon.

The former "in itself" belongs to common cognition; the latter is a metaphysical hypothesis, founded or unfounded. Without the "in itself" in the former sense, common cognition would not exist. This is the reason why the assumption of which we were speaking seems obvious; indeed, it does not even seem to be an assumption, but an integral part of cognition. But because it is impossible to deny the in itself in the former sense, it does not follow that it is impossible to deny, nor that it is legitimate to assert, the in itself in the latter sense; for the two senses differ *toto cœlo*. Common thought, within its own sphere, is right; but those philosophers who transfer it just as it is to the philosophical field transform it into a philosophical error.

4.

APPEARANCE AND APPEARING. COMMON DISTINCTIONS, AND LIMITS OF THEIR VALIDITY.

In a phenomenon we distinguish appearance and appearing. That is to say, the phenomenon is always at the same time objective and subjective; the appearance, for instance the blue seen, is the objective aspect of the phenomenon; the appearing, my seeing blue, is its subjective aspect. That these elements are not separable, is manifest; the object seen is nothing without the seeing, the seeing is nothing without the object seen. By the distinction mentioned we have therefore not transcended the phenomenon.

It is further said that the phenomenon implies both a thing which appears, and a subject to whom the thing appears. This also is manifest: the blue which I see is the blue of the sky; the sky is a thing which appears blue to me; and I am the subject to whom the thing appears blue. But the question is, whether, by recognising such an implication, we have gone beyond the phenomenon.

As concerns the thing which appears, we answer immediately, No. The reasons have been alleged by us in the preceding paragraph; let us add some further developments. I make a judgment based on appearance. The judgment, in general, goes beyond the appearance which serves as its foundation; but it does not go beyond the field of appearance. *E.g.* of a coin which I receive, I say (and if I do not say, I assume) that it is good; that is to say, it passes current. I see, I touch, etc. the coin; but I have not yet tried to spend it. As coins are made in order to be spent, my judgment refers to the capacity of being spent; that is to say, to an order of phenomena which with regard to that coin I have not yet experienced, but still to an order of phenomena. It may happen that those phenomena, the order of which constitutes the capacity of being spent, and which I infer from the apprehended phenomena (form, stamp, colour, brilliancy, ring), cannot be experienced in spite of the relation in which I suppose them to stand to the apprehended phenomena. Then I say, the coin seemed good to me, and it is counterfeit. To the appearance I oppose the thing which appears. Obviously, my opposition is not unjustified; but it is an opposition of the results of a vaster experience to the inferences drawn from a narrower experience—it is an opposition of certain phenomenal formations to each other, not an opposition of something non-phenomenal to the phenomenal.

The same may be said concerning the subject. I am not the noise which affects me at this moment. The noise (so I think, and that rightly,) is an impression indirectly produced on me by a carriage passing in the street, much as the image is impressed on the wax by the seal. All this has, within the phenomenal order, an intuitive evidence; but it is not manifest, it has no meaning, except within the phenomenal order. Let us leave the carriage, with which we have no longer to occupy ourselves, and consider the subject. Of what am I made ? If I confine myself, as I ought, to the recognition of what I know, I must confess that the matter of which I am made can be resolved precisely into those phenomena, of which I say that I am severally aware ; each of which separately, or each group of which separately, is opposed by me to myself, as the apprehended object to the subject which apprehends it. The distinction between extended and unextended phenomena, however important it may be under another aspect, does not mark the boundary between a matter which is not mine and a matter which is my own ; are not extended phenomena, then, apprehended by me, are they not my own, like the others ? If all phenomena were to vanish, the subject which apprehends them would vanish also.

The subject therefore is really nothing but the system, the unity of its phenomena. Certainly the unity is not a phenomenon, and perhaps it will open us the way to escape from the phenomenal; but this point we shall discuss further on. For the present, it has been made clear that the distinction between any one (or any one group) of the apprehended phenomena, and the subject which apprehends them, takes place within the system of phenomena. As we cannot say of any phenomenon that it is external to the system, or that it implies something external to the system; so it is not permissible (excluding the conclusions which might be reached by considering more carefully the form of unity) to speak of the subject as of something external to its phenomena.

Since the subject is simply the system of its phenomena, the opposition commonly made between the subject and one of its phenomena is significant and justified in so far as it is the opposition between the system and one of its constituents; but not otherwise. The common man is not wrong; but (here again) the philosopher who should transfer a common distinction unchanged to the field of metaphysics—who should interpret as a going beyond experience that which in substance is a simple systematisation of experience—such a philosopher would be in the wrong.

It is moreover to be remarked that, although phenomena are essential to the subject, perhaps no one is essential to the subject. Phenomena are accidental; and many of them have only a very small importance for the subject. These circumstances must be taken seriously into account, even in philosophy; they also explain the common conviction better; but they do not justify us in simply transforming this conviction into a metaphysical doctrine.

5.

INSEPARABLENESS OF SINGLE PHENOMENA FROM THE SUBJECT-UNITY. ONE SUBJECT AND ANOTHER SUBJECT.

"The ultimate reality of things, therefore, which the common consciousness seeks in their purely unrelated or independent being, and which science seeks in their existence as essentially related to each other, is only to be found in what we may call their ideal character, as unities of correlative differences, or unities which manifest themselves in difference, yet in this difference are still one with themselves."[1]

[1] E. CAIRD, *Hegel*, p. 175. Compare F. H. BRADLEY, *Appearance and Reality*, 2nd edition (5th impression; the 1st edition appeared in 1893), p. 552: "Reality is one experience, self-pervading and superior to mere relations."

No single phenomenon and no limited group of phenomena, or in short no distinct fact (no concrete, and *a fortiori* no character of a concrete) is possible except as a constituent of a higher unity, which in its turn is constitutive of each one of these elements. Every fact of experience or of consciousness, under both aspects, subjective and objective (every content and every containing, for each subject can be resolved into the unity of a containing, of a power of apprehending), implies all the others. It is therefore connected with all the others by relations which are essential to all.

But these relations, just because they are essential to the elements connected by them, cannot be considered as something external to the elements, like for instance the mortar which binds the bricks of a wall together. Relations, because essential to the elements, are constituents of them; they are characters of the elements; so that, consequently, to speak of relations is still to speak of elements, and nothing else.

We must be able to understand; for what could not possibly be understood (what is absurd) would be neither real nor possible. This, which is the constant test of common thought, must be *a fortiori* the test of philosophic thought;[1] for philosophic thought implies common thought which it claims to transcend, and succeeds in transcending in so far as it introduces into the latter a greater coherence, and is a more rigorous and more conscious application of the same test. The single phenomena are not separately comprehensible; the relations by which we recognise them to be connected are in

---

[1] "We were judging phenomena, . . . and throughout we proceeded as if the self-contradictory could not be real. . . . Thus we possess a criterion, and our criterion is supreme. . . . Our standard denies inconsistency, and therefore asserts consistency. If we can be sure that the inconsistent is unreal, we must, logically, be just as sure that the reality is consistent" (BRADLEY, *op. cit.*, pp. 136-7-9).

substance nothing but the forms by means of which we express their inseparability : if we wish actually to understand the inseparableness of single phenomena, that is to say, if we do not wish to declare the single phenomena which we experience impossible, we must reach a unity of which every phenomenon is a constituent, and which in its turn is constitutive of every phenomenon.

Every subject is such a unity for its own phenomena, that is to say for those of which both the content of its consciousness and its own consciousness (awareness, and that of which we are aware,) are the result. The subject-unity is no phenomenon; but, as such, it is neither outside, nor above, the phenomenon; for it is precisely the phenomenal life of the subject and nothing else. It might imply a non-phenomenal reality. But, when we consider it in its pure and simple appearance to itself, in that appearance to itself which is essential to every appearance within it, and can be resolved into appearance within it, we must recognise that it is no non-phenomenal reality. It is a form or law of phenomena—a law, without which there would be none of the phenomena of which it is the law, but which vice versa would not exist without a complex of phenomena, since it is nothing but the law or form of those phenomena. We have seen on another occasion that the necessity essential to every thought and fact included in the subject-unity, has as its foundation the subject-unity itself.

But the particular subject is not singular. It cannot be singular, for it recognises an essential constituent of itself in the existence of other subjects, of other unities. The process by which a subject is led to think itself reflectively,[1] to recognise itself, leads it at the same time to recognise

---

[1] Note the adverb carefully : a subject which does not think itself, is impossible ; but between thinking itself, and thinking itself reflectively there is a difference, as there is between clear consciousness and subconsciousness.

the other subject—to recognise, in the analogous process of the other subject, an indispensable element of its own process : it is sufficient to observe, that without some kind of language we have no reflective consciousness of ourselves.[1] On the other hand, the necessity which every developed subject recognises in its own thought, does not belong to its thought in so far as it is its own ; it is universally valid, *i.e.* it applies also to the thought of any other subject, if any other subject exists. Have we in this way proved only the possibility of the other subject ? It may be ; but the possibility, besides being something in itself, deprives captious doubts, which might be raised against the foregoing proof of fact, of all value.

### 6.
#### THE ABSOLUTE AND BEING. THE ABSOLUTE AND THE PHENOMENAL UNIVERSE.

The many subjects cannot simply co-exist with one another ; they are connected by relations essential to each of them, for otherwise one subject would neither know nor imagine anything about another ; therefore (as consequence of the reasoning which we have previously mentioned, § 5) they are all elements of one and the same higher unity, constitutive of each. Obviously the higher unity of subjects is also the higher unity of all phenomena without exception; for there are no phenomena which are not connected in the unity of some subject, if not of every subject.

According to the doctrine which we have set forth, the higher unity of phenomena and of those particular unities of phenomena which are subjects, the supreme unity, is

---

[1] "The process, which conducts you to other selves, is not weaker sensibly, if at all, than the construction by which your own self is gained" (BRADLEY, *op. cit.*, p. 257). Properly, that "process" and this "construction" are simultaneous and co-essential ; they constitute together one and the same systematisation of experience.

that quite indeterminate Being, of which every concrete, and every character of every concrete, is a determination.

Must we therefore conclude that Being is the Absolute?

Being, as we said, and as everybody understands, is nothing but a concept which exists only in so far as it is thought, and can be thought only by some subject. And only developed subjects can think it reflectively. But the thinking in which the existence of a concept consists may also be unreflecting. The thought then of Being, at least the unreflecting thought of it, is an essential constituent of every subject, knowing or capable of arriving at cognition. In fact cognition can be resolved into judgment; and judgment always necessarily implies Being as predicate.[1]

Being includes all its determinations. Therefore a subject, when it thinks Being, implicitly thinks the universe; that is to say, it implies the universe, it is a centre of the universe. And the existence of the subject consists in its being thus a centre of the universe; for the subject would not exist, if it did not think Being (reflectively or unreflectingly). I suppose that by now it will no longer seem a riddle how a relation to every other subject is essential to every subject.

Being, though every subject thinks it as a whole (for Being, as wholly indeterminate, can have no parts), is not

[1] "When I say . . . that a certain being exists I should not understand what I am saying, unless I already knew what a being is" (ROSMINI, *Philosophic System*, section 15). It is useless to multiply quotations, for this doctrine of Rosmini is well known. He who does not understand what it is to think Being with or without reflection will do well to study all Rosmini's works diligently: some, perhaps not useless, hints will be found in the *Great Problems* and also in the preceding pages of the present work. The doctrine, which I am working out, is not the same as that of Rosmini; but this fundamental point of it belongs to Rosmini, who, by establishing it, made perhaps the most important advance in modern philosophy. My doctrine, I believe, is simply a logical development of the Rosminian principle. But in order to compare the two doctrines—in order to make clear, not the differences (which are obvious), but the reason of the differences—I should have to write a whole book. It is impossible to lengthen this note, so as to make it into a book; it will be better therefore to cut it short at once.

exhausted in being thought by a subject; its existence consists in being thought by every subject. And every subject exists, in so far as it is a particular thought (one among many) about universal Being. In this sense we say that each subject is a determination of Being; which, as essentially thought by each subject, is common to all—is that, by which the unity of all is constituted.

But, conversely, if there were no single subjects, Being also would not exist, for its existence consists in being thought by all. So that consequently Being, or the unity of the phenomenal universe, is not something subsisting independently of phenomena and of those secondary unities formed by them which are subjects. Even of the supreme unity we must say what we have said of the secondary unities: the supreme unity is the form of a matter—a form which cannot subsist without a matter, as on the other hand matter could not subsist without the form.

And therefore the Absolute cannot be reduced to Being as such. According to the doctrine expounded (as to which we are inquiring, whether it needs or admits of any modification), the Absolute is the universe in the unity of its form, which implies necessity, but at the same time in the multiplicity of its matter and of its secondary forms—a multiplicity, which implies accidentality. To sum up, the Absolute is the phenomenal universe—one indeed, but at the same time manifold also.

### 7.

#### POSSIBILITY OF PHENOMENA.

For the common man the universe is a phenomenal multiplicity. Obviously, the manifold phenomena to which both the content of consciousness and the fact that it is a content (the known and the act of knowing) can be reduced, or into which the existence of consciousness can be resolved, must be possible. We have to understand, how they are possible; this is the *raison d'être* of philosophic reflection.

The possibility of the manifold phenomena has their unity as its condition. And this unity cannot be that of a thing which has to be known; for then we should still have a multiplicity: the thing known on one hand, the knowing subject on the other. It must be the unity of cognition. In every cognition (we are speaking throughout of common cognitions) the known object and the act by which it is known, both of them phenomenal, that is to say both of them facts of consciousness, constitute together one strict unity, although, or rather because, they are distinguishable: they condition each other. And their unity is the unity of the knowing subject.

We cannot however be satisfied with this unity. For the cognitions are many; and, considering the way in which we commonly possess them, it does not appear clearly how they can constitute a unity. While, on the other hand, it is undeniable that they must constitute such a unity: there is no cognition which stands by itself; a cognition is possible in so far as the system is possible, *i.e.* in so far as the unity of all exists.

The unity of all, the unity of cognition or of phenomena, is certainly not outside common cognition, of which it is a constituent (otherwise there would be no common cognition); the function of philosophy can be only that of apprehending it clearly and distinctly.

From all this it follows that if we succeed in reconstructing the universal unity by simply recognising it as the unity of phenomena, or as the form of that matter in which phenomena consist—a form essential to matter, but essentially implying matter—then the burden of proving that the unity so reconstructed is not the true one, or is not ultimate, falls on him who denies the value, the ultimate value, of the unity reconstructed. Thus we have determined the position of the doctrine expounded in relation to any other.[1]

In order to show that the supreme unity must be a non-phenomenal reality, many writers have maintained that the concept of phenomenon is itself contradictory. The method would be decisive, if it were not defective; but it is really defective.

Let us observe in the first place, that contradiction pure and simple cannot, as such, be transcended or overcome in any way. Let us suppose that I addressed the following argument to my opponent: (1) Your doctrine is true, but, nevertheless, it is false. (2) Consequently, I am in search of a doctrine which may overcome, or eliminate, the contradiction just pointed out.—The opponent would reply that my words as reported in the first clause are altogether meaningless; they are not a proposition, true, hypothetical or false, from which I can draw a consequence.

I spoke of contradiction pure and simple. It would be another thing, if I were to say: Your doctrine seems true to me from one point of view, and false from another; I cannot, *hic et nunc*, decide between the pro and the con; and therefore I proceed in my search.—The reasoning is sensible, even if I could not produce the precise reasons for which the doctrine seems true to me, and the contrary reasons for which it seems false to me; it is enough, that I should apprehend confusedly both sets of reasons together. The contradiction, in this case, can be overcome; but it is not a contradiction pure and simple. I have not said yes and no; but I have reasons for saying yes, and reasons for saying no. Have I any reasons for

---

[1] I mean those which recognise the impossibility of dispensing with unity; doctrines which are satisfied to remain fragmentary do not deserve to be taken into consideration.

asserting that phenomena happen? Yes; at least this, that even if I were to deny that phenomena happen, my denial would be itself a phenomenon. Phenomena are absolutely undeniable.

Let us proceed. I analyse the concept of phenomenon; and (let us suppose) I recognise it to be intrinsically contradictory.

If I make the meaning of the assertion—phenomena happen—thoroughly explicit to myself I recognise (let us suppose) as necessarily implicit in it the negation— these phenomena (the same) do not happen.—So that I am reduced to saying: it is true, and it is not true, that phenomena happen.

To propose to oneself to overcome this contradiction, *i.e.* to discover the meaning of a phrase which in its essence is meaningless, is much the same as to propose to oneself to discover how many vertices a temperature has. And to have recourse, in order to overcome the contradiction, to something which transcends phenomena, is even worse. For, to transcend phenomena, to reduce phenomena to something which is not phenomenal, is to deny phenomena. And to deny phenomena is, in the first place, to adhere to one only of the two opposites, instead of reconciling them as was intended. In the second place it is to leave as they were the reasons (just mentioned) which make phenomena absolutely undeniable. So that, after all, we find ourselves still entangled in the contradiction; the attempt to overcome it has failed.

### 8.

APPARENT CONTRADICTION IN THE CONCEPT OF PHENOMENA, AND ELIMINATION OF IT.

Let us consider particularly the contradiction which is asserted to be implicit in the concept of variation. The discussion, of which we shall make it the subject, may serve also as a model for others, more or less analogous, into which we think it useless to enter.

A (particular, finite) being of any kind A varies. At a given moment it is in an intrinsic condition or state $A_1$; at a succeeding moment it is in an intrinsic condition or state $A_2$, $A_1$ and $A_2$ being different. The variation, whether continuous or discontinuous, necessarily implies that, at one and the same moment, A must be said to be in the state $A_1$ and in a state different from $A_1$, *i.e.* not in the state $A_1$. Here the contradiction is manifest: at one and the same moment A is, and is not, in the state $A_1$. And in order to overcome it, we must (so it is asserted) recognise the variation as only apparent.

It is not difficult to recognise the insufficiency of this device. In fact, if we were to accept it, we ought to say: A seems to be at the same time $A_1$ and not $A_1$. In other words, A at the same moment is and is not $A_1$ in appearance. The contradiction exists as before, exactly as before; it consists in fact, not in the predicate, $A_1$ *sic et simpliciter*, or $A_1$ in appearance, or whatever else it may be; but in the double copula " is " and " is not," which has not disappeared in consequence of the change of the predicate.

We think variation; therefore the thought of variation must not be absurd. It seems absurd; it must be possible to recognise it as not absurd. And to recognise behind variation an absolute permanence in which the thought would not be absurd (even if we suppose that this recognition is more than a fiction), is not to recognise *this* thought as non-absurd or to make it so.

The difficulty can have only one solution, which consists in showing that the absurdity apparently implied by the concept of variation is implied by it only apparently. Not the variation, but the absurdity of the concept of variation is a mere appearance. A mere appearance must be capable of being overcome ; let us see how it is possible to overcome that of which we are speaking.

We have the very old and rooted habit of considering things as permanent. " Real " things, according to the vulgar conception, are in the end bodies. And we are well aware that a number of bodies, if not all, vary. But we recognise at the same time that, in a great number of cases, though some or many qualities of a body vary, a certain complex of other qualities remains unvaried. And to this complex we ascribe a special primary importance ; for the need of immediate practice, which dominates common thought, obliges us to do so.

I go here and there, I sit down, I stand, I pluck a fruit, I eat it, I lie down, etc. ; my body varies unceasingly. But nevertheless it is always my body. The water of a receiver becomes warm, and nevertheless it is still, warm as it is, the same water which was before cold. Why do I say this ? Because the water is still in the receiver ; and the receiver was not emptied to be refilled. And so on ; to adduce other examples would be useless.

There are exceptions : the wood on the fire is consumed ; here is a variation, under which we do not see anything permanent. But, first of all, common thought is not thoroughly coherent, and for that very reason man was not satisfied with it ; incoherence, however, does not prevent common thought from being what it is, nor from exerting a durable influence on scientific and philosophic reflection. Further, the assumption (empirically justified, as we said,) that under the variations of bodies there are true permanencies, led to a second assumption (also empirically justified, as we have observed above,)—to the assumption that variation, at least in many cases, is violent. The vulgar do not perceive any essential difficulty in the concept that while violence mostly changes only some qualities of a body, it may, by becoming more intense, reach that nucleus which usually remains permanent—may end in the destruction of the body. The coherence of common thought, though not such as to satisfy a strict skepsis, is even greater than it appeared at first.

## 9.

### CONTINUATION.

The assumption that the variation of a body implies a permanence of the varying body, *i.e.* of a complex of its qualities which is considered as the true nucleus, has acquired a primary value in the general systematisation of experience; has become, we may say, the centre of it. Not without reason. The assumption cannot stand the test of philosophical criticism; but it is justified, it is imposed, by such experience as the vulgar have and by the reflection which the vulgar are capable of exercising on their own experience. Its empirical or practical validity is beyond question. By accepting it, *i.e.* by implying it, the vulgar make no mistake; while the mistake is made by the philosopher, who transfers immediately to the field of metaphysics a concept whose true place is in the field of common practice.[1]

The only permanence which is necessarily presupposed by variation, the only permanence therefore which may be called absolute, is the permanence of the subject; we mean, of the subject as unity of experience,[2] as form: the permanence of the content would exclude variation.[3]

---

[1] Here it is well not to neglect a simple but instructive reflection: the philosopher ascribes to every being that which the vulgar say of every body; one understands how the vulgar identify being with body; but the philosopher?

[2] Naturally, the permanence of that unity which is the single subject implies the permanence of that supreme unity which is the system of subjects. This must be always understood; but here it is enough that it should be understood.

[3] Permanence of form implies a certain permanence of content, but not the absolute permanence of any content. The subject would vanish, if the whole content were all at once replaced by another; but it persists, even if

In order that I may say that the water has become warm, I must know that the water is always the same; but (without considering that the permanence of the water is never absolute, even if we neglect the temperature,) the change of the water does not prevent me from recognising a variation of temperature. Variations are always possible, on condition that the formal unity of consciousness persists. Not only so, but we must exclude the permanence of anything except this formal unity, for every content is a phenomenon and, as such, consists in a variation.

Bearing this well in mind, let us return to the judgment expressing variation. A is and is not, at the same time, $A_1$. If we conceive the being of the thing in the common way, as a permanence, no doubt the judgment is contradictory. A is $A_1$, is then understood as if it meant, A is permanently $A_1$; so also A is not $A_1$, is understood as if it meant, A is permanently not $A_1$. For example, of a moving point M of which the fixed point P is a position, we may say, M is and is not in P; if to be in P is interpreted as to be constantly in P, the judgment is contradictory.

But from the reflections already made it follows, that nothing permanent exists, nor can exist, save the formal subjective unity which is not contemplated in the judgment supposed to be contradictory. Strictly speaking,

the whole content changes, on condition that the latter changes gradually. The permanence of the subject implies reminiscence; and (as I have shown in the *Great Problems*) the possibility of recollecting a phenomenon is still a certain permanence of that phenomenon. But, first of all, it is not an integral permanence; to recollect is not precisely to live over again. Further, it is not at all necessary that reminiscence should go back *ad infinitum*; for none of us do recollections go beyond early childhood. And if the possibility of recollecting were to vanish completely (as it practically vanishes as regards the greater part of the content) after a definite time, for instance, after ten years, our life would certainly be different from what it is, but the continuity of the subject would remain (so it seems to me) untouched. The only permanence which may be called absolute is the permanence of a form; which is no doubt the form of a matter, but which can remain the same, even when the matter varies.

therefore, there is no place for the application of the category of permanent being.¹ And, when we dismiss this inapplicable category, the contradiction also vanishes, for it arises simply from applying a concept outside its conditions of applicability, or validity.

The category of which we have to make use, when we are speaking of variations, is not that of being, in the sense of a permanent *quid*, but that of variation. We must say, not that A is $A_1$ and is not $A_1$ at the same moment, but that A, in a given moment, passes through the state $A_1$. In the example of motion, we must say, not that M is and is not in P at the same moment, but that M, at a given moment, moves through P.

The passing, the moving, or simply the varying, are irreducible to being in the sense of permanent being; but this does not mean that they are not concepts. They are concepts which have to be considered such as they are, without professing to reduce them to others, to which they cannot be reduced. It is true that, if we try to express variation in terms of permanent being, we fall into contradiction; but we should also fall into contradiction if we tried to express permanent being in terms of variation. Of these two contradictions, the latter does not justify the negation of the invariable (formal) unity of consciousness; in the same way, the former does not justify the negation of the variability essential to phenomena, *i.e.* to the content of the invariable unity.

### 10.

#### THE PHENOMENAL SUBJECT AND THE SUBJECT IN ITSELF.

Let us return to the concept of "thing in itself," in order to examine another and more important application of it.

---

[1] Strictly speaking; for we do not deny that this category allows that rough application which common thought makes of it, but this does not signify.

The assertion was (this proposition has already been discussed), that the phenomena of which a subject is conscious, and which together constitute its experience, are the modes under which a reality which remains unknown, the thing in itself, appears to that subject. We may add that the subject which is conscious of the phenomena, and which is simply their unity, is also phenomenal—is therefore the mode under which a "subject in itself" becomes manifest or appears.

The two propositions, most obviously connected with each other, seem however at first to be distinct; but it is easy to recognise that they can be reduced to one. The subject in itself does not differ from the thing in itself. We must notice that the thing as well as the subject in itself appears under the form of a complex of phenomena—of one and the same complex of phenomena, *i.e.* that, by which the experience of the phenomenal subject is constituted. It is not credible that spatial phenomena should be referred to the thing in itself, non-spatial to the subject in itself; for the two classes of phenomena are inseparable from each other, and the former, as well as the latter, are constitutive of the phenomenal subject.

Moreover, we can say nothing of the thing in itself, for categories are not applicable to it; consequently, to assert or even merely to suppose that there are two or more things in themselves (even the subject in itself is of course a thing in itself), is nonsense; the distinction between two things implies distinctive characters, which cannot possibly be assigned in this case. And further, we must not forget that necessity, manifest even in the field of objective phenomena and of phenomenal subjective knowledge, implies the unity of objective and subjective phenomena, the real unity of the universe. Having assumed any kind of multiplicity (more than one thing in itself, or

## The Absolute

more than one subject in itself, or several of both, or even only one thing in itself besides one subject in itself), we ought then to go back to a principle of unity, numerically one. And such a principle will be at the same time both the thing in itself and the subject in itself.[1]

There ought to be therefore one single reality, which can be considered under one aspect as thing in itself, under another as subject in itself. But first of all, by having ascribed to the thing in itself the further character of subject in itself, we have not in the least removed the difficulties, previously recognised in the concept of thing in itself (present chapter, §§ 3, 4). A phenomenon is subject to conditions which cannot be simply resolved into other phenomena (matter implies a form ; whence however it is not to be inferred that form is something subsisting by itself, outside all matter) ; but no phenomenon is ever the appearance of a thing, which there is any ground to believe different from that appearance, or phenomenon. And the argument is absolutely true even of the subject. No doubt, the phenomenal subject appears, consists in appearing. But there is no reason, any more than in the former case, to believe that the appearance constituting the phenomenal subject is the appearance of a *quid*, of the subject in itself, other than that appearance, than the phenomenal subject.

There are moreover some very serious difficulties, special to the second case. The subject is, in its very nature, the being which knows itself. It may be doubtful, and more than doubtful, whether the subject ever knows anything except itself ; but certainly, either it knows

---

[1] "I will . . . make a remark as to the plurality involved in things in themselves. . . . Their diversity and their relations bring us back to those very difficulties which we were endeavouring to avoid. And it seems clear that, if we wish to be consistent, the plural must be dropped. Hence . . . we shall confine ourselves to the Thing in itself" (which is one, and therefore not only the *thing* in itself, but at the same time also the subject in itself). BRADLEY, *op. cit.*, p. 129.

itself, or it knows nothing, and therefore does not exist as a subject. The phenomenal subject (it is said) is the subject in itself in so far as (as, such as) it appears to itself. This is hard to understand. The subject in itself is not, according to the hypothesis, phenomenal. The phenomenal subject is phenomenal. Therefore phenomenal consciousness is not the consciousness which the subject in itself has of itself. And the subject in itself does not know itself, is no subject. We might say at most, that the X which is (wrongly) called subject in itself, has the power of deceiving itself by constructing a phenomenal consciousness, which imagines itself to be a consciousness of itself. It remains to know, whether these phrases have a meaning; whether they constitute a theory of knowledge, and serve to determine exactly the concept of self-consciousness.

On the other hand, subject is a category,—not entirely objective, but also not entirely extra-objective. The subject is always conscious of itself, otherwise it would not exist; but it recognises itself as subject, only in so far as it reflects on itself. Now, by reflection, the cognition even of oneself assumes an objective character. It is true that in this objectivity the subject reconstructs its own subjectivity; but it is also true that subjectivity is reflectively reconstructed only by means of objectivity. And the subject recognises itself reflectively as subject, only in so far as it recognises by the same reflection other subjects which are objects for it. Whence it follows in the most obvious way, that subject is a category which has also an objective, though not a merely objective, value —a category therefore which is not applicable outside the field of phenomena. The thing in itself (supposing, what I do not admit, that there is a thing in itself,) cannot be a subject.

Not so—is the reply.—From what you have said it is to

be concluded, not that the non-phenomenal subject is impossible, but that there is only one non-phenomenal subject. The category (if we wish to call it so) of subject has an objective aspect only in so far as it is predicated of many; in order to suppress its objectivity, and so make it applicable beyond phenomena, it is enough to exclude its manifold predicability.

This argument, which is offered as a defence, is the avowal of an error of method. The category of subject is applicable in the phenomenal world, and is severally predicable of many things. The two characters are at once constitutive and co-essential characters of it. Without the smallest reason, against all reasons, the second character is left out, and it is pretended that in this way the first is transformed, and that the category thus becomes applicable outside phenomena. But by leaving out the second character, the first is, not transformed, but destroyed; and the category is reduced to a word which has no longer any possible meaning.[1]

## 11.

### THE UNITY OF THE UNIVERSE AS UNITY OF ONE SINGLE (UNIVERSAL) SUBJECT.

Although the doctrine which resolves the unity of the universe into the unity of one single subject, cannot be accepted under that form of it which we have just discussed, it might still be acceptable, or even inevitable,

---

[1] It is, in fact, Spinoza's error. The category of substance is valid in the phenomenal universe, and is manifoldly predicable in it. By dropping the manifold predicability S. thought he could make of it a category, to speak in our own language, of the noumenon. That his error has marked an advance in some essential respects we do not deny. So we do not deny that the error just attacked marks an essential advance with respect to S.'s conception and others. But we cannot stop even at the point which we have reached by this advance. Our "confutations" are, in reality, attempts to transcend certain doctrines—attempts in which the doctrines transcended are taken into account, and in which a doctrine is transcended by the means furnished by itself when considered in relation to others.

under some other form. We must examine its intrinsic merits.

The universal Subject must be conceived as a unity of consciousness; for a subject which is not a unity of consciousness, is an absurdity.

That unity of consciousness which is the particular subject, implies the whole phenomenal universe; but does not imply all the elements of it in the same way. As content, the universe, with regard to each particular subject, can be divided into two spheres between which we must distinguish, although it is not possible to distinguish them exactly, the sphere of clear consciousness and the sphere of subconsciousness. And although the two spheres together always constitute the phenomenal universe, the line of division between them is different for each subject: this difference is a characteristic of the particularity of each subject.

For the universal Subject, all the elements of the phenomenal universe must be contained in its consciousness in the same way: no division can take place between a sphere of clear consciousness and a sphere of subconsciousness. The universal Subject must be clearly conscious of every phenomenon.

In fact, each of us must recognise that the phenomenal universe is an essential constituent of himself, is implicit in him; and that, for the most part, it is only implicit in him, while, for some elements (*e.g.* the pleasures and pains of others), even the possibility of ever making them clearly explicit to oneself is excluded. Now, the implicit and subconscious are certainly indispensable; but, no doubt, they are not clear concepts. It would be a real gain to eliminate them, especially to eliminate that implicit and subconscious which must always remain such. And the hypothesis of a universal Subject has theoretically no other office, no other meaning, than that of eliminating them.

A universal Subject for which there were still a subconsciousness would be a useless, or rather a contradictory hypothesis, for subconsciousness, as we just remarked, is characteristic of the particular subject.

But the universal Subject must not only include, as its content, every content of a particular consciousness or subconsciousness; it must also include as content every particular consciousness or subconsciousness. That is to say, the universal Subject must be aware not only of all that of which every particular subject is aware; it must also be aware of the awareness of every particular subject. It includes the universe; and it includes all those inclusions of the universe, to which the particular subjects can be reduced and into which they can be resolved. It thinks, it knows, even the thoughts and the thinking of each of us.

This is intuitively obvious. Every phenomenon, the complex of phenomena, is a matter of which each particular subject is a unity, a form. And matter cannot subsist without form, as form cannot subsist without matter. No phenomenon would happen, if they were not all, in various ways, phenomena of each of those unities which are the particular subjects. Therefore even the particular consciousness implies both its own unity and the other unities. None of us is altogether clearly conscious of himself; the clear consciousness of that in which the intimate life of another subject consists, is wholly absent from each of us. But this happens because none of us particular subjects is in one and the same relation with all other particular subjects and with all phenomena. Each of us is in great part subconscious : this is the reason why particular consciousnesses are each outside the other.

Subconsciousness can have no place in the universal Subject; it follows that the universal Subject is also conscious of the consciousness of every particular subject.

The universal Subject cannot but be fully conscious of everything,—and of itself. It is therefore personal. We also are persons. But we easily recognise, that in our personal unity only a part of that which forms the vaster unity of consciousness and subconsciousness is organised; we are imperfect, because limited, persons. The personality of the universal Subject, not being limited, is perfect.[1]

## 12.

### HOW THE UNIVERSAL SUBJECT MUST BE CONCEIVED.

We have seen that the existence of particular things, phenomena and subjects, is conditioned by their supreme unity: there is nothing which is not a determination of Being; nothing exists, except as a determination of Being. Since we have admitted that the unity of the whole is a universal Subject, we shall have to conclude that the existence of every particular thing consists in its being thought by the universal Subject.

There is, or there ought to be, no need of repeating that "thought" does not mean here "abstract thought." There is no phenomenon, which is not a fact of consciousness—of the consciousness of a particular subject, immediately. But as this consciousness would not exist without its essential relations with other analogous consciousnesses, and ultimately with all the analogous consciousnesses, so, and for the same reason, it cannot be reduced to any of those elements which can be abstracted from it.

The stone over which I stumble is a resistance opposing me. I am aware of it. My being aware consists in an act on my part, partially obstructed and partially determined

---

[1] "If the term 'personal' is to bear anything like its ordinary sense, assuredly the Absolute is not merely personal. It is not personal, because it is personal and more. It is, in a word, super-personal" (BRADLEY, *op. cit.*, p. 531).

by the obstruction to which it is correlative and which is a constituent of it; in a suffering on my part; further in a knowledge on my part, that is to say in a system of concepts and judgments belonging to me. No one of these distinguishable elements exists or can exist separately from the rest. The thought on my part, to which my phenomenon can be reduced, is my vital action in its intrinsic fulness and in the complexity of its extrinsic relations. We do not pretend to reduce the matter of the phenomenon to that form of it which is abstract thought (we are not idealists, in the sense in which many, perhaps most people, understand idealism); and that for the very reason for which we do not believe that the form of the phenomenon, abstract thought, can be reduced to a product of unformed matter (for the same reason for which we are not empiricists). And in both cases in substance nothing but an abstracting takes place; there is a breaking up of the phenomenon, which is a phenomenon in so far as it has all together the characters which can be abstracted from it, in so far as it is the unity of those characters.

To imagine that the consciousness of the universal Subject is less rich, less energetic, less vivid, than the consciousness of the particular subject, would be an extravagance. It has been said that the world exists in so far as God geometrises. And we do not deny that a reasonable sense may be given to this conception; but it is necessary not to give to it an unreasonable sense. The world is infinitely too various and too complex to allow the doctrine of it to be reduced to any kind of geometry. Not only so, but the world absolutely cannot be reduced to any doctrine of the world, if a system of abstractions is understood by the word doctrine. We can and must say that the world is one and the same with the doctrine, or with the cognition, which God possesses of it; not however in the sense that the world is nothing but (abstract) thought, but in the sense that there can be nothing in the world (no element, no character), which is not a divine cognition, or thought. We mean, not that a divine thought, as adequate as we like, but different or other than reality, corresponds to reality, but that reality IS precisely the divine thought of such reality. The distinction between thought and phenomenon, since the two, in their fulness, in their actuality are coincident, has not an absolute value even with regard to the particular subject; it has, as we have recognised, a certain value with regard to it, but a value correlative to its particular limited being, as a compound of consciousness and subconsciousness; with regard to the universal Subject it becomes an absurdity pure and simple.

Therefore, the existence of particular subjects, and consequently of the phenomenal universe, can be reduced to their being thoughts of the universal Subject: *scientia Dei est causa rerum*. There is a universal Subject, in so far as Being (of which every phenomenon and every secondary unity of phenomena is a determination,) has consciousness of itself, or rather is consciousness of itself. The phenomenal world exists, in so far as self-conscious Being actualises the determinations in itself. Whether to actualise the determinations in itself by thinking them coincides or not, is or is not one and the same with self-consciousness, is then a point which for the present remains undecided.

### 13.

#### IDENTITY OF PHENOMENA AS INCLUDED IN THE PARTICULAR OR IN THE UNIVERSAL SUBJECT.

A phenomenon is always the same, whether it be considered as included within the consciousness of the universal Subject, or as included within the consciousness of a particular subject. A phenomenon of which I become aware, is certainly something in so far as I am aware of it; in other words, this my awareness and its content which is inseparable from it, are facts which happen—which happen really, though to be sure not independently. No phenomenon is possible outside the universal unity; if we admit that the universal unity is the consciousness of the universal Subject, no phenomenon is possible outside the consciousness of the universal Subject. Just for this reason it must be concluded that a phenomenon of mine is the same, both as my phenomenon, and as a phenomenon of the universal Subject.

In fact, let us suppose that a phenomenon has, in so far as it is mine, certain characters; and, in so far as it is a phenomenon of the universal Subject, certain other characters. Then, my phenomenon and the phenomenon of the universal Subject will be two different phenomena, let us say H and K. And that existence which cannot be denied to my phenomenon H, because H is a phenomenon of mine, will not consist in its being included in the consciousness of the universal Subject; for H, according to the hypothesis, is outside the consciousness of the universal Subject, in which, on the contrary, there is K.

Perhaps it will be said that the existence of K is the cause or condition of the existence of H. But it is not the same thing, to recognise that each phenomenon (I am speaking of those of which we are aware or can become aware) has a condition or a cause, is subject to something else, and to recognise that phenomena essentially constitute a system, a unity, outside which they are not possible. And the preceding investigations have compelled us precisely to recognise the system or unity of phenomena, of these everyday phenomena of ours. The possibility of inferring a cause or condition transcending phenomena has as its indispensable presupposition the recognition of the unity of phenomena; for, if this is denied, it is no longer possible to suppress the fragmentariness of common cognition, a doctrine of the whole is no longer possible. If we wish to say something intelligible, we ought neither to assert that unity consists in the cause, nor to conceive the cause so as to exclude unity.

It is objected, that to the human phenomenon H there corresponds in the universal Subject something different K, the condition *sine qua non* of H. Now, what is K? We expressed ourselves just now as if K were a phenomenon, though a phenomenon different from our own. But it cannot be so. If the consciousness of the universal Subject admitted what we call a phenomenon, a various multiplicity of phenomena, it would admit our own phenomenon, and there would be no reason for supposing a phenomenon K in the place of a phenomenon H. The supposed K can be only non-phenomenal; and cannot even be a form of phenomena, for form is inseparable from matter; it is therefore an absolute unknown, or rather an absolute unknowable. So the theory of knowledge ends in agnosticism; and the fundamental identity between reality and cognition, which we have recognised as undeniable, vanishes.

Moreover, since the H's of particular finite consciousnesses become K's (become other) in the universal consciousness, this latter cannot be said to be unity of the H's, but at most the cause of them. The universal consciousness which we had introduced in order to understand the unity of the H's, the concept of which ought to have been the concept of such a unity, has become transformed for us into a cause, unknown in itself, and of which we do not even know in what way it is a cause—into a cause, of which we know with certainty only this, that it is not the unity of the H's. The attempt to understand the unity of the H's better has destroyed it.

## The Absolute

After this, it is no longer possible even to admit, that universal consciousness is the cause of the phenomenal universe. Since a consciousness which is only theoretical, is nothing but an abstraction, it is clear that if the universal consciousness were the unity of the phenomenal universe, it would be also its cause; that is to say, it would be not only cognitive, but at the same time creative too. Reciprocally, unless it is a cognitive unity, it will not be creative either; for mere practical doing is no less abstract than mere theoretical thinking. And further we have still to learn, whether there is any meaning in defining as a subject an X, of which we know absolutely nothing, which indeed we see to be absolutely useless.[1]

[1] I have discussed in this paragraph some assertions of Mr. Bradley, *op. cit.* I quote a few of the more remarkable passages: "There is but one Reality. . . . In this one whole all appearances come together, and in coming together they . . . lose their distinctive natures" (p. 453). "And reality in the end belongs to nothing but the single Real. For take anything . . . which is less than the Absolute, and the inner discrepancy at once proclaims that what you have taken is appearance. . . . The internal being of everything finite depends on that which is beyond it. Hence everywhere, insisting on a so-called fact, we have found ourselves led by its inner character into something outside itself." (I too subscribe to these two last sentences; but I do not see how the consequences inferred by the author can be derived from them.) "And this self-contradiction [?! compare below, § IX] . . . is a clear proof that, though such things are, their being is but appearance" (pp. 456–7). It does not seem to me that the author is quite in agreement with himself. In fact, while he says, as we have quoted him: "There is but one Reality," immediately he adds, "and its being consists in experience." Further, "Everything is experience, and also experience is one" (p. 457). "There is no reality at all anywhere except in appearance. . . . And existence, on the whole, must correspond with our ideas" (p. 550). "The reality itself is nothing at all apart from appearances" (p. 551). We deny (compare below) that phenomena are the appearance of Reality (p. 552), if the appearance is opposed to being: the Reality consists of the phenomena, though none of these is possible outside their unity, which perhaps may also contain non-phenomenal elements, but contains *also* phenomena, such as they appear to us (there are no others). Consequently we deny that time is unreal, or illusory (pp. 206–7); though time, being a form of variation, has, like every single phenomena, no existence in itself.

## 14.

### THE PARTICULAR OR UNIVERSAL UNITY IS NOT A RESULTANT.

Unity is no resultant, in which the elements of which it is the resultant can and must lose their own individuality. This seems a paradox, and on the contrary it is the most simple, the most obvious of things; the constituents of a real unity preserve in it their own particularity, not although, but precisely because, they do not exist apart, because they exist only as constituents of the unity.

Every resultant about which we have any information is a resultant of things which are independent of it. Two forces are compounded into a resultant, in which it is no longer possible to distinguish them, to recognise them; from the combination of hydrogen with oxygen we obtain water—a body, the properties of which are wholly different from those of hydrogen and of oxygen. But these very propositions, of the truth of which no doubt is possible, presuppose that each of the two forces in the first case, and each of the two gases hydrogen and oxygen in the second, is a thing independent of the other which it happens to meet, and of the third which results from their meeting.

Let us consider on the other hand the proposition: the elements A and B exist only as constituents of the group AB. In order that this proposition may have a meaning, it is necessary (1) that the consideration of A or B apart should be a mere abstraction; (2) that the real constituents of the group (real in the group and not apart) should be precisely A and B. To suppose that, in the constitution of the group, A and B are transformed, so as to become, for instance, $A_1$ and $B_1$, is doubly contradictory. It is to suppose, against (1), that A and B do not exist only as constituents of the group, and, against (2), that the group in question is composed of the elements $A_1$ and $B_1$ instead of the elements A and B.

The unity of the subject (I mean the particular subject) is not a simple resultant. It is true that between the many elements of which it is the unity, there are causal connections, and that consequently each element is subject to the influence of the rest, changes with the changing of the rest, or even of one only of them; but on the other hand it is true that the causal connection of the elements is conditioned by their unity, and is not a condition which can be realised outside the unity, and produce that unity.

A boy learns a rule of grammar and a theorem of geometry. It is quite obvious that the rule and the theorem do not remain inactive side by side with each other, like two coins in a safe; but it is no less obvious that the cognition which the boy has of the rule and of the theorem does not consist in the mutual modification of the two cognitions; whereas rather that closer connection of the two cognitions, which can be considered under a certain aspect (but only under a certain aspect) as implying causal interference, presupposes that they are both cognitions possessed by the boy, that they are connected in a unity, which is not the resultant but the condition of the interference.

What is true of every partial unity, may be said of the total unity. In becoming causally connected, phenomena modify each other more or less; but this connection and modification presupposes unity, does not produce it. Unity is also a resultant; but it is a resultant in so far as it is a unity, and not vice versa. We do not mean that there is first the unity, and then the resultant; but the unity is the logically prior. In so far as they are elements of a unity, facts logically imply each other, do not modify each other causally; although it is true that, since each fact is, as such, a varying in time not reducible to a pure logical process, the mutual implications give rise to casual connections, to mutual modifications.

And if everyone has not understood, we must have patience. It is not easy to overcome the habit of practical thinking, on which our common inability to see any unities other than resultants depends. But philosophy cannot be reduced to practical thinking. That reflection is philosophical which is not satisfied with presupposing, but wishes to understand, the possibility of practical thought. And practical thought would not be possible if those unities which are resultants were not preceded logically by particular unities and by a universal unity, which are not resultants.

The difference between a particular subject and the universal Subject can be reduced, with reference to our present problem, to this that the first is clearly conscious of some phenomena, and the second is clearly conscious of all. To suppose that to be conscious consists in combining or amalgamating phenomena, so as to make them other than they would be outside their unity, is nonsense, both with regard to the particular subject, and, *a fortiori*, with regard to the universal Subject. The unity of consciousness of certain phenomena is the unity of consciousness of those phenomena, and nothing else. Phenomena vary, and vary together; in this sense we may say that they become combined and amalgamated. But this connected varying is a consequence of the existence of one single consciousness of them all, in which each appears such as it is (for its existence consists in its appearing), and is essential both to their variable existence and to their variable appearance.

## 15.

**INTELLIGENCE AND BEING. THE SYSTEM OF SUBJECTS; HOW IT IS INTELLIGIBLE WITHOUT THE HYPOTHESIS OF A UNIVERSAL SUBJECT.**

" Intelligence is not one thing among others, but is the principle, in reference to which only the world exists. It is not a being which is distinguished from others by certain definite qualities; we must rather say of it, in one sense, that it has all qualities, in another sense, that it has none. In fact, a known determination is a determination of intelligence (possessed by intelligence). Vice versa, all determinations of which it is possible to speak in any way are intelligible; therefore none can belong to intelligence so as to exclude another, for then the other would not be intelligible."

" No doubt, the particular subject which thinks is one among others. But his individuality as thinking implies universality. So that the particular subject, while on the one hand conscious of himself as opposed to others and to another, is at the same time, *eo ipso*, conscious of himself as essentially related to others and to another, and therefore of his oneness with all and with everything. Whence it follows, that the subject, though particular under one aspect, is under another aspect free from every individual or generic limitation."[1]

The doctrine recapitulated in the lines here quoted cannot be rejected by anyone capable of understanding it. It only requires to be a little developed, in order that its consequences concerning the point now under discussion, *viz.* the existence of the universal Subject and its relations with particular subjects, may be seen clearly.

It is easy to recognise that the " system," according to

---

[1] CAIRD, *op. cit.*, pp. 153-4. I have introduced some modification, even in the order, and some addition which seemed to me to be required by clearness.

the concept of it which we have expounded,[1] constitutes the development of which we are in search. The particular subject thinks, in so far as it thinks Being. Of indeterminate and universal Being we can and must say that it has all qualities, and that it has none; both the affirmation and the negation are true; for Being, as indeterminate, has no determination, and every determination is a determination of it.

Since it is a concept, Being exists only in so far as it is thought: its existence consists in being thought. It is thought only by particular subjects; and, since it is universal, it cannot be thought by one single particular subject. This is to say that Being necessarily implies a multitude of particular subjects; each of which in its turn implies Being, *i.e.* implies all the others, and is implied by every other. For each particular subject intelligence is resolved into the concept of Being; therefore, each subject is intelligent, exists as subject, because its existence consists in being a particular element of the system of all analogous particular elements.

Nothing exists, which is not in relation with intelligence; or rather, to exist is simply to be in relation with intelligence. But the existence of intelligence consists in the existence of a multitude of consciousnesses; which are distinct as consciousnesses, but have all, in the end, one and the same content. However, this single content can be resolved into the system of distinct consciousnesses.[2]

These few hints will be enough to make it plain to those

---

[1] Chapter on *Unity and Multiplicity*.
[2] To consider the content as something subsisting by itself, outside the consciousness in which it can be included, is to misunderstand our doctrine entirely. If many distinct consciousnesses imply each other, none would exist if the others did not exist also. It is therefore essential to the content to be in relation with every consciousness; but we must add that the consciousnesses must be many, for each implies the rest; each would be without content, unless the rest existed.

who have followed us so far attentively that the monadology which we accept is a development of the outline cited above (at the beginning of this paragraph)—a development which perhaps may be and will have to be integrated, but on condition that the integration does not disfigure or destroy it. Particular subjects exist; and they exist in so far as they constitute a unity: to deny this is to deny the possibility of cognition. The objection that the system of subjects falls short of real unity, or has only an objective unity, *viz.* Being, has no foundation. Every subject is the unity of the system, and Being is not a " thing " the existence of which does not consist in its being known; it is the thought of every subject; the unity of Being can be resolved into the mutual implication of subjects, into the fact that each is the unity of all.

### 16.

#### DIFFICULTY ARISING FROM SUBCONSCIOUSNESS, AND IMPOSSIBILITY OF ELIMINATING IT.

A difficulty which we have recognised, and which it is perhaps desirable to eliminate, consists in the impossibility of separating clear consciousness from subconsciousness. The hypothesis of a universal Subject allows us to base subconsciousness on consciousness, while for particular subjects the contrary is true; it has consequently a manifest advantage. It is requisite, however, that we should not form an absurd conception of the relations between the universal Subject and the particular subjects: between an absurdity and a difficulty, the choice cannot be doubtful.

Every doctrine is always the construction of a particular subject; or of several particular subjects in cooperation. Indeed, since the particular subjects are solidary, it must be said that in a certain sense they all co-operate in the construction of any doctrine, true or false. Still, it remains true that a doctrine exists in so far as it is thought by particular subjects, few or many; and not otherwise.

A true doctrine is true in so far as it is implicit in, and essential to the thought of, every subject. The learned man who discovers it does not accomplish something exclusively his own, does not add a simple accidentality to the several others, which distinguish him from other men; rather he develops that universal, in virtue of which he is one with all or with the whole. Just so; but what he does, though not only his own, is however his own too. And the discussion of the doctrine, by him or by others, is an inquiry whether what he has done is only his own (a product peculiar to himself, or, perhaps, to a school, etc.), or has a universal value.

The discussion presupposes two things. First, a universal infallible criterion, which may not be known explicitly, but is implicit in every man, and which every man knows more or less how to use; to admit this criterion is then further to admit that the true doctrine is implicit in all, and that its truth consists in its being there implicit. Second, the matter, the value of which is discussed, the doctrine as it was formulated and propounded. It is clear that, in the discussion, the doctrine is considered as a formation peculiar to that man (to that school, etc.), and cannot be considered in any other way. In fact, it is manifest that the doctrine is a thing of this kind: the doctrine is thought by some person, and, so far, it might even be an aberration of that person; whether then the doctrine is more than a thing of this kind, whether it possesses a value transcending the particularity of the individual who has formulated it, is precisely what we are inquiring.

Hence we may draw a consequence as instructive as it is

simple. He who denies the reality of phenomena, he who recognises no value in phenomena as such, excludes at once the possibility of transcending them. For, the transcending of phenomena is, first of all, itself a phenomenon; and we shall have to say of it what we say of any phenomenon. The transcending of phenomena (*i.e.* a transcending which is not a mere fiction) is a phenomenon, since it is a fact of the phenomenal personal consciousness. It is a phenomenon which has a higher value than another; for instance, than a caprice; but why? Because of its implications. And I recognise its value in so far as I recognise its implications. But what real implications can a phenomenon have which is not itself real? What implications can I recognise, if that other phenomenon which is my act of recognition is not real?

It will be said that no one has ever denied phenomena as phenomena. But there is no reason why we should discuss only explicit negations. We agree that no phenomenon is possible outside the unity of all. Since it is so, we say that a phenomenon which has appeared implies unity in so far as it has appeared; it implies Being of which it is a determination; and has consequently a value, which can be recognised in it only by penetrating deeply into its relations with the whole, but by means of such penetration becomes recognisable in it. We say, in short, that a phenomenon is real, although, or rather because, it is relative and inseparable; that, in so far as it is real, it reveals to us something (supposing that we know how to interpret it) of Being of which it is a determination; that, therefore, a proposition, a doctrine, a book, which are certainly phenomena, can be true. Our opponents must say the contrary unless they are opponents only in name. No doubt, they do not expressly deny the phenomenal as phenomenal, which is not denied even by sceptics. But by equivocating on the obvious impossibility of making an absolute of the phenomenal, they deny the reality of the phenomenal; and this is, according to our view, to deny the phenomenal implicitly. In any case, by denying to the phenomenal that value of which we have spoken they exclude cognition, which is simply a form of phenomena; they exclude the possible truth of assertions, and therefore also of their own assertions.

From this we also infer that the reduction of subconsciousness to consciousness, obtained through the hypothesis of the universal Subject, has an importance which, though not negligible, is not decisive. The subject which asserts, which theorises, which recognises the universal Subject, is still the particular subject. From this subconsciousness cannot be eliminated in any way. The reduction of subconsciousness to consciousness is itself obtained by means of subconsciousness. And therefore it would have no value, it would be an illusory and fictitious reduction, if subconsciousness were an absurdity.

### 17.

THE INDISPENSABLENESS OF UNITY DOES NOT ALLOW US TO INFER A NON-PHENOMENAL REALITY.

It is impossible to stop at mere scattered phenomena. Therefore (it is said) we must go back, by means of our reason, to " deeper " realities, to substances. Subjects and bodies appear as phenomena, and exist as substances. A body is divisible, hence it is not properly a substance, but a group, a (conditioned) system of substances. Every subject is a separate substance. And separate substances can be distributed into two classes—material and spiritual, which are distinguishable clearly and surely (if we leave on one side the difficulty or impossibility of knowing a substance in itself), by the fact that bodies appear only to subjects, while a subject not only appears to another subject, in the same way in which a body appears to a subject, but also appears to himself.

This statement, though at first it seems satisfactory, cannot be maintained.[1] We must not think that by merely superposing the concept of substance upon that of phenomenon we have satisfactorily removed the difficulties implicit in the phenomenalist view of things. A distinction between phenomenon and substance is already made in common thought (there is no one who does not distinguish, for instance, between the stone and that which appears to him of the stone); and, as such, it has no doubt a precise meaning and a remarkable importance. But, in so far as it is a common distinction, it does not transcend the phenomenal field: it serves to organise experience, it does not determine the condition which makes experience possible. If we wish to determine this condition, we cannot content ourselves with resorting to the common distinction, which loses all meaning when we apply it for a purpose which is not its own. The true reason why we cannot stop at mere phenomena, is their fragmentariness. Either we must overcome the obstacle of fragmentariness, or we have done nothing; to substitute a fragmentary complex of substances for a fragmentary complex of phenomena is to be satisfied with a verbal solution which leaves the true problem still in the same obscurity. It is impossible to do without something non-phenomenal; but this something non-phenomenal must be a *quid* which is absolutely ONE.

But we must remark that the necessity of going back to the One, of transcending the phenomenal datum in its fragmentariness, does not allow us to infer a non-phenomenal Reality. The One, since it is the condition of the

---

[1] Compare above *Unity and Multiplicity*, §§ 14–16, and also the notes at pp. 167, 175.

course of events as well as of cognition, is certainly implicit in experience. The cognition which we have of it is not experimental, in so far as it is not the cognition of any datum of fact ; but it can be drawn from the cognition of fact, in so far as this presupposes it. To experience in the full and true sense of the word, to know, does not mean merely to apprehend unconnected material elements ; it means rather to apprehend the matter together with the form which is inseparable from it—to apprehend, in the fact, the One which is an essential constituent of it. Hence, though the hope of constructing the One (the supreme form, or rationality,) by means of detached elements, of drawing it from strictly empirical cognitions, taken in their fragmentariness, is vain, we are not therefore to infer that to arrive at the One we must leave the field of experience. Without the One which is necessarily implied by experience, there would be no experience. Hence the mistake of the empiricist, who sees the simple result of a process in that which is on the contrary the foundation and condition of the process, who imagines that he can work with the elements of a fragmentary experience, whereas his labour is possible only in so far as the experience is his own, or in other terms is one. But if the One is necessarily implied by experience, it may still exist only in so far as it is implied by experience (in the same way as, for instance, while we cannot speak of variation if we make abstraction from time, vice versa the existence of time is only the existence of variation).

The One is Being ; which is known to us, at present, as wholly indeterminate. Being certainly exists as the supreme unity of experience, as the universal form. We are not positively sure that it has also a further existence in itself. Let us try to penetrate deeper into that of which we are positively sure, to understand its meaning thoroughly, and to develop its consequences.

## 18.

### THE UNIVERSE AS THE RESULT OF A LOGICAL PROCESS INTRINSIC TO BEING.

We may say, in a certain sense, that the universe is the result of a logical process intrinsic to Being,—of a process by which Being becomes conscious of itself. Being, as necessary, cannot but be. But in itself it is indeterminate, and cannot subsist without its determinations; it is a concept, the existence of which, since it can be resolved into the act of being thought, presupposes some thinking being. Being therefore, in consequence of its own necessity, *i.e.* by means of an intrinsic logical process, produces in itself those determinations which are the primitive unities, the elementary subjects. Each of these realises Being in so far as each subject thinks it in its indeterminateness, and is at the same time a determination of it; each subject is Being in so far as it thinks itself by becoming determinate, or in so far as it posits itself, in so far as it becomes conscious of itself.

But we must guard against misunderstandings. A first gross misunderstanding would be to represent to ourselves as temporal what we have shown to be a logical process. We must not believe that first Being exists, and afterwards primitive unities are produced by Being, almost in the same way as our volitions are produced by us. The absurdity of such a representation becomes obvious to him who reflects that since Being is simply the character common to all its determinations, it exists only in these, does not precede them, does not produce them temporally. The true meaning of what we have said is that primitive unities have always existed; but that they have always existed as determinations of one and the same Being, which has always existed as their common character. To suppose the said unities to be non-existent is to suppose the non-existence of Being—an absurdity. The *raison d'être* of primitive unities can be resolved into the impossibility that Being should not exist; this, and no other, is the sense in which the unities must be understood to be founded on a logical process intrinsic to Being.

Another misunderstanding (more subtle, but still a misunderstanding,) consists in supposing that the distinction between subjects is "only" phenomenal, and that the "profound" (noumenal) subject is the same in each phenomenal subject, is one alone. Have we not said ourselves, just now, that in the universe, *i.e.* in each subject, "Being becomes conscious of itself"? It seems therefore that "the conscious being" is one alone, always the same. This point must be discussed in detail.

"The subject, in so far as it takes thought as its object, arrives at itself, for its pure self is thought";[1] when I think of Being, I think myself; therefore my true "self" is Being. This is certainly, in a sense, an axiom; but only in a sense; and we must guard carefully against confusing the true sense with another. The subject is Being, in so far as it is a determination of Being: any determination implies indeterminate Being. But the subject, in so far as it is "one" (particular) determination of indeterminate Being, is always distinguished both from every other determination of Being and from Being taken in its indeterminateness.

The subject is a particular consciousness of universal Being. The content (and, it must be noticed, the real content; but here we simply consider it in its most universal form,) is common to every subject; but each subject is a recipient different from every other, as recipient,—a particular consciousness.

Will opponents say that in this way we hypostatise (that

---

[1] HEGEL, *Encyclopædia of Philosophic Sciences*, §. 11. Hegel says "spirit." It is not necessary for me to explain why I prefer to say "subject."

is to say, materialise,) the content, while we fall back more or less into the inexactitudes and inconsistencies of Platonism, and neglect the results of criticism, which has clearly shown the inseparableness of content from consciousness ? He who were to urge this objection against us, would give proof of not having understood anything of what we have said. The content and consciousness are certainly inseparable even according to us, because according to the doctrine set forth, the content is simply what single particular consciousnesses have in common, and because these, in their turn, are the logical consequence of the content, of Being; they are necessarily implicit in it, for they constitute its existence. But the content (indeterminate universal Being) and each of the single particular consciousnesses, though they imply each other, or rather because they imply each other, are distinguished and opposed.

The single consciousness and Being are inseparable, that is to say, if either of these elements were to vanish, the other would vanish also. And nevertheless they are distinguished, for the existence of Being consists precisely in the existence of the many particular consciousnesses, to which it is common. Each single consciousness is, as such, different from the others with which it is necessarily connected (in so far as they are all determinations of one and the same Being); the existence of a content which is not reducible to any one of them, though it is essential to each, consists precisely in the existence of the many single consciousnesses.[1]

---

[1] Compare the following passages (which I choose among many analogous ones) of HEGEL, *op. cit.* "The universality (of spirit) is also its determinate being. In so far as it is in itself, the universal becomes particular and remains in this identical with itself. The determinateness of spirit is, therefore, its manifestation. Spirit is the infinite idea; finiteness is an appearance which the spirit opposes to itself as a barrier, in order to be able to become manifest by overcoming this barrier" (§§ 383, 386). "Consciousness constitutes the stage of reflection of spirit as appearance" (§ 413). It is almost

## 19.

### EXTRA-TEMPORALITY OF THAT PROCESS AND TEMPORALITY OF THE COURSE OF EVENTS.

The process through which Being becomes realised in a multiplicity of connected distinct subjects, is intrinsic to

obvious that these propositions can be interpreted in the sense of the doctrine set forth, or rather that they cannot be interpreted in any other sense. (Note also § 384: "The revelation of spirit is a positing [by the spirit] of nature as its own world—a positing which, as reflection, is at the same time a presupposing of the world as independent nature. To reveal, in the concept, is to create the world; in which spirit gives itself the affirmation and the truth [that is to say, the reality] of its own freedom." This in substance expresses the logical dependence of the universe on Being already indicated; though this universe is not the creation of the particular subject.) We must, however, also take into account this other passage: "Self-consciousness" (which is "the foundation of consciousness," or its "truth," § 424), "that is to say, the certainty that its determinations are objective,—determinations of the essence of things,—as well as thoughts of its own" (compare above, *Thought;* especially at the end; identity of the two considerations, objective and subjective), "is reason; which is this identity, since it is not only the absolute substance, but truth as knowledge. This truth, which knows, is spirit" (§ 439). Observe that self-consciousness is the "foundation" and the "truth" (that is to say, the reality) of consciousness, in so far as consciousness and self-consciousness are in the end *unum et idem*. If apprehension were not (we may say with Bonatelli) transparent to itself, it would not be apprehension. Sight, as such, is neither recollection, nor reference, nor suffering or enjoying, nor thinking, (conceiving, asserting), nor doing. Hence, sight, as mere sight, is consciousness of objects, not self-consciousness. The same is to be said of the other indicated facts or elements of consciousness, considered in their purity. But all these elements, as pure, are abstractions; each element is always associated with the rest, though the rest are more or less vivid, more or less subconscious; and therefore consciousness is always, though in a great variety of degrees, self-consciousness. A non-phenomenal consciousness is a *contradictio in adjecto;* the same is therefore true also of self-consciousness. (I am speaking here of human consciousness and subconsciousness; if a superhuman self-consciousness exists, which I do not deny, this will be the condition of the human, but it is not the human.) To speak of a numerically single and human self-consciousness, since a man's self-consciousness is not his consciousness of the consciousness of another, is to use the term self-consciousness in a meaning different from that of which it cannot be divested without declaring all cognition vain and impossible. Consciousness and self-consciousness, though they are essentially phenomenal and manifold, imply a non-phenomenal unity, that is to say, they are essentially solidary, as determinations of one and the same Being. But Being and the consciousness of Being, though they are not to be separated in the Platonic way, must however be distinguished. We have pointed out how it is possible to transcend the Platonic separation without sacrificing the distinction; the defect of the doctrine which we are examining is its failure to understand the possibility of reconciling the transcending with the distinction. Since "*for us* [only for us] spirit presupposes nature," that is to

Being, *i.e.* logical and outside time ; it does not appear as a temporal course of events [*accadere*]: it is apprehended by each single subject, more or less clearly according to the

say the phenomenal universe, while *in itself* it "is truth and therefore the absolute first" (§ 381) ; we must conclude that between *ourselves* and spirit *in itself*, *i.e.* between ourselves and Being, there is some distinction. This can be resolved into the multiplicity, and therefore the relative and correlative limitation, of self-consciousnesses. When the idea (Being) is considered in its being by itself, object and subject become identified (*ibid.*) ; my thought of Being is both a thought of mine and the essence of things (§ 439, already quoted) ; in other words, my thought and Being are one. But my thought is Being in so far as it is my thought, Being plus that determination of it, which is its being thought by me—a determination which is essential to it, for Being exists only in so far as it is thought. "In so far as it is by itself, the universal becomes particular"; its universality not only does not exclude, but implies the multiplicity of consciousnesses, in which it "is by itself"; while we must notice that Being, in this process of becoming particular, "remains identity with itself." This is intuitively obvious. Peter and Paul both think blue : it is true that the blue thought of is one only ; it is true that the thinking subjects are two ; and it is true that the two truths mentioned do not exclude each other, or rather that they imply each other. From all this it results that the phenomenon (inseparable from the multiplicity of subjects : "consciousness constitutes the stage of reflection of spirit as appearance") is not less essential to Being than Being to the phenomenon. An isolated phenomenon is a contradiction, for nothing occurs outside the unity of all that occurs ; but this unity, Being, is simply the unity of all that occurs, or of phenomena, and would not exist without them. (Otherwise we ought to say, in opposition to what is asserted by the doctrine in question, that the course of events is not necessary, is not the appearance in which the dialectic process of the idea becomes manifest.) "If language always expresses the universal, I cannot utter that which is only my feeling. And the ineffable, the feeling, is not indeed the most excellent and truest of things, but the most insignificant and the least true" (§ 20). Why? Pure theory is nothing but pure form ; it leaves out matter. But although matter is "not true" in so far as it could not exist without form, it is nevertheless an element without which no form could exist. And, in this sense, it is neither less "excellent" nor less "true" than form. Pure form and pure matter are abstractions ; only the universe is real. It is a mistake to hypostatise matter, as if each phenomenon were a self-contained truth, whereas it is simply a distinct occurrence. But it is a mistake (in substance, the same mistake,) also to hypostatise form. "When I say—I—, I mean myself as a certain subject which excludes every other; but every other is precisely what I call—I—, that I, which excludes from itself all the others" (*ibid.*). Well? What I express is only the form of that being, composed of form and matter, which is I ; but from the fact that I can express only the form (for my being able to express myself is simply my power of abstracting the form), it does not follow that form exists alone, or is more important than the matter, without which it would not exist. Every one says of himself what I say of myself. That is to say, the form which we all express is one alone ; but the expressions of this one form are many ; the multiplicity of expressions is just as real as the uniqueness of their formal content (a uniqueness which is inferred from comparison, which implies multiplicity) ; therefore, besides the one universal form, there are many par-

development of the latter, as what it is, that is to say as logical necessity, which extends to everything, which dominates and connects everything.[1]

ticular matters, so that besides the uniqueness of formal meaning, we have the multiplicity of expressions. As form is implicit in matter, so matter is implicit in form, and we must dispense neither with the one nor with the other. To close this long note, it seems to me not out of place to recall in brief some other arguments against the hypothesis that the multiplicity of phenomenal subjects is only apparent, and that reality can be resolved into one single, extra-phenomenal (noumenal) subject. (1) The hypothesis is in contradiction with the premises, from which it is sought to be inferred (§ 20). (2) "Subject" is a category which loses all meaning, if we pretend to separate it entirely from phenomena. (3) If reality could be resolved into a logical process (this is a necessary consequence of the hypothesis considered), the course of events would not even be possible as appearance; given, what we do not admit, that to call the course of events mere appearance has any meaning. (4) We cannot say that two subjects are only superficially two, and one and the same in a profounder sense. In my consciousness there is nothing more profound than my "I know," and my "I will," which are inseparable: to be self-conscious means to know while willing and to will while knowing. And my "I know," as well as my "I will," are neither the "I know," nor the "I will," of another person; I may be ignorant of the knowing and the willing of another, and my willing may be opposed to the willing of another. (5) It is impossible to segregate from one another individual consciousnesses, each of which implies all the rest. For this very reason individual consciousnesses are irreducibly many.

[1] The opposition between the thing (as it is) in itself and the thing as it appears, an opposition not less familiar than justified in the field of common thought, becomes absurd and meaningless when we transfer it to the field of philosophic reflection. The ring which seems to me of gold is in fact of brass. That is to say, from certain characters which appear to me, which I apprehend, and which the ring actually has, I infer mistakenly certain other characters which do not appear to me, which I do not apprehend, and which the ring does not possess. In all this there is nothing which is not clear and simple. But to suppose that the intrinsic brassy quality of the ring appears to me under the form of the golden quality is a contradiction. In fact, what appears to me, if you assume that it is the golden quality, is not the brassy quality; the brassy quality does not appear to me in any way, and therefore it cannot be said that the golden quality appears to me under the form of the brassy quality. In the same way, it is a contradiction to imagine that an intrinsically logical process appears to me under the form of a course of events: that which appears to me, which I apprehend, is according to the hypothesis a course of events, not a logical process; and if the logical process does not become known to me by some other means, it remains entirely unknown to me, it does not appear to me in any way. And if the logical process is known to me by some other means, it is known to me, *i.e.* it appears to me; but by this other means, not under the form of the course of events. It will be said that something, in consequence of some character of its own which is in itself a logical process, produces in me an impression which is an occurrence; this is the appearance of the logical process to me under the form of the course of events. This, I say, is a meaningless statement. First of all, the theory of knowledge which it implies is precisely that on which primitive philosophy is based; we have spoken about it on another

The course of events had no beginning; its principle consists in the spontaneities of the single elementary subjects—spontaneities which manifest themselves as they become necessarily connected with each other in consequence of the unity of Being. The course of events therefore is always partly determined and partly undetermined; for the two parts, or rather the two moments, are inseparable from each other, and reciprocally co-essential. If we consider any sphere, however limited, we see determination or indetermination predominating in it, according to the relations which the preceding course of events has established between the subjects constituting that sphere. And consequently the greater or less development of certain elementary subjects and of certain limited systems of subjects (*e.g.* of humanity, or of a limited human society) depends on these conditions.

The course of events which appears, is always real in so far as it appears. Nevertheless, between the course of events which appears and the real course of events a difference can be established—in so far as the real course of events is not wholly included in the consciousness of each subject;[1] and on the other hand, the course of events of which a subject becomes aware in any way, being

occasion, and we have seen that it has no value. Then we ask what the impression received by me can be, if it is not an occurrence? That which appears to me as an occurrence is therefore "really" an occurrence, and nothing else. Lastly, if we admit the hypothesis just now formulated, though it is neither reasonable nor possible to do so, my representing to myself (in consequence of the impression I receive) as an occurrence that character of the thing, which in itself is not an occurrence, does not constitute an appearance to me of the said character, for it is rather an appearance to me of something quite different. And my belief that what appears to me is a character of the thing is on my part self-deception, as when I believe the ring to be of gold, while in fact it is of brass. In what way then it can be possible for me, while I found myself on this deception—a deception which, as we must bear in mind, would be invincible, to reach the "true" character of the thing by overcoming the deception, is a mystery of which it would be vain to ask an explanation.

[1] Each subject is for the most part subconscious, and most of the subjects are almost exclusively subconscious.

partly an effect of the general course of events, is more or less different from it.

Since the course of events has had no beginning, it cannot tend towards an ultimate end. For the end would be already attained *ab æterno*. It follows that, although the universe is always changing in each of its parts however limited, nevertheless, or rather for this reason, it remains always as a whole in the same general conditions.

Vice versa, the subjects, each of which is a secondary but essential unity of the universe, tend to develop; that is to say, the action of each subject is purposive. Purpose in the spontaneous doing of each subject, and the absence of purpose from the general course of events which results from it—the tendency of each subject to develop and the absence of development from the system as such—are both equally essential to Being, to the universe considered in its supreme unity. This, which seems a paradox, is on the contrary a necessary result of the logical character essential to Being, and of the way in which Being consequently is realised or actualised as it becomes determinate.

Being is realised only by becoming determinate: it exists only as the form of the course of events. In order that Being (which cannot but exist) may exist, there must be a course of events. Consequently, the end (if we wish to call it so improperly), for which Being creates the course of events, is simply to realise itself. It is an end which cannot but be attained, which is always actually attained, whatever the form of this or that part of the universe may be; the universe, in its unity, is always that which it can and must be, the full realisation or determination of Being; it cannot, as a unity, have a temporal development.

But the plenitude of Being is realised in the course of events. In order that it may be so realised, it must necessarily break up *ab æterno* (we need not say that the breaking up is only relative) into a multiplicity of spontaneous principles, which are all included in its unity, and of which each is the (secondary) unity of the others. Each of these principles, that is to say each more or less developed subject, changes by helping to change the others, and by varying in consequence of the changes of the others. Apart from those changes which are to be referred to the changes of the others, it changes *spontaneously*. Since the reason of spontaneous change can be found nowhere else except in the subject, it must have a reason intrinsic to the subject. In other words, the subject would not be spontaneous if its being this or that, and its varying thus or thus, were not experienced by the subject itself as a good or as an evil. Spontaneity is inseparable from feeling: the subject which suffers struggles to escape the suffering, and because the struggling is in itself and immediately a pleasure.

Without feeling there would be no spontaneity; without spontaneity there would be no course of events; and without the course of events there would be no Being, and Being cannot but exist. Therefore Being, the only end of which (more properly, not an end, but a logical exigency) is to exist, must, precisely in order to attain such an end (in order to satisfy its own logical exigency), create in itself those determinations which are the spontaneous subjects, which are not contented with mere existence, but tend to well-being or diminution of ill-being, that is to say, which tend to develop, because the good for a subject is the unimpeded manifestation of activity.

### 20.
##### THE LOGICAL EXIGENCY AND THE PRACTICAL EXIGENCY. FINALITY. HAS THE UNIVERSE AN END?

Between the logical exigency of Being—which, having as its end (as its aim) Being only, is always satisfied and preserves the universe throughout its varying and by means of its varying, in a total state of invariability—and the practical exigency of the particular subject—which tends to develop that subject, to develop it indefinitely in time—there is not that which we, who are dominated by the same practical exigency, should care to call harmony. To recognise that the practical (subjective) exigency is the indispensable means for satisfying the logical (universal) exigency, is to recognise that the practical claim is subordinated, impeded, and in short violated.

No doubt, this subordination to the logical exigency is not, for the subject, a mere extrinsic bond, a hindrance; it is at the same time, especially when it is conscious, the means by which the subject develops.

Primitive feeling—pleasure or pain, which are weak and insignificant at first—attains by development degrees of intensity which defy and disturb imagination; but at the same time becomes impregnated with a rationality, which makes it superior to itself. Since the subconscious agitation of the primitive monad is provoked by an obscure feeling, it is radically teleological, but its finality is only implicit: in order to act according to a determined end, we must know. Only the man who knows is capable of proposing ends to himself with clearness.

And the man who really knows and wills (will and cognition are inseparable, or rather one and the same), who has wrought his reasoning and active power into a stable unity, who, in so far as he is such a unity, is truly master of himself,[1] understands that his true end is not his immediate and primitve feeling, but the said unity—the full agreement of his strength and of his reason. I

---

[1] "The really free spirit is the unity of the theoretical and of the practical spirit" (HEGEL, *op. cit.*, § 481). I must limit myself to a few hints. For a further development, compare *The Great Problems*, and especially *Values* (the whole chapter), *Being* (towards the end), the *Conclusion*, the whole note *Metaphysics and Morals;* other places here and there.

mean himself, not however as a mere simple subject, but as a person,—a self, which cannot be realised without realising at once, in his own person, both the fellow-citizen and the man; for the form of unity, which is himself, is universal. I realise myself only on condition that I recognise the universal value of personality; vice versa, my recognition of the universal value of personality is the means by which I realise myself, my highest value, and attain my end.

All this is incontrovertible. But, on the other hand, the logical exigency—which, as always satisfied, preserves the universe in a state of total invariability—inevitably renders every effort of individuals, and groups of individuals, of mankind or any analogous formation, in the end transitory, that is to say, vain; it resolves history into an immense tautology, which may be called inconclusive, for its ultimate meaning is to provide for the eternal existence of Being.

A young man, or a man who is conscious of belonging to a young nation, or who at least is conscious of belonging to humanity, as long as humanity remains young, has a right to look with confidence towards the future. For the goods which the future allows him to procure (with labour; but this is just what makes them good), are real, though hopelessly transitory. And it is no use to object that, besides these goods, and inseparably connected with them, there are evils, that beside divine pleasure, there is monstrous pain beside glory, undeserved and (what is infinitely worse) deserved shame; beside virtue, vice. We may answer, that life is beautiful just because it is full of risk; that, without evil, that supreme good, that supreme value, which is conscious courage, would not exist.

But everything grows old; and mankind will grow old too; and all our work will have been in vain. In vain;

for, although a time in which a more or less analogous work is not being accomplished will never come, in any case our own work will not help the succeeding analogous work at all, as it was not helped at all by the analogous work which came before it. It is true that the accomplishment of this infinity of work, which remains in substance always the same through continual repetitions, is the condition which allows Being to remain always conscious of itself—which makes the existence of Being possible. But to say this is to say that the existence of time can be resolved into a loss of time. Being cannot but exist: it is a necessity, which however is not presented to us with the characters of value.[1]

## 21.

### CONTINUATION.

The conclusions which we have reached, coincide more or less with those of materialism, which considers consciousness as a product of the physical course of events. Hence, it will seem to many that, materialism once refuted, the said conclusions also are implicitly refuted, without requiring any further consideration.

This is a mistake. If Being implies necessarily, that is to say logically, the course of events, or in short if Being

---

[1] "This I know and feel:
That from the eternal revolutions,
That from my frail being,
Perhaps others may draw
Some good or benefit: for me life is evil."

Leopardi, though a great poet, was less than a mediocre philosopher. Life is not absolutely an evil for the individual ("for me" cannot mean anything else). Considered as a whole, it seems to have no meaning; and it has no meaning, if the only determinations of Being are those which we have recognised. So we have found the fundamental reason of pessimism—a reason, which certainly is not empty, though it does not justify pessimism. The contrast between the logical and the practical exigency, though they are co-essential, is (supposing it to exist) tragic; but it is not to be confused with the tribulations, of which each of us has more than a portion; which, though they have ultimately their root in that contrast, can be converted by each of us into values, at least by enduring them, if in no other way.

exists only in so far as a course of events takes place, the course of events cannot have had a beginning, and therefore cannot tend toward an end; in other words, the phenomenal universe, and the Being which is realised in the phenomenal universe, have no value.

Each subject has a value; (the value of the developed subject is transitory, for the developed form of the subject is transitory); and it has such a value, in so far as it is an element of the Whole, inseparable from the Whole and from the other parts; and yet the Whole, as such, has no value. It seems that there is here a contradiction; but this is not true. In the same way it is not true that there is a contradiction between ascribing spontaneity to each subject, as included in the unity of Being, and denying the spontaneity of Being.

If Being necessarily gives rise to the course of events, it is not spontaneous, for spontaneity is the contrary of necessity; but the course of events, which according to the hypothesis cannot but take place, implies single spontaneities connected with each other; these therefore depend on that same logical (non-spontaneous) exigency, in consequence of which Being gives rise to the course of events. So the second of the two antinomies is solved. And the first also is solved in the same way; for spontaneity, finality (at first only implicit) and value are, in substance, one and the same, and develop together.

No doubt, all spontaneity, all finality and all value would vanish, if they were separated from that unity, which is Being. Moreover, they are determinations of Being; therefore we may say that all spontaneity, all finality, all value are ultimately the spontaneity, the finality and the value of Being. Just so; but Being is enriched with these determinations only in so far as it becomes determinate, in so far as it develops, without breaking up absolutely, into a multiplicity of subjects; the developed forms of those determinations all belong to the phenomenal world (to Being, but in so far as it is realised in the phenomenal world), and therefore they are all transitory, while this varying gives rise to no intrinsic development of the whole, which remains always the same.

The hypothesis that " real " consciousness is the same, numerically one, in each and every phenomenal subject (supposing it to have a meaning[1]), does not allow us to change one syllable of what we have established—unless it be profoundly modified as we shall presently explain. For, if the phenomenal breaking up into a multiplicity of consciousnesses is essential to the existence of the only real consciousness; if, in other words, God is conscious of Himself only in so far as He constitutes the conscious being of each particular subject—in this case, we cannot say either of each subject or of the universe anything more than what we have said of them; and God Himself is simply an arbitrary name to denote what we have more properly called Being.

### 22.

#### THE BEGINNING OF THE COURSE OF EVENTS AS CONDITION OF UNIVERSAL FINALITY. CONDITION NECESSARY TO THE BEGINNING OF THE COURSE OF EVENTS.

In order that the course of events [*l'accadere*] may tend toward an end, that it may have a value, it must have had a beginning. But a course of events which has had a beginning, is not essential to Being, is not the result of a logical exigency of Being. Thus, the determina-

---

[1] It has no meaning, as we have seen. The true value of this hypothesis consists in its being a first attempt to understand, in an epistemologically correct way, the relation between the One and the many—an attempt which encounters several difficulties. The elimination of these difficulties transforms the hypothesis into the doctrine which we have developed.

## The Absolute

tions essential to Being will be something other than phenomena. What will they be ?

Being (our common concept of Being) exists only in so far as it is thought; its existence consists in being thought, it is the existence of a thought. Therefore, its existence—supposing that it does not logically imply the course of events, *i.e.* that it cannot be resolved into its being thought by a multiplicity of single subjects—will consist in thinking itself. I mean, in thinking itself in itself, by itself; for that thinking (we might say, that mediate self-thinking,) which is realised in the consciousnesses of the single subjects, and presupposes these consciousnesses, is not essential to it. Either Being logically implies the consciousnesses of the single subjects, that is to say the course of events ;—or it is a consciousness independent of the single consciousnesses, distinct from them.

The single subjects exist; and, since their existence had according to the hypothesis a beginning, they do not exist in consequence of a logical exigency of Being. Their existence will therefore be produced by the intrinsic spontaneity of Being; it will be created. It must be possible to assign a cause of that which does not exist necessarily, which does not exist *ab æterno;* and the cause, in our case, can be only Being. If we suppose that Being does not logically imply phenomenal reality, it produces that reality; that is to say, it is active. Of course, I mean active in a sense analogous to (though higher than) that in which every subject is active, and independently of the activities of the single subjects. According to the contrary hypothesis, the activity of Being exists only in so far as the single activities into which it breaks up exist; Being cannot be called active in the former sense.

On the other hand, that essential constituent of consciousness which is its theoretical character (cognition

as such) cannot be separated from its practical character.
A being which was not active, would not be self-thinking.
We, who must vary in order to act, have no means of
representing a spontaneity the existence of which implies
no extrinsic manifestation, does not consist in a varying;
(to each of us, who are particular beings, it is essential to
be in a variable relation with something else). But we are
not without the means of conceiving it. We conceive the
invariability of thought; or rather, we can conceive no
thought, which does not imply something invariable.
Now, the activity or spontaneity of Being, its doing, is in
substance nothing else but its thinking, its being in itself,
Being itself. When we ascribe spontaneity to Being, we
simply recognise that its thinking (that being conscious
of itself, in which its existence consists,) cannot be resolved
into an abstract thought: it is an absolute reality, an
eternal life.

An analogue of that which for us is feeling (and, in a
higher sphere, sentiment and emotion), that is to say
value, must needs be associated with that doing-thinking,
by which the eternal intrinsic life of Being is constituted.
As vivid and real consciousness implies knowledge and
spontaneity, so it implies also value, which is the unity
of the other two moments. Consciousness, spontaneity
and value can be distinguished, but not separated; in the
same way as, in a polyhedron, the faces, the corners and
the vertices can be distinguished, but not separated. If
value is taken away, there can be neither spontaneity,
nor (consequently) cognition: a *quid*, which has no value
by itself (in relation to itself, intrinsically) may be an object
of cognition, an end of action, for others, but it is not a
subject which thinks itself, and which thinks.

The determinations which (according to this hypothesis)
we must recognise as essential to Being, as constitutive
of Being in itself, are therefore such that we must con-

ceive it as a person. (Let us say, in an "eminent" sense; we shall not inquire, what this sense may be.)

That Being, which is common to all distinct phenomenal realities, or of which each phenomenal reality is a determination, which is the unity of the phenomenal world, and which, in the thought of each single subject (a thought more or less clearly apprehended, but essential to the single subject), is a most indeterminate concept;—that same Being has an existence in itself. It has an existence in itself, independent of the single subjects which are essential to the course of events, *i.e.* to the phenomenal world, but not foreign to the single subjects, for every single subject, as a secondary unity of the phenomenal world, necessarily implies the thought of Being, which is an essential constituent of it.

Being is therefore, in the truest sense of the word and without any equivocation, God.[1]

The existence of God removes all doubt as to the purposiveness of the phenomenal world. Let us not try to represent this purposiveness clearly to ourselves; one thing is certain, and we may be contented with it: he who sacrifices himself to the universal order does not sacrifice himself in vain.

All this, however, is true upon the hypothesis that the course of events has had a beginning—an hypothesis which again presupposes the purposiveness of the whole course of events.

---

[1] The word "God" has been and is used in many different senses, which are generally not carefully determined. He, who uses it in a sense different from that which we have defined, endeavours to express a supreme concept, without giving to himself a clear account of the real exigency of the concept itself. So it seems to me. And I have said why it seems so to me. To express a different opinion with equal clearness will perhaps be less easy than is sometimes imagined.

## 23.

### THE THEISTIC AND THE PANTHEISTIC HYPOTHESES; DEFINITION AND MEANING OF THEM.

We must in the end choose between two hypotheses: the phenomenal universe either has had, or has not had, a beginning. From the first hypothesis we infer the (personal, or super-personal,) existence of God; an existence, which on the contrary cannot be reconciled with the second. The former is theistic, the latter pantheistic.

Theism resolves phenomenal reality entirely into a content of explicit thought (a thought which is not abstract: as we need not repeat); this is, theoretically, an undeniable advantage, as we have remarked. But, as we have also remarked, such an advantage does not seem to be decisive. For the explicit thought into which reality would be resolved is not, as essentially explicit in itself, our own. A theory which we wish to construct must not exclude the possibility of our constructing it; it must be capable of becoming our own cognition. Now, our cognition implies a thought which is essentially for the most part implicit: if we were not also subconscious, and chiefly subconscious, we should not be conscious. A known reality (a reality, of which we may speak with an intelligible meaning), absolutely different from cognitive thought, is not admissible. Just for this reason we do not think ourselves justified in identifying reality with a completely explicit thought, while we know well that (our) cognitive thought is for the most part and essentially implicit.[1]

---

[1] Even if we admit that the multiplicity of subjects is "only" phenomenal, and that the "true" thinking being is one in all, the difficulty here mentioned is only apparently solved. Let us set aside the considerations which we might make, which we have made, concerning that "only" and that "true." If the one consciousness exists only in so far as it breaks up ("only" phenomenally, it may be, but in any case necessarily,) into a multitude of particular subjects, to found philosophy on the one consciousness is to found it on an equivocation: subconsciousness remains, uneliminated and incapable

## The Absolute

A partial system in which the full development of some subject is possible is teleologically ordered. The phenomenal universe includes at least one partial system teleologically ordered—our own; according to all probability, it includes at present other systems also (who knows how many!), as diverse as you like, but not less teleologically ordered. And though it is true that no partial system can be preserved perpetually so ordered, it is true on the other hand that the universe must always have included in the past and will always include in the future more or less analogous systems. The phenomenal universe is therefore, even as a whole, teleologically ordered in some degree.

But we cannot draw a decisive argument from this in favour of the theistic hypothesis. In fact—

Being cannot but have its essential determinations. If phenomenal determinations have had no beginning, and are therefore essential to Being, Being, in order to exist and in order to be always the same, needs must always have all its possible phenomenal determinations; which, without being lost, must be constantly transferred from one to another of the subjects and partial systems of which the supreme unity is the result. They must be transferred, because in that way only can they be perpetually realised.

The order which we have just mentioned, and on which it depends that the universe is never without teleologically

of being eliminated. If God exists, the existence of a particular subject consists in its being thought by God: just so. But if God has to exist, He must be, for each particular subject (we mean, with regard to the consciousness of that subject), as "different" as, for each particular subject, He is different from the other particular subject. (The "consciousness" of the one and of the other, the "recipients" as such, are two, irreducible to one; and this is also true in part of the "contents." There is, in any case, a common content, something divine; but, if we disregard the personality of God, the existence of a common content is resolved into the mutual implication of the contents—a mutual implication which is subconscious, although, or rather because, it can be inferred from reflective consciousness, which recognises it as a *conditio sine qua non* of itself.)

ordered partial systems (though no partial system remains teleologically ordered for ever), has therefore its root in that same logical exigency of Being, in consequence of which Being necessarily breaks up into a multitude of spontaneities, which necessarily interfere with each other. It is not properly directed toward an end; or, we may also say, the end toward which it is directed is always attained; it is the reality of the universe which always remains identical with itself in its varying, by means of its varying.

That which has its root in a logical exigency, exists always. It has no purposive value in the sense in which purpose must be understood in order that the personality of Being may be inferred from it.

The pantheistic hypothesis is not inconsistent with those purposes, of which we are certainly informed, and which are all particular and limited in time; indeed it implies them. It excludes the perfectibility of the whole; and it excludes the possibility that any part of the whole should either attain a perpetual ultimate perfection, or continue to advance towards perfection *ad infinitum*.

A subject has a history by which it profits, that is to say, it perfects itself, as long as its body lives. With the death of the body, it returns to subconsciousness, without profiting any longer by its past history. It may, under favourable circumstances, begin to develop once more, to perfect itself; but only by forming itself over again. A society of subjects, which lives much longer than a subject, may draw a correspondingly greater advantage from its history. But, like every subject, every society, every limited system, dies sooner or later. And with the death of a system, the elementary subjects which compose it lose the possibility of drawing a lesson from the past. The history of man goes back to yesterday. That of the day before yesterday is lost for us. That of to-day will serve to-morrow, but will be lost for the formations of the day after to-morrow.

The course of events implies a multitude of spontaneous primitive unities. A primitive unity would not be spontaneous, if a value, however subconscious and elementary, did not belong to its essential constituents (if all varying were not a good or an evil for the unity which varies). As prerequisites of the course of events, these primitive values are indestructible. But they are capable of development. And each primitive value, as it develops, passes outside the sphere of the corresponding unity; the development gives rise to the formation of values, each of which is realised in a determinate unity in so far as it is common to all the unities of a group,—to the formation of collective values. Development implies the existence of primitive values which develop; it is, nevertheless, conditioned, or determined by the course of events.

Such being the case, it is necessary that there should always be values developed to a maximum, and that the developed values should vanish in the end without exerting any influence on succeeding developments. The prerequisites of the course of events necessarily persist. The formations produced by the course of events, after lasting for a longer or shorter time, are dissolved. To suppose otherwise is to suppose that the course of events is directed toward an end; that is, that the determinations of Being cannot be resolved into phenomena; it is to give up pantheism. Pantheism does not exclude values; but, by excluding the universality of value, that is to say the purposiveness of the whole course of events, it excludes the possibility that the developed values may continue for ever under any form.

One who could show that universality and perpetuity

are essential to value, would have refuted pantheism, which perhaps cannot be refuted in any other way.[1]

## 24.

### SUMMARY.

Independently of any hypothesis, the conclusions of the inquiry which we have instituted can be summed up as follows:

Every subject is a centre of the phenomenal universe, is the unity of all phenomena,—a secondary, that is to say a particular, unity; *i.e.* not unique, but one among many ordered among themselves, but still, a unity of the whole phenomenal world. This latter is a system of more or less developed subjects. And phenomena are interconnected variations of the single subjects. Every subject varies in so far as it is spontaneous, but also in so far as its spontaneous variations interfere with those of all the rest. The course of events implies both a-logical factors, which are the spontaneities of the single subjects, and a logical factor, on which the interfering of the single spontaneities according to necessary laws depends. This logical

---

[1] Compare the *Great Problems*. Some values last much longer than the persons who have realised them; the person of Aristotle no longer belongs to the phenomenal world, in which nevertheless the Aristotelian thought still continues to assert itself. But that a value may persist, perpetually, under any form, the course of events requires an order such as it can derive, not from pantheistic necessity, but from Providence and from Providence only. Now, if Providence exists, it will not take care of some values only, and neglect the others. The single person is without doubt immortal, if God exists; while if God does not exist, no value will continue perpetually under any form. This is the reason (which still seems to me valid) why in the *Great Problems* I have identified the permanence of values and the permanence of individual persons. I take the opportunity to reaffirm resolutely the doctrine of values, of which I have laid down in the book mentioned only the main lines, which however are laid down in it with exactness. The value of the individual consists in the individual; that is to say, in the perfect rational organisation of individual practical capacities. He who denies the value of the person, or does not recognise it as the principle and the fulcrum of every known value, does not know what he is saying. And the value of the whole as a whole stands or falls with the permanence of such a value.

factor, on which the necessity of thought is founded, is the supreme Unity of the universe—a Unity which, while it connects the subjects, is constitutive of each, so that each subject exists only as belonging to the system. The supreme Unity is Being—that which is common to every concrete, and of which every concrete is a determination. Subjects are, as unities (with regard to their form, not to their content), fixed determinations of Being; phenomena are variable determinations. And Being is simply the most common concept of being. It exists in so far as it is thought. And it is thought essentially, in a more or less explicit way, by each subject. For the existence of a subject consists in thinking, not, to be sure, in abstract thinking, but in a living which implies abstract thinking as an essential moment of itself, or from which it is possible to abstract pure thought. And without the thought of Being, or of the universal, there is no possibility of thought. Therefore, the reality of the universe coincides with its knowableness. Or rather, the reality of the universe consists in its being known. The cognition of reality by a particular subject is nothing but reality itself, in so far as it is included in the subject as a constituent of it; and reality is properly nothing but what is included and necessarily included, though under a more or less explicit form, in each particular subject.

It is not difficult to perceive that the propositions above formulated, while they will seem paradoxical and rash to those who do not understand them, simply express with precision something which we all think and know,—something which no one can but think or know, for not to think or not to know this would be to think or know literally nothing.

Obviously, every subject is the unity of a certain experience or multiplicity of phenomena : it is the centre of its own phenomenal world. Its existing, or its being such a centre, is a living; in which the two moments, cognitive (theoretical) and practical, are inseparably connected. This living of the subject can be subdivided in a double way. The facts constituting its phenomenal world are—external (extended), or internal (unextended). And the former as well as the latter are either clearly conscious or subconscious. A recollection is an internal fact which was my own even before becoming actual again, *i.e.* which formerly was indeed my own, but subconscious. A stone thrown at me, of which I become aware the moment it hits me, belonged even before to my external phenomenal world; it was a subconscious element of it. In my phenomenal world I exert an activity which meets resistances in it, that is to say, which interferes in it with other activities. Consequently, my phenomenal world implies both that centre of activity in which I recognise an essential constituent of myself, and other more or less analogous centres of activity. Some of these centres are considered by me as subjects like myself. Nor can I possibly doubt of the accuracy of this my conviction; for the process through which I come to recognise the other subject is a part of that same process through which I am able to conceive myself as subject the two processes, or the two parts of the same process, have the same value. It follows that my phenomenal world is not only my own; it has as its centre, not myself only, but also many other subjects analogous to myself. On the other hand, when I reflect on what it means to be a centre of the phenomenal universe, by exerting an activity which interferes with others, or in short by living in the universe, I become convinced that only a subject analogous to myself can be a centre of activity, although its consciousness may be much less explicit than my own. And to recognise this is to recognise that the phenomenal world, which is not only my own, though also my own, can be resolved into a multiplicity of more or less developed subjects, the activities of which interfere with each other. Since the phenomenal world is a tissue of facts (though of polycentrically unified facts, as we have said), it implies spontaneities; for without many spontaneities there would be no course of events; and we easily recognise that the manifold spontaneities are precisely the activities of the subjects. But while the course of events implies the manifold spontaneities, it also implies their unity. For, without unity, in the first place there would be no interference, and therefore no course of events: even the single spontaneities would not exist, for each of them exists only in so far as it is opposed to the rest. In the second place, without unity there would not be the necessity which I recognise in my thinking as well as in the course of events. Each spontaneity therefore is the unity of all; that is to say, spontaneities imply each other; and they imply each other in so far as they all have something in common, to which it is essential both to be a constituent of each and to be not only a constituent of each, but of all. This *quid* is indeterminate Being—that Being which a subject cannot but think in order to exist, and of which every subject and every fact is a determination. Being cannot be indeterminate; and therefore it has necessarily those determinations which are essential to it.

At this point the necessity of choosing between the two hypotheses which we have mentioned becomes apparent. Those determinations by which the phenomenal world is constituted either are or are not essential to Being. In the first case, to assume that Being has other determinations is gratuitous and idle; we are within the sphere of pantheism. In the second case, it is inevitable to assume that Being has other determinations which constitute it a person; we are within the sphere of theism.

Here we stop. We do not believe that the ascertained elements are sufficient to justify a choice. But we do not therefore believe that our labour has been in vain. The problem has been stated in decidedly clearer and more precise terms than has been the case hitherto. We can arrive at a definite choice only by working on a solid ground—*viz.* on that which we have, not indeed discovered, but freed from a quantity of lumber which did not allow us to recognise it and to traverse it safely.

# APPENDICES

## I

### EXPERIENCE, RELIGION, PHILOSOPHY

Our purpose was of an extreme simplicity. We intended to reflect on ordinary thought, on common cognitions, and to make the presuppositions of them evident, so as to eliminate their fragmentary character.

We have not set this problem before ourselves according to our fancy, just to give ourselves the air of doing something; by trying to make common thought coherent, to make it agree with itself, we satisfy a demand of common thought itself. Even the uncultivated man, wholly absorbed in immediate practice, if he wishes to attain his practical end, must endeavour to think with order, systematically.

The uncultivated man can arrive only at a rough systematisation, whence it follows that very often he does not succeed in attaining his ends, however modest they may be (or rather, because they are too modest).

The cultivated man sets before himself more complex, more distant and more elevated ends—that is to say, ends which would seem to be more difficult of attainment, and in fact cannot be attained, or rather cannot usually be even represented, by the uncultivated man; whereas in virtue of culture, that is to say of an improved systematisation of thought, they are attained by the cultivated man more easily than the uncultivated man attains his own. (Indeed those ends not seldom make the attainment of his own ends easier to the uncultivated man himself; for instance, codes have no less influence, though a less direct influence, on alimentation than ovens.)

Man is irresistibly drawn toward the formation of culture, or the more and more complete systematisation of thought, even by the mere exigency of human practice ; that is to say, of a practice which, however uncultivated, is in any case rational. This is quite clear. And it is no less clear that the systematisation of thought never ends. And it does not end, because, so long as thought does not end, there is no thought which must necessarily remain unsystematised. To imagine thought broken up into parts, so that the elements of one part, though reducible to a system among themselves, can be systematised only among themselves and can form no system with the elements of another part, is nonsense : man can avail himself, for ends both of practice and of culture, of all that he knows or thinks.

Now, this *fact*, that we are gradually systematising (that is to say, arranging, connecting,) our thought without ever ending, because new thoughts always arise, and yet without ever meeting absolutely insuperable obstacles (that is, of course, as long as we remain within the field of what we know and of what we think),— this fact must be *possible*.

And our object was precisely and exclusively to understand such a possibility, to define its conditions exactly.

These conditions are, no doubt, essential to thought, even to the most common thought ; they are implicit in it. The common man does not know them, that is to say, is not capable of formulating them ; but he fulfils them, he realises them, for he thinks, and his thought, though not explicitly systematised, admits of systematisation, that is to say, is implicitly systematised. In order to arrive at a formulation of them, we have simply to construct the theory of that fact which is ordinary thought, or common cognition.

He who imagines that we meant to do anything else, has not understood what our purpose was ; he who imagines that we have done anything else, has misunderstood our book.

But to construct a theory of common cognition means, in other words, to construct a theory of experience.

When one speaks of experience many persons think at once of physics, and will be astonished that we profess to have constructed a doctrine of experience without having entered the field of physics. But we must not forget that physical experience, that is to say, extended experience, is not the only one ; and that physics considers only the objective aspect of extended experience, an aspect which is never alone.

Physics, in so far as it is a doctrine of extended experience objectively considered (that is to say, in so far as it is physics), may be, if we like, absolutely exact.[1] But it is not a doctrine of experience in general, though it is founded, or rather because it is founded, on its own experience; for physical experience is simply an element of that total experience which is the true experience—an element distinguishable, but not separable, from the others. A doctrine of real experience must be complete, not indeed in its particulars (no doctrine is or ever will be complete in this sense), but in its general outlines; that is to say, in the sense that no element of experience must be neglected in it. Such is the doctrine which we have expounded; and there can be no other.

We have simply identified experience and cognition; and this will seem strange to some. No doubt, cognition properly so called, judgment, is not the same thing as experience properly so called, the apprehension of a fact. But cognition properly so called and experience properly so called are inseparable. There is the unity of both; the elements which can be distinguished in the unity are distinguishable only in the unity, exist only in the unity.

Experience properly so called, fact, is the matter, of which cognition properly so called, judgment, is the form. Form is

[1] This opinion, which was held by Kant, and is still held by many, is no longer defensible. Many fundamental physical doctrines have had to be corrected; it is enough to observe that mass, the permanence of which seemed till yesterday an indubitable axiom, to-day seems to be at least in part a function of velocity (compare, *e.g.* RIGHI, *op. cit.*, especially Chaps. VI and VII). And everything leads us to believe that physics will require perpetual correction, and that therefore it is not absolutely true, not even with respect to its own limited field (it is almost unnecessary to mention in this connection the works of Duhem, Mach and Poincaré). Even if it is not absolutely true, physics remains a " science," that is to say, an indispensable element of culture; for instance, the Ptolemaic system fulfilled an important function, and only a foolish person can consider it as a complex of follies, though it was not fated to last. But all this reasoning is, for us, useless. We must neither discuss, nor (much more) correct physics. It is enough for us not to forget that physics, whatever its value may be in its own field, considers only one part of experience—a part which, though it can be studied separately in the same way as we can study arithmetic separately, cannot be separated from total experience. I had already observed in *Scienza e Opinioni* (before the appearance of the works of Duhem, who rightly insists on this point,) that knowledge is founded on " the general pressure of experience," that is to say on the complex or totality of experience, not on this or that among the parts which can be distinguished in it.

nothing but the form of matter; vice versa, matter is not given and does not exist independently of form.

Hence, experience and common cognition (that is to say, the cognition of phenomena, whether it be vulgar or scientific; the distinction does not matter here), if they are considered not abstractly but as they are in fact, are one and the same thing. Cognition means ordered experience. But human experience is always ordered, always known: who could found anything on an experience which were unknown to one, who could consider it as his own experience?

We do not profess to extract reason from fact, nor fact from reason; we distinguish between cognition properly so called and experience properly so called; but we remark that the distinction must not be an hypostatisation; that to consider these two elements separately is simply to abstract; that each of the two implies the other; and that consequently by constructing the theory of common cognition as it is, we also construct the theory of experience as it is.

The doctrine which we have expounded is a doctrine both of that which appears to consciousness and of its appearance to consciousness; a doctrine of the phenomenal universe, of experience.

It is manifest that every religion is a more or less successful attempt to go beyond the phenomenal. The most perfect religion by far, Christianity,[1] is no doubt in its theoretical doctrine a transcending of the phenomenal. According to the Christian doctrine, the universe, including the multitude of subjects, is altogether distinct, absolutely different, from God. It is created by God freely, that is to say, independently of any necessity, even an internal one. Relation to the universe is no essential constituent of the Creator. God is certainly not one among the many phenomena, of which the universe is the result. And He cannot even be reduced to the system of phenomena, to the universe as a unity. God is the foundation of the unity of phenomena as well as of every phenomenon; but He is not simply such a unity: He is something else. And therefore He is not phenomenal; He excludes all phenomenality; He is outside variation, outside time,

---

[1] I do not assert that Christianity is only the most perfect religion; that therefore it is not the perfect and absolutely true religion. The superiority of Christianity is out of question; the absolute truth of Christianity cannot be presupposed by a philosophy which is conscious of its own office.

outside all essential relation to other things : He is the Eternal and the Absolute. The same may be said of Christianity practically considered. Moreover, the ultimate practical valuation and the ultimate theoretical conception imply each other, and in substance coincide.

Christianity is relatively very recent, and its development as a doctrine was largely the result of a philosophical reflection on which the already existing philosophical doctrines exerted no small influence. In the other religions, and especially in primitive religions, the concept of the non-phenomenal, of the supernatural, is far from being equally well determined. The gods of Homer are simply men—superior (to a certain degree !), but still men.

But every religion, however crude, implies, at least vaguely, the concept (a concept clearly apprehended only through the feeling which accompanies it and is determined by it), that common cognition or experience is not sufficient to itself, and that it is necessary to go beyond it. Beyond, in what sense ? The uncultivated man would not be able to answer this question with exactness. Nevertheless he understands, or, if we prefer, feels, that not only has each man need of other men, for no one would know anything if he were left to himself, but that all human knowledge (that, of which he has an idea) must be transcended and integrated, implies problems of which it does not contain the explicit solutions, presupposes an order which is not formulated in it.

We do not mean to go into descriptive or explanatory details. Man wishes to rise to a yet unknown order, as that which supplies the foundation and justification of the order which is known to him and of which he makes use. Such is in its purely logical character (we are not concerned about anything else) the *raison d'être* of religion,[1]—a reason, the value of which cannot be reasonably denied.

---

[1] The uncultivated man is essentially directed toward practice. He takes special notice of the practical character of the order which is known to him ; for the same reason, the higher order which he would like to know, has a specially practical value for him ; to search for it is to search for a practical order. This is as much as to say that a primitive religion is especially a moral code. This is, moreover, true of every religion ; practice, for the cultivated man, is no longer the immediate practice of the uncultivated man ; however, even the cultivated man is always directed toward practice (toward *his own* practice). It could not be otherwise : to lose sight of practice, or to consider it as something secondary, is to loose sight of reality, or to consider it as something secondary, for the practical element is the most real (if I may express myself so) among the elements of reality.

But let us reflect further. The undeniable insufficiency of that order which is known to us (we mean that which is known to us apart from religion or philosophy) proves the necessity of a higher, more comprehensive order, of an order which is more properly an order; but it does not prove that such a higher order is to be sought outside the known order, the insufficiency of which has been recognised. Explicit thought implies presuppositions, without which it would be dissolved; these presuppositions must be made clear. In order to reach this result, we shall have to transcend explicit thought, but it is not self-evident that we must go outside the field to which explicit thought belongs.

Common cognition (whether vulgar or scientific) of phenomena, —it matters not whether they are few or many—is not such that it can satisfy us; it has a reason, but it does not contain it clearly formulated. The reason which we are seeking is certainly not one of the cognitions which we possess, nor a complex of many or of all; it is not a cognition of phenomena. It might nevertheless be a cognition of the phenomenal; I mean, the cognition of a law, implicit in phenomena, and essential to phenomena, and yet such that phenomena are essential to that law.

The fact that religions have always existed proves that men have always had a more or less vague consciousness of the fragmentary character, and therefore of the insufficiency, of common cognition, —of the necessity and possibility of removing this defect from it.

According to H. SPENCER (*First Principles*, p. 37, 6th ed., 1900,) " the accompanying code of conduct . . . is a supplementary growth in a religious creed." It is difficult to find, even in Spencer, a more radically mistaken opinion. *Formulated* morality (which must not be confused with the *principle* of all morality formulated or capable of being formulated—a principle which can be resolved into rationality,) varies with culture; consequently it may happen that the moral value of certain beliefs escapes us; but it does not follow that the beliefs themselves had no moral value for those who accepted them. Man is *always* directed towards practice: the geometer would not geometrise, unless he were conscious, perhaps in an involved manner, that this is for him a duty. But the practice of man is rational, and therefore inseparable from cognition. The cognition of a supreme practical (ethical) order is itself cognition, it belongs to the theoretical order. And it is cognition of an order which is not only supreme in practice, but supreme also in theory, and would not be supreme in the former unless it were so also in the latter. (The reciprocal proposition is also true.) Whence it follows that in sketching more or less successfully the outlines of a moral code (I do not say, in collecting and arranging certain rules which have become customary; but in endeavouring to find for ourselves a valid explanation of them, and so to arrive at really ultimate rules), one draws at once, and more or less successfully in correlation, the outlines of a metaphysics also (meaning by metaphysics the cognition of a supreme theoretical order, *i.e.* an order which is sufficient to itself).

But it does not prove, or at least does not prove immediately, that the removing of the defect requires the cognition of something other than the phenomenal universe.

Religion was the first solution of a problem which was presented to thought by its intrinsic necessity. But this necessity was at first apprehended only in a very confused manner. Therefore, though religion satisfied the sentiment of primitive man, it could not appear satisfactory to a more conscious reflection. A rational transformation or explication of religion was the necessary consequence of the development of reflection.

But, at the same time, religion was transformed in a quite different sense by an historical process. Two or more nations are brought into contact and sometimes fused: their respective religions exert some influence on each other and even become amalgamated. The religions which collide in this way are perhaps identical in substance, but the diversity of languages and of other customs makes them appear different. And appearance, in these cases as in too many others, has the same result as reality. The vulgar are not capable of penetrating beyond the form. Even among those who do not belong to the vulgar, very few are capable of overcoming passions which cannot however be called ignoble, of excluding the consideration of interests which are in great part legitimate; they also therefore adhere to the form; and in this way they help to preserve, to exaggerate the value of it. Articles of faith, traditions, rites, customs, having different origins, casually brought together, and firmly consolidated in consequence of a reciprocal attrition of which no trace remains, have no longer any precise meaning; notwithstanding all this, or rather in great part because of all this, the mixture is considered with the deepest respect, and faithfully transmitted as a sacred property. Faithfulness does not exclude the modifications which are gradually introduced and always in the same way, unconsciously or almost unconsciously.

No very great learning is required to perceive that when inquiry properly so called, or rational research, began, scholars were confronted everywhere by religions, no doubt very various, but all having the characters which we have summarily indicated. It was not possible that men, now convinced that it was necessary to understand, should imagine that simply to follow one of those religions was the same thing as to understand. Possibly, or even certainly, religion implied that conception of the universe for which they were seeking because they had *recognised* the rational necessity of it (which at first was only *felt*, as we said). But to make that conception explicit by means of reflection on religion (by means of a reflection which, presupposing the truth of religion, should aim at bringing this truth under a clearly intelligible form) necessarily appeared a hopeless undertaking with respect to those religions. Therefore the first inquirers followed, as inquirers, a different way.

To follow a different way does not mean necessarily to oppose religion. It means to seek, by a purely rational method, that solution which may be implicit in religion, but does not appear explicitly in actual religion. Supposing that religion is true, the result will be a rational reconstruction of religion; but the method, in order to be rational, must not admit the truth of religion as a presupposition.

We have expounded, if not the historical origins, the logical *raison d'être* of philosophy.[1]

[1] A fact always implies a law; but it also always implies an accidentality which by itself is *ex-lege*; therefore, the problem of origins and the problem of reasons are irreducible. At the time when inquiry began, it would not have been possible to have that clear concept of the ends of inquiry which we ourselves have of them. The incentive to inquiry had a reason which was felt, but not apprehended as a reason. On the other hand, we can set before ourselves two quite different objects in our inquiry. One is to extend vulgar cognitions by arranging them in well connected systems; by means of such an inquiry, that which we now call science is constructed. Another is to go back to that unity without which there would be no cognition; by means of such an inquiry, that which we now call philosophy is constructed. But the distinction between science and philosophy, though it is not recent, cannot have been original. Science, as well as philosophy, is constructed by means of reflection. Philosophy is (according to us, and not according to us only,) the doctrine of cognition, that is to say, of reason. Now, the purely irreflective (we were just going to say, unconscious) use of reason, sufficient for vulgar practice, is not sufficient for science; science also is therefore to a certain degree a doctrine of reason; but at first it is not so easy to determine how it is properly distinguished from philosophy. This is so true that the distinction, even at present, seems a subtlety to many, even not ignorant, persons. (Among these there are even professors of philosophy; for, as we said, there is always in a fact an accidentality *ex-lege*.) The first inquirers were not able to distinguish that which belonged to philosophic reason from that which belonged to scientific reason; in other words, they philosophised also, but without understanding clearly what they were doing, or the reason why they did it. We cannot blame them. We ought to blame, or rather to pity, those moderns who obstinately repeat a useless labour in going over the same road, by which the oldest inquirers have already passed.

## II

### HUMAN KNOWLEDGE

"THE true office of every serious Philosophy has been, is, and will always be that which Dante well defines—to describe the foundation of the whole universe.—What is this foundation? What relation has it to ourselves? May we deal confidently with the things, actions, affections, by which we are surrounded? ... The vulgar do not even suspect the existence of the problem.... We are obliged to solve it in some way."[1]

There is only one means to arrive at a solution of it, which consists in giving to ourselves a clear and exact account of human knowledge—in studying cognition, in making manifest the relation between the cognitive process and reality.[2]

This relation, according to Hegel, is the relation of identity: "Spirit is the Absolute of Cognition. ... Now, since the organ of cognition is logic, Spirit ... must be absolute λόγος, or real logic; i.e. *Principium* not only *cognoscendi*, but *essendi*." And yet, "If an interpenetration of the world and God takes place in man, ... the interpenetration must take place in the whole man, that is to say in man considered as *Thought, Emotion, Action*, and not in the fractional man of mere thought."[3]

"I also claim to be a dialectician. I also begin the logical inquiry with *Being* and with *Nothing*, and proceed with all the theses, antitheses and syntheses of Hegelian logic. ... But those Syntheses ... in which the Antithesis is perpetually resuscitated ... show me ... the permanence of the manifold in the field of phenomena. And I believe that manifold to be altogether

---

[1] A. TARI, *Saggi di Estetica e Metafisica*, edited by B. CROCE, Bari, Laterza, 1911, p. 258. I take into consideration only papers VIII and IX, already published in the years 1872 and 1882 respectively in *Proceedings of the Royal Academy of Mor. and Pol. Sciences* of Naples, but little known (unknown to me) up to the present moment. The idea set forth in the passage quoted has also been formulated almost in the same way by myself more than once, and is common to every one who does not misunderstand philosophy seriously. The verse quoted does not admit the interpretation given to it by the author; however it is usually understood in this sense.

[2] Kant maintained that philosophy must be preceded by the *critique* of knowledge; Fichte has shown that philosophy is constructed by means of the *theory* of knowledge.

[3] *Op. cit.*, p. 260.

irreducible, or reducible only to the triad of Knowing, Willing, Enjoying. . . . Thus I also admit logic, but a dualistic, not a monistic, logic."[1]

The author rightly insists on the impossibility of reducing everything to pure and simple cognition. "Knowing, Willing, Enjoying" are "first elements, irreducible to each other."[2] To be sure, Will in its true and proper sense is an "intellectual formation," so that Spinoza could say: "*Voluntas et intellectus unum et idem.*" But "Impulse, . . . the cell of this polymorphous Will, is . . . autonomous, . . . excludes all direction by Intellect"; in other words, Will implies an absolute spontaneity. "Nor does the capacity of enjoyment seem to me less original."[3]

All this deserves to be examined with some diligence.

I know that my volition, my enjoyment are elements not reducible to pure and simple knowledge. Volition and enjoyment therefore are not outside knowledge; they constitute, together with knowledge, that indissoluble unity which is myself. I will and enjoy only in so far as I am, more or less clearly, more or less directly, conscious of it.[4] The consciousness which is an element of volition and enjoyment, may not be properly a knowledge in the explicit form of judgment, but it is, no doubt, "the cell of polymorphous knowledge." Vice versa, while at least a germ of knowledge is implied in volition and enjoyment, knowledge in its turn implies a germ of volition, a germ of enjoyment; otherwise it would not be *my* knowledge.

A volition which is volition pure and simple (unconscious and indifferent spontaneity), an enjoyment which is enjoyment pure and simple, a knowledge which is knowledge pure and simple—are abstractions.

I am no aggregate, but a real (indecomposable) unity which develops into a multiplicity of facts. Each one of these my facts is characterised at once, though not always in the same way, as activity (volition), as feeling (enjoyment), as consciousness (know-

---

[1] *Op. cit.*, p. 273.
[2] *Ibid.*, p. 181.
[3] *Ibid.*, pp. 183-4. The author gives the name enjoyment to what is usually called feeling.
[4] We have said "more or less," for the subject implies, over and above clear and immediate consciousness, a subconsciousness which merges insensibly into unconsciousness.

ledge). No one of the three characters can be reduced to another, but none is separable from the others, although, in the developed subject, one of the three characters generally predominates in a determinate fact.

If by cognition we mean (as we often do) only the cognitive moment which is a simple abstraction, it is certainly not permissible to identify reality and cognition; for my real living is not a theorising. But those elements of reality which absolutely cannot be confused with abstract knowledge, are nevertheless (or may become, and with the development of the subject, and in proportion to its development, do become) elements of real knowledge.

Reality, according to the author, cannot be "constructed doctrinally; it is an "idea" only "*sub specie* of cognitive symbolism"; it is "an original, autonomous content."[1] Obviously; the inventory is not the estate. But the estate is after all something of which it has been possible to make an inventory.

Reality, you say, has characters, in consequence of which it cannot be reduced to cognition. Either your words are a mere *flatus vocis*, or you know these characters, and you know that they are characters of reality. The same arguments by which you would like to show that reality transcends your cognition, imply that reality is, not properly only your cognitive act (an act which by itself alone would not be cognitive, or rather would not exist), but the end of the act—that, of which you become conscious by means of the act, and which therefore is not beyond your cognition.

"If Absolute Knowledge is identical with Reality, it is difficult to understand how a Philosophy (a Cognitive Process) can arrive at it; for Reality has no Premisses or Conclusions of any kind. It will therefore be necessary to declare that the Process is *Formal*. But here again it is difficult to understand how a *Reality* can be inferred from a *Formality*. . . . And we are always at the same point. Either you mean to have Knowledge; and you must say with me, that it is . . . pure and simple Relativity to Life. Or you mean to have Life, and you can only *Live through it*."[2]

---

[1] *Ibid.*, p. 216.
[2] *Op. cit.*, p. 182, note. Lotze (quoted by the author, p. 208, n.) had written: "What is science? Not properly truth; for this is always valid, without requiring that man should endeavour to construct it." So he had distinguished, in the same way as the author (compare the preceding quotation), between COGNITION which

But, suppose life should imply knowledge ? Suppose life without knowledge should be a simple abstraction, as (human) knowledge without life certainly is ? That living of which we speak, and of which the author speaks, is obviously connected with the knowledge of living. The cognitive process is formal; but is it only formal ? To affirm, to deny, to infer, in general to know, are facts as real as to feel. Vice versa, we admit that reality is not only formal; but what should have been proved is that reality is not formal at all, so that the formality of knowledge would be something foreign to reality ; whereas the author is content to assume this.

It is impossible to deny that there is a known reality ; in that case the term reality would be meaningless, and the idea of inventing it would not have crossed anyone's mind. Each one of us calls his own phenomenal world—the complex of facts of which he is aware, or has become aware, or expects to become aware in any way—real. This phenomenal reality is, as phenomenal, absolutely beyond all doubt.

We wish to know whether a noumenal reality exists above or under phenomenal reality. The inquiries, the controversies, or, if we prefer, the philosophical *nugæ* about reality can only refer and do only refer to noumenal reality. And one thing ought to be clear : we shall be justified in asserting noumenal reality only if it is found to be necessarily implicit in phenomenal reality.

If we wish to arrive at a conclusion, we must therefore penetrate deeper into the concept of phenomenal reality.

The author says : " The world is neither nothing nor reality, but an absolute phenomenon " ;[1] which last, " if it is indeed a phenomenon, is indeed inserted between nothing and being."[2] A concept of reality, different from that of phenomenal reality, is here obviously presupposed ; whereas, in any case, it can be only the goal. And being and nothing would seem to be the elements of non-phenomenal (noumenal) reality ; which is another presupposition.

---

is the result of a process, and THAT which we wish to know (truth or reality, according to the point of view), which is not a result of the process itself. The author, without being aware of the coincidence between his own thought and that of Lotze, adds to the quotation this postscript: "A Truth without men who assert it!!" To speak of a non-asserted truth is as reasonable as to speak of an unknown reality

[1] P. 305.   [2] P. 306.

"Cognition is masked reality; and its true theoretical culmination is reality unmasked, but unmasked only as far as the recognition of an actual and definite vassallage and of an indefinite and indefinable virtual principality."[1] The cognition of which the author is speaking here, is cognition of the phenomenal. Let us even admit the noumenon, without forgetting that the author was content to presuppose it. But what is there to prove that the phenomenal is a counterfeit, a " mask " of the noumenal ? What is there to prove that the noumenal is not only not known through cognition of the phenomenal, but is not knowable at all ?

And what is the meaning of "vassallage"? "My totality appears to me as myself pregnant with the not-self which is the limit of reality."[2] No doubt, the non-ego is a limit, but a limit of the ego, not of reality. And it is a limit constitutive of the ego, not a violence which oppresses it. I know the limit; therefore let us not speak of cognitive vassallage. In practice it is a curb, very often an inconvenient or painful curb. But the necessity which compels me to adapt myself to it in my actions is just that which makes my actions, my operating activity, valuable; which transforms blind spontaneity into rational will;[3] therefore let us not even speak of practical vassallage.

The author is not without the right concept of a phenomenon: "The phenomenon, as phenomenon, is and appears, and is only in so far as it appears."[4] But his thought is dominated (this is a case of real heteronomy) by the Kantian hypothesis (an incongruous hypothesis, which had already been recognised as such) of the " thing in itself "; the phenomenal is, of course, a " human Reality "; it will be therefore a " limited Reality."[5]

We were saying that we require a doctrine of phenomenal reality. The doctrine can be summed up in a few words.

My phenomenal world is the complex of facts which have been, are and will be included in the unity of a consciousness (and of a

---

[1] P. 255.      [2] P. 241.

[3] In substance, even the author thinks the same thing: "In the nothing of theoretical thought I see gleaming before me practical Reality, not as an empty X, but as a vivid and true humanisation of this X" (p. 240). The substance is good; the form is defective. It is impossible to "see" anything "gleaming" in "nothing." Let us designate by A that known element, which the author calls "humanisation." Supposing that X is something absolutely unknown, how shall we be able to assure ourselves that A is an humanisation of X, or that any relation exists between X and A ?

[4] *Op. cit.*, p. 317.      [5] *Ibid.*, p. 189.

subconsciousness). This unity can be divided (it does not break up) into two groups: a non-spatial group, the ego in the proper sense (the ego in the wider sense is the above indicated unity), the subject, and a spatial group, the external world. There is further an intermediate group, which is non-spatial from one point of view, and spatial from another—my body.

The ego (in the proper sense, of course,) receives impressions from its external world by means of its body. That is to say, spatial facts are followed, according to certain laws, by non-spatial facts; for instance, my becoming aware of a spatial fact is a non-spatial fact. And the ego receives impressions from all parts of its external world; a spatial fact which made no impression on me would remain unapprehended by me, would not belong to my external world.

Therefore we can and must say that, while the ego in the wider sense is the unity of its phenomenal world, the ego in the proper sense, the subject, is the centre of its external phenomenal world.

There is more than one subject. And the body of each belongs, or may belong, to the external world of every other. Subjects communicate with each other by means of their bodies and their external worlds. Therefore we must deny that the external worlds (we are speaking throughout of phenomenal external worlds) are as many as the subjects, and as separate from each other as the subjects.

The vulgar belief that the external world is numerically only one, is therefore fully justified, and the only justifiable belief. Differences, commonly recognised, exist between the external worlds of two subjects; but they are not greater than those which are determined in the external world of the same subject by ITS OWN variations of place or of other conditions. The mistake of the vulgar lies in not reflecting that the external world, common to all, that in which we live and of which we know something, is a phenomenal world.

Since (1) each subject is the centre of its own external phenomenal world, and (2) only one phenomenal world exists,—it follows that the external phenomenal world, spatial reality, has a polycentric structure. Its centres are subjects—unities including not only spatial external facts, which are the same for all subjects, but also non-spatial facts, of which each subject has its own, internal to it, and on which it depends that one centre is not another, that the centres are many and not one only.

From what we have established it is obviously not to be inferred that every centre must be a developed subject, such as men, or rather some (few) men, are ; and it would not be difficult to show that this is not true. Whether developed or not, subjects are as essential to reality, as reality to subjects.

Let us hear what the author says. " Two capital errors have so far infested Science, the *Geocentric* . . . and the *Anthropocentric* error." This " famous aphorism " of Huxley, " false if it denies the *phenomenal* centrality of the thread thought in the cocoon world, is true if it refers to the hyperbolic *real* centrality of man, that *vanitas vanitatum*, and vanishing infinitesimal of the universe."[1]

But the " famous aphorism," which according to Huxley himself is the expression of " modern naturalism,"[2] refers precisely to the phenomenal world, the only world which is taken into consideration by the natural sciences.

Any subject, any group of subjects, whether developed or not, is as nothing compared with the universe ; experience assures us of this. Vice versa, the subject is central, that is to say, essential, to the universe ; the theory of knowledge proves it.

We have not to inquire here how two characters which seem obviously opposed may be reconciled. Let us only observe that both characters are relations between the subject and the phenomenal universe. Nothing has yet been found which allows us to assert, or even only to suppose, a noumenal reality.

Phenomenal reality is certainly not inaccessible to human knowledge. Those who pretend to recognise a gulf between human knowledge and reality, must do something more than refuse the name reality to the phenomenal world ; they must prove the existence of something which is not a phenomenon.

---

[1] *Op. cit.*, p. 188.
[2] *Ibid.* " Modern naturalism " has not been needed to convince man that, compared with nature, he is something insignificant ; " *vanitas vanitatum*," " *folium quod vento rapitur*," etc., are formulæ which boast of a respectable antiquity, and many others, even more ancient, might be added to them. Experience, I mean vulgar everyday experience, is painful and mortifying. But experience, whether modern or ancient, scientific or vulgar, makes us acquainted only with the phenomenal world.

Since all that is known in any way is for that reason a phenomenon, since "existence" is a category of human knowledge or thought, which, as even our opponents are ready to acknowledge, does not transcend phenomena, it is indeed difficult to understand how the existence of the noumenon can be proved,—or even assumed as an hypothesis for discussion; for noumenal reality is not the expression of a concept; it is an ill-assorted collection of words, without any objective meaning.

We must distinguish between reality and human knowledge. The question is, how the distinction can be made. Reality is said to be "an unqualifiable superhuman X"; knowledge, a "human," but only human, "elaboration"[1] of the same X. But if human knowledge is without value with respect to reality, this distinction also will have no value.

Man is not outside reality; we cannot therefore admit that thinking is "invisible emergence" out of reality. Thinking is no "emergence" out of reality; it is a real process—*i.e.* a process which we can, or rather do, live through.[2]

I am not outside reality: I am something real. But I am not the whole of reality. In fact, I am a centre of phenomenal reality, not however THE (only) centre, but ONE among its innumerable centres. Every centre, as distinct from every other, has something exclusively its own; vice versa, the centres, as centres of one and the same reality, have all something in common. Those elements of reality which belong particularly to the other centres, remain outside my immediate consciousness. It is possible for me to know something of them indirectly, in so far as—(1) the centres, as centres of one and the same reality, must resemble one another even in that which belongs particularly to each of them; (2) that which belongs particularly to each centre, does not remain without effect on their common reality.

No doubt indirect cognition must be distinguished from reality.

---

[1] *Op. cit.*, pp. 216–17.
[2] *Op. cit.*, p. 236. Compare the passage already quoted: "Either you mean to have Knowledge, and you must say with me that it is pure and simple Relativity to Life. Or you mean to have Life, and you can only *live through it.*" This opposition of life and of knowledge fails to recognise that knowing, thinking, are facts of life; and that the life of man consists precisely in thinking, in knowing, though certainly not in an ABSTRACT thinking, in an ABSTRACT knowing: the life of man is conscious life.

I infer the pain of another person from certain external manifestations; but I do not feel it; its reality does not consist in that which I know of it.

And a distinction must be made also with respect to that cognition which is founded on immediate consciousness. I see a mountain: there is in my consciousness an element, a coloured form, which belongs also to the mountain. But this is the only element of the mountain of which I have immediate consciousness; it is not however the only element of the mountain. Further, even this element is not strictly the same in my consciousness and in the mountain: I see the form of the mountain as it is visible from the place where I am looking at it, and according to the greater or lesser excellence of my eyes.

In short, the distinction between human knowledge and reality can be resolved into that between consciousness and subconsciousness, which are both constitutive of a subject, and into that between living or concrete consciousness and the abstract consciousness of order.

Human knowledge is always the knowledge of a determinate person; for instance, myself.

All that belongs to my subconsciousness, belongs to reality, and not to my knowledge. But the elements of my subconsciousness are fundamentally the same as those of my consciousness; they may reach consciousness; though the conditions required for reaching it perhaps are never realised for some persons. Under this aspect, reality differs from cognition; but it is nevertheless something essentially knowable.

All that belongs to my living and concrete consciousness belongs also to reality; under this aspect, reality and cognition coincide. However, reality is not a simple mass of elements which can be singly included in my consciousness: it is an ordered complex. In order that my consciousness should be consciousness of reality, should be cognition, or known reality, it is necessary that the explicit consciousness of order should be associated with the consciousness of the single elements.

Since not a few elements of reality are, not, indeed, absolutely outside myself, but outside my consciousness (for they belong to my subconsciousness), and since, on the other hand, the true order of real elements is a total order which includes them all, and can be understood only as the order of all, it is manifest that if I wish to know, if I wish to infer the system of the whole of reality from the reality which I apprehend immediately, I must necessarily do something on my own part, *i.e.* undertake an inquiry the result of which is not always assured; I must construct for myself the instruments which, though real as my instruments, are not however elements of that objective reality which I propose to know.

For instance, the concept of NOTHING is indispensable to the processes by which we endeavour to arrive at a knowledge of reality. If we wish to identify human knowledge and reality *sic et simpliciter*, to identify them in such a way as to exclude all distinction, we shall be obliged to admit that NOTHING is a constituent of reality, just as much as BEING. This supposition, logically developed, leads (it has led the author) to deny that reality is knowable.

Really, "nothing" is only a human (a strictly human) concept, indispensable to us, but indispensable because we, who are a mixture of consciousness and subconsciousness, cannot but have recourse to artificial means if we wish to consider the totality of things.

Human knowledge, as knowledge, coincides with known reality; it is this reality, included in the consciousness of the subject. But it coincides only with known reality; it cannot be identified with reality; for a part of reality is always unknown, in so far as it belongs, not to consciousness, but to human subconsciousness.

Vice versa, the reality included in subconsciousness is of the same kind as that included in consciousness: it is *knowable*. Human knowledge coincides with reality *potentially*, though not *actually*. Therefore, the possibility of constructing a doctrine of the whole of reality in its main lines and only in its main lines is beyond question.

## III

### THE "GREAT PROBLEMS" AND ITS CRITICS

#### 1

##### SUPREME PROBLEMS

We distinguish good from evil; on what grounds do we distinguish, and what is the real meaning of the distinction?

Will the psychical life of man last, or will it not last, after the death of the body?

The experience of our forefathers is not lost for us. Even the experience of those forefathers who have vanished for ever from our memory, is not lost; we profit by it only indirectly, at second-hand, but still we profit by it. For, in short, the historical development of man is continuous, connected in itself; although the connection does not always appear manifest to our reconstructive inquiry, although it has not been such as we should like it to have been, yet it exists among all parts or phases of development; no doubt is possible with regard to this. Even the history of the universe is, in a certain sense, continuous. But is the sense in which it is continuous such that we can believe that the universe has a development analogous to the development of humanity? Will human experience, human history, have an end? Supposing that they should end, will they leave a trace, whether recallable or not, by which other beings may profit, in the same way as we profit by the traces which our forefathers have left? Or must we not rather believe that the influence of the past on the future, without being ever destroyed, becomes useless in the long-run? that a humanity (or a society of intelligent creatures of any kind), which may in a remote future take the place of our own, must begin its development anew, without being able to avail itself of a past experience? In short, does the universe tend toward an end of its own, yes or no?

The question just formulated is connected with the other above formulated, whether the psychical life of man lasts after the death of the body or not, and in what way they are connected with each other.

Does the varying of the universe, with its necessary laws (concerning which we shall not consider whether they are, or not, such that the varying tends toward an ultimate end), fatally determine the end of every man and all men? Or is every man capable of doing something to determine his own end and in part also the end of others a little in his own way? Are we, or are we not, free? If our freedom exists, is it limited, and what are these limits? If it exists, we shall be able to make a right and a wrong use of it. How is the right to be distinguished from the wrong use? This is a question which brings us back again to the first.

Does God exist? I mean, a God who justifies hope, or confidence in the attainment of our ends. Supposing that a personal God does not exist, can there be in the universe a true and ultimate finality? And does the personality of God assure us of such a finality? Supposing that God exists as a person and guides the universe toward an end, supposing further that man is free (within certain limits, no matter what), man will obviously be able to co-operate with divine Providence, or to oppose it. What consequences will come to him from co-operation? What others from opposition? How will man have to work in order to co-operate with Providence?

The problems which we have just mentioned, are really "great." A man who does not care about them, may attain a number of ends, and even obtain universal admiration; but he is not an honest man. The ultimate end (if it exists) must be kept in view in every act, not as a means to the particular end of the act, but because every act must be subordinated to the ultimate end. To neglect the ultimate end if an ultimate end exists, to pursue an ultimate end if an ultimate end does not exist, means to deprive life of its character as an organic whole. Not to care about the supreme problems is to leave the field open, on the one hand to the blindest superstition, and on the other hand to the most vulgar grossness; it is to abandon the destinies of civilisation to chance.

Such is in short the course of reflections by which my book was suggested to me.

2

TWO CLASSES OF PROBLEMS. PARTICULAR AND UNIVERSAL PROBLEMS

We may distinguish, every one distinguishes, two classes of problems.

A problem of the first class is given, when we try to know a fully determined particular fact. For these cases it is only necessary to add a very small particular to a system of facts and of cognitions which is already ordered and possessed by us. Note that such a system is presupposed. Hence the solution is obtained by means of a simple immediate experience. Let us give a familiar example: is it raining (we mean, here, now)? In order to have the solution, I have simply to look out of the window.

A problem of the second class is given when we try to penetrate deeper into some part of that system, that order (of facts and of cognitions), which was presupposed in the problems of the first class. Even in the problems of the second class presuppositions are not wanting. The other parts of the system (those, with which the inquiry is not concerned, and which give us the means of inquiry,) are presupposed; or, in general, some general characters of the system are presupposed. In conformity with the difference of the object and the presupposition, the manner of solution is also different, for it can no longer be resolved into a simple immediate experience, but becomes much more complicated. The question, by what laws do heavy bodies fall to the ground, cannot be answered by observing the fall of a heavy body.

Manifestly, every problem of those reducible to either of the classes mentioned is limited; it refers to a limited field, outside which it not only cannot be solved, but cannot be raised under a significant formula; (a problem is absolutely insoluble only when it cannot be raised, that is to say, when it does not exist). The limitation, though most obvious in the problems of the first class, is no less real in those of the second. The laws of the fall of bodies, for instance, are not the same on the earth and in the interior of a hollow sphere. The laws of gravitation seem to be the same everywhere and always; but (not to say that this universality is presumed, not ascertained) they are not applicable to thermotics; and more generally, they are applicable only to physical reality.

Are there problems which can be raised, and therefore also solved, universally? That is to say, such that in order to understand them we are not obliged to confine ourselves to a limited field, which remain significant independently of all variations of place, time, circumstances of whatever kind?

No doubt. And they are the supreme problems mentioned above.

Will our opponents say that these problems are significant only for man? My answer is that they are significant for every active intelligent being which lives through the exercise of its own activity and intelligence as having a personal value. Will our opponents press their point by saying that such beings might even not exist, and in any case are only a very small part of the universe? From my book it follows, as we shall explain again further on, that this objection, in spite of appearances to the contrary, is puerile;

meanwhile I note that the existence of any problem can be resolved into its being raised, or capable of being raised by one of these beings, and that consequently the supreme problems, which are the problems concerning the beings themselves as such, exceed all others by far in generality, in independence of possible variations, in importance.

### 3

FICTITIOUS PROBLEMS. THE PROBLEM OF THE SOUL'S IMMORTALITY

But there are fictitious problems; such is *e.g.* the problem, whether the lunar concave is, or is not, smooth.[1] It may be that some (and why not, all?) of the problems considered as supreme are fictitious also. The phrase in which we believe a supreme problem to be raised, might have no meaning. And that this is true in many cases, cannot be denied.

For instance, is the soul immortal? Before seeking an answer, we have the right and the duty to ask whether he who puts the question knows what "soul" means. Man is alive, and is mortal; this is quite clear and quite certain. A living man accomplishes many functions, some of which are common to all living beings, others are common to all animals, and lastly others are peculiar to him. Every function implies conditions which make it possible: living bodies have something which distinguishes them from lifeless bodies; animals have something which distinguishes them from plants; men have something which distinguishes them from other animals. Nothing prevents us from designating this last "something" by the name "soul."

If the term soul is understood in the above sense (and in what other sense is it possible to understand it?), the illegitimacy, the emptiness of the problem in question appears obvious. He who asks

---

[1] Lunar "concave" means the concave of the sphere, in which the moon was supposed to be fixed. The problem, raised by L. SARSI (*i.e.* by Father GRASSI) in the *Libra philosophica*, was discussed even by GALILEI in the *Saggiatore*, of course from controversial motives. GALILEI, who had succeeded (it seems incredible!) in making the discussion instructive, finished by quoting the verses of the "witty poet":

"For Roland's sword which they do not possess,
And perhaps will never possess,
They give each other blindly such blows."

(The verses, with a trifling difference, are from BOJARDO in the *Orlando innamorato*; GALILEI must have had before him the reconstructed version by BERNI.)

whether the soul is immortal supposes tacitly but necessarily that the soul is a living being; supposes in substance that the soul is a body, whereas it is simply the complex of conditions which make certain functions of a living body possible.

Even a vegetable has something which distinguishes it from inorganic matter; and we might even give (some one has given) the name soul to this something. The question, whether the soul of the vegetable may perhaps continue to live after the body, will be allowed by everyone to be a most foolish one. The vegetable has a soul in so far as it fulfils certain functions, including *e.g.* nutrition; to suppose that the soul of the vegetable continues to live is to suppose the continuation of those functions when the vegetable no longer exists—is to suppose, for instance, that a tree continues to absorb nutriment after it has been burnt.

We have recognised that a vegetable has something more than an inorganic body, that an animal has something more than a vegetable, and that man has something more than an animal. That is to say, we have recognised the impossibility of resolving vital processes into simple physical becoming, feeling into simple vital process, thinking into simple feeling. But when these truths have been recognised as unquestionable, we have not yet done anything which can give a meaning to the proposed problem. Vegetable life is not reducible to inorganic becoming; but the concept we have formed of inorganic becoming, which obliges us to consider the vegetable as the result of the superposition of a vegetable soul upon inorganic becoming, this concept, we ask, what is it? An abstraction obtained by breaking up the unity of experience and by mentally separating from it certain facts which in reality are not separable from it. If the physical world is conceived as a reality standing by itself, certainly it is no longer possible to understand vegetables without introducing a new reality, the vegetative soul. But, since vice versa the vegetative soul never does appear (nor could it appear) separately, the impossibility mentioned does not prove that the vegetative soul is something existing by itself, apart; it proves only that the physical world must not be conceived as a reality standing by itself. More or less, the same argument holds good of the soul of a brute, and of that of man.

In short, the concept that a special existence and a special life must and can be ascribed to the soul, so that to be associated with the body is not essential to it,—is a crude interpretation of experience which cannot resist criticism, is an illusory concept. But the problem of immortality necessarily implies such a concept. Therefore the problem of immortality is only apparently significant.

4

IN WHAT SENSE THE PROBLEM OF THE SOUL'S IMMORTALITY HAS A MEANING AND ADMITS OF A SOLUTION

The reasons stated above (which it would have been easy, but useless, to develop further,) are, even in my opinion, irrefutable. That is to say, they prove that the problem of immortality, in the form under which many writers have presented it and many continue to present it, is fictitious. But they do not prove that the problem cannot be presented under another form, such as to make it significant and capable of solution.[1] *I present it under another form.* To oppose to me reasons which I know and accept, but which are valid only against a position of the problem different from my own, is a real waste of time. I shall sum up my doctrine.

All that is in any way known to a man, is known to him in so far as it constitutes a unity—the unity of the personal consciousness of that man. *Nihil est in intellectu quin prius fuerit in sensu*, is an aphorism of which no positivist will doubt. Now, sensible impressions are facts evidently connected in the unity of subjective consciousness; the form of impressions, whether it be inherent in the impressions or dependent on their unity (on the subject), is also included in the same unity of consciousness. I have not said[2] that all that exists or happens "in reality" is included in the unity of the subject; but all that is or happens "in cognition" is certainly included in it; even my knowledge (if you suppose, what I do not concede, the existence of such a knowledge,) that something exists or happens outside and independently of me, belongs to my knowledge; or, in other words, presupposes that unity which is myself, to which it belongs.

---

[1] I am not the only nor yet the first person to do so. HUME (who did not write yesterday) remarks that the problem of immortality does not necessarily fall with the hypothesis of substantiality. In other words, and perhaps with less exactness, he says in the end what I say myself.

[2] I have shown above that it can and must be said; but here it is not at all necessary to repeat it.

This being so, the hypothesis that one of the said unities is produced or vanishes, is absolutely meaningless. To say that *my* facts may happen independently of me, may while they happen in that way, combine, be associated so as to constitute that unity which is myself, is the same thing as to say that a local movement is possible without a space, that a number can exist without numerable elements.

The unity of consciousness can develop or become enveloped. That is to say, its content can increase or diminish in multiplicity and in variety ; its form, or internal organisation, can increase or diminish in delicacy, in order, in distinctness ; but that is all. Since the increase or diminution of the content, and the correlative refinement or simplification of the form, obviously depend on the interference of an activity belonging to the unity with other distinct activities, such an interference presupposes that the unity exists, and therefore it can neither produce nor destroy this latter. It can only have as its effect the development or envelopment of the unity, as we have said.

That unity which in a certain (very variable) condition of development constitutes a person, existed before what we call the (visible) body of that person was formed, and will continue when the body is dead and dissolved. Before, that unity was in the absolutely lowest stage of development. And afterwards ? . . . This is the problem. It may be that the unity will fall back into a condition like the preceding ; that the experience made during the life of the body will be entirely lost, will not serve for a further development in case circumstances should determine such a further development, which would then be a new beginning. But it may also be that the experience achieved will not be lost, that the unity will preserve in its indestructible life at least a part of the treasure accumulated during bodily life.

## 5

### THE HYPOTHESIS OF ULTIMATE UNITIES

Will our opponents say that unities are "non-verifiable" hypotheses? They would give the surest "verification" of their incapacity to understand the matter. Unities are not, and it is impossible that they should be, "observable things"; they are the conditions of that fact which is observation, or, in general, knowledge. Developed unities, subjects, are certainly so. Now, it is positively certain that subjects develop or become enveloped. It is not positively certain that a subject is formed, or dissolved in an absolute sense; this is indeed a non-verifiable hypothesis. An hypothesis, let us add, which analysis not only fails to define with precision, but clearly shows to be devoid of signification—an indefensible hypothesis.

Perhaps positivists will succeed in showing that the experience garnered during the life of the body is wholly lost at the death of the body, for the unity which had garnered it; that, in short, the personal subject does not outlast the functions of the organism. Let it be so. By doing this they will have discovered the true solution of the proposed problem. But the problem, whether the true solution is this or another, remains significant. It was not so as long as it was made to consist in determining the properties of a thing—the soul—of which the very existence, in the way in which it was vaguely conceived, appeared to be unquestionably problematic, and worse than problematic. But the form under which the problem has now been raised is new; to imagine that considerations which refer to the old form and are conclusive in so far as they refer to the old form, can be valid against the new form, shows a singular *naïveté*.

The so-called problem of immortality constitutes a serious preoccupation for everyone who has not solved it or eliminated it. To distract one's mind in order not to feel the weight of it is wrong and foolish. We must, not indeed distract our minds, but free ourselves. And a real deliverance can be obtained only by means either of a solution or of an elimination.

Traditional spiritualism had stated the problem, and had consequently solved it in a certain way. Positivism eliminates the spiritualistic position, and the consequent solution. In practice, the positivistic elimination is identical with the materialistic solution (which last is theoretically untenable). It "delivers us," provided it is a "definitive" solution. Now, we have seen that it is not definitive; in fact it is so only with regard to the spiritualistic position; whereas the problem must be stated in a wholly different way, and one which positivism had not considered.

"Deliverance" therefore has not yet been obtained; and we must continue to seek it by more adequate means.

Such is the *raison d'être* of my doctrine, so far as the problem of immortality is concerned. I think it useless to insist on the other "great problems"; what has been said of one, is applicable to the others also, with a few simple variations. I shall only remark that they all bring us back in the end to one single problem—the problem of the personality of God.

### 6

#### AGNOSTICISM PHILOSOPHICALLY ABSURD

It is obvious that the supreme problems are not problems belonging to any particular science. But this is not sufficient by itself and immediately to eliminate them as fictitious. If we take our stand on the sciences only, we shall arrive at something quite different from the final solution or elimination of the supreme problems. We shall arrive at the conclusion that these problems are both "real" and "insoluble." Agnosticism, if philosophically absurd, is scientifically inevitable; and this very fact proves the impossibility of constructing philosophy by assuming as a "criterion" the complex of the sciences. Agnosticism is scientifically inevitable; for every science implies a presupposition with which it cannot dispense, but which on the other hand it is not able (nor is it its business) to discuss, interpret, estimate, or understand. The man who is acquainted with one science only, may believe that the corresponding presupposition, unknown to him and at the same time incapable of being denied by him as the foundation of his science, may become known by means of other sciences. But the man who is acquainted with the principles of all the sciences, understands that the scientific cognition of the world leaves us necessarily in the presence of an X which cannot be eliminated or penetrated. Men of science—the true men of science who, not having undertaken, and not wishing to undertake, philosophic inquiries, wish to give their opinions about philosophic questions by making use of their scientific cognitions only—all with one voice declare that things have a ground, and that this ground is unknowable. They are wrong in declaring it absolutely unknowable; but, in so far as they declare it unknowable by scientific means, they are right.

It is therefore necessary to undertake a philosophical inquiry which assumes as its starting-point the fact of cognition and presupposes nothing but cognition. Note, not this or that cognition, but simply cognition—the fact that there are cognitions. This is a known and necessary fact, for one who denies cognition contradicts himself as much as one who supposes it to be unknown (who supposes a knowing which is no knowing).

The cognition which we presuppose, which we must necessarily assume as the first thing known, must be possible. In what way is it possible?

7

THE PROBLEM OF THE POSSIBILITY OF COGNITION

Such is the problem which we mean to solve. Let us observe that—

The problem cannot be included in the field of any science.[1] Every man of science knows or possesses a criterion by means of which he is able, within the field of his own science, to distinguish cognitions from mistaken or problematic or meaningless propositions. But to distinguish, to apply a criterion, is to know—a process, the possibility of which is not and cannot be investigated by any particular science. The subject must be able to know the object, the object must be capable of being known by the subject. A potentiality of the subject, a potentiality of the object, a relation between the two potentialities—such is the common presupposition of all sciences, the only one which is common to them all. Science does not and could not investigate this presupposition, precisely because it is assumed by science as a necessary presupposition, because science implies it and makes use of it. To construct a science is to study objects, not cognition. It is one thing to see, and another thing to create the theory of vision. Therefore science, not only does not and cannot inquire into that presupposition, but is forbidden to make such an inquiry if it means to fulfil its own office; the office of the eye is to see things, not to see itself. Science

---

[1] To think that, though it cannot be included in the field of any science, it can be included nevertheless in the field of "science" is the same as to say: A certain book has not yet been printed by anyone, but nevertheless it has been printed.

derives no inconvenience from not investigating its own presupposition; science derives no advantage from an inquiry into that presupposition (an inquiry which, though not to be accomplished by science, can nevertheless be accomplished). A seamstress has no need to know how needles are made; and her trying to know how needles are made is not the same as sewing.

The problem, if foreign to science, is not however foreign to intelligence. The subject can know the object, the object can be known by the subject; I should like to know in what these two potentialities properly consist, and what relation they have to each other. The word "cognition" has, no doubt, a meaning. I should like to know what its meaning precisely is. I should like to form an adequate concept of cognition; that is to say, a concept such that in thinking it I think with clearness the cognition such as it is in fact and such as we all understand it without much clearness or much precision. Will you say that what I ask is meaningless? that, since we can see without knowing the anatomy of the eye, the anatomy of the eye is an absurdity? The absurdity would be my own, if I were to answer you.

The problem, foreign to science but not to intelligence, is fundamental. We can, without solving it, obtain a great number of fragmentary cognitions—common cognitions. We can even systematise a class of cognitions, so as to construct a science; systematise another class of cognitions, so as to construct another science, etc. We can moreover systematise all together the constructed or constructible sciences. And if this work is well done, if in accomplishing it we have duly applied the rules which we possess and can know even reflectively, by means of which truth is distinguished from what is problematic, false and absurd;—we shall have obtained in this way a knowledge, which it will be impossible to call in question in any way and by whatever inquiries—objective knowledge.

## 8

SCIENCE AND EPISTEMOLOGY

Now, the question is whether another field exists beyond the one of which we have just now formed a concept.

That a man cannot see the Alps while he remains in Rome, is

true; but this proves nothing against the Alps. That a man of science cannot, as a man of science, go outside the field of which we have spoken, is true; but this proves nothing against the existence of another field. The man of science knows only his own field. But he knows that science necessarily implies a presupposition which science itself cannot penetrate; this knowledge prevents him from ascribing a negative value to his own ignorance of another field.

The philosopher knows moreover what the presupposition necessarily implicit in science and impenetrable by science is; this presupposition is THE POSSIBILITY OF COGNITION. Whereas the man of science is reduced merely to recognising the existence of the presupposition as the existence of something which is at once the foundation and the limit of science; the philosopher knows enough about that presupposition to be able to undertake the study of it. And this study will make it possible for him to transcend scientific agnosticism. That which is merely an unknown for the man of science, will be either penetrated or resolutely denied by the philosopher.

It is easy to show in a few words that the theory of knowledge must lead necessarily to the result mentioned, and that this cannot be obtained in any other way.

We can—(1) obtain cognitions of objects, that is to say construct science; (2) study cognition in itself, explain to ourselves how science is possible, that is to say construct a theory of knowledge. And we have absolutely not the faintest idea of a knowledge which cannot be brought under one of these two heads; the hypothesis that a third kind of knowledge is intrinsically possible, though inaccessible to us, is gratuitous and unfounded. That which neither science nor the theory of knowledge can admit as positively certain, is therefore mere unjustified and unjustifiable fantasy; it is not, and cannot become, cognition; it must be abandoned, excluded, as a chimera.

Vice versa, though the theory of knowledge cannot invalidate or modify science, which it seeks only to explain, it is yet true that as long as the theory of knowledge is not constructed, a field which ought to be explored remains still unexplored; and therefore it is illegitimate to draw from science alone conclusions having a definitive character; it is illegitimate in particular to infer that only the field of science exists from the fact that science is acquainted only with its own field. We do not presuppose that another field must exist; presuppositions can be ascribed to us only by one who has read merely the title of the *Great Problems*, and has interpreted the book fancifully according to an arbitrary presupposition of his own. What we assert is, that a question which has two aspects (the scientific, and the epistemological), is not solved as long as only one of the two aspects has been examined.

And in doing so we claim to remain faithful to that which may be said to be the leading, correct and important idea of positivism (though afterward disfigured and falsified in its applications)—the idea that philosophy must not be constructed on a foundation of arbitrary or in any way unjustified presuppositions.

Impartial and intelligent criticism has already recognised that the claim is legitimate. "M. Varisco, par cet important ouvrage [the *Great Problems*] s'assure une place originale dans la philosophie italienne. Il s'éloigne du positivisme dans sa forme doctrinale; mais il conserve une méthode positive. . . . Et c'est pourquoi à certaines observations . . . il s'est cru en droit de répliquer :— . . . Une doctrine qui ne se justifie pas rationellement n'est pas la philosophie——"[1]

9

EPISTEMOLOGY AND METAPHYSICS

Over and above the limited problems which imply certain presuppositions, that is to say over and above the problems of science, there are, as we said,[2] others which are possible and can therefore be solved universally, *i.e.* are such that they remain significant independently of any variation of time, of place, of all circumstances whatever—the problems of philosophy. It is by now

---

[1] *Rev. de metaph. et de mor.*, Paris, 1910, n. V, pp. 25–6. From this important review I transcribe a few more lines: "M. V. veut nous présenter un système indépendant de toute préconception. . . . [Il dit que] la réflection philosophique reconnaît une même valeur positive . . . à tout ce qui est donnée de connaissance . . . il rejette le mystère et l'inconnaisable.—Quand on a fait, dit-il, la théorie des choses et la théorie de la connaissance, on a fait la théorie de tout ce qui existe, de tout ce qui est possible. L'intelligence ne peut aller au delà, non que les forces lui manquent, mais parce qu'au delà rien n'existe plus."

[2] Compare above, § 4.

intuitively evident that these problems exist. And they are those which are found to be implied by the fact of cognition; they can be resolved into one single complex problem, that of explaining how cognition is possible. The only presupposition of such a problem is the cognitive fact; and since this fact is necessary and necessarily known, it cannot be called a presupposition in the sense in which we speak of scientific presuppositions.

Some may think that the question has been misplaced. —You wished to speak and had begun to speak about certain "great problems,"[1] and you have ended by speaking about the problem of cognition, which is something quite different. While we were expecting (for you had promised to give it) a metaphysics, you now mean to give us only an epistemology.

My answer is that metaphysics can be constructed only by means of epistemology, and can be certainly constructed by means of epistemology.

The cognitions of which science is constituted, and also those of which vulgar knowledge is constituted, are objective cognitions— of the object as object. The cognition of the object is inexhaustible; but, even if we supposed it to be exhausted, it would still be a cognition of the object. It is never a cognition of reality "in itself": the object is an object only for the subject, for it is that which confronts the subject as something else which is known by the subject. We shall never be able to know whether a reality "in itself" exists or not, and what it is, supposing it to exist, so long as we limit ourselves to assembling and ordering objective cognitions, whether vulgar or scientific; the man of science is, from this point of view, at the same level as the uncultivated man; for though the cognitions of the former are more extended than those of the latter and much better ordered, they still are however, like those of the latter, cognitions of objects.

Objective cognition exists; how is it possible? This is the problem of epistemology—a problem which, first of all, must not be misunderstood. We do not ask what causes or conditions, extrinsic to cognition, may produce cognition. Under this form the problem would imply a vicious circle: the extrinsic causes or conditions of cognition belong to reality in itself; and we do not yet know of reality in itself what it is or whether it exists. Our

[1] § 3 and again, § 4.

object is simply to make clear those conditions of possibility which are intrinsic to our concept of cognition.

I shall try to explain myself by an example (the example must be understood with discretion; for the cognitive fact is unique in its kind). A triangle A B C is inscribed in a semicircle; I wish to know how this fact is possible. Observe that I do not wish to know who has placed the triangle in the semicircle. This last problem cannot be solved by means of the simple cognition of the fact; and even if it were solved, would leave us in the same obscurity: whoever placed the triangle in the semicircle, was able to do so because the triangle was inscribable; to suppose on the contrary that the capacity of the triangle to be inscribed is a consequence of its having been placed in that way, is nonsense. My question is quite different. Let us represent by H my concept of A B C. My concept of A B C is the concept of a triangle inscribed in a semicircle; I know explicitly a character of H which we may represent by K. Well, in order that H may have the character K which it has really and which is known explicitly to me, it must have further some other character X, without which it would not have K, that is to say, without which H would not be H, would not be possible. What I ask, what I am seeking, is to know X explicitly. (The answer is familiar: it is necessary that the triangle A B C should be right-angled.) Manifestly, I do not go beyond my concept; the conditions of possibility which I am seeking, are inherent in the concept, necessarily implicit in the concept, and therefore also necessarily explicable with greater or less facility.

I hope to have made myself clear. I consider cognition. I consider it (that is to say, I wish to consider it, success in the attempt being more or less easy,) in its full and living reality of fact. I seek the intrinsic condition of possibility of this fact. I have a concept of that fact which is cognition, a concept which is partly explicit, but only implicit as concerns another part. I wish to make explicit to myself that part which at first is only implicit; I wish to think explicitly that which is necessarily implicit in my concept, which is necessarily implicit in it because without that element my concept would not be the same concept, and neither my concept nor the fact of which I have this concept would be possible.

## 10

### THE PROBLEM OF REALITY "IN ITSELF" MUST BE ELIMINATED

And reality "in itself"?

The first result of epistemological inquiry—the first result which is also the most important, for it marks the starting-point for further inquiries,—is this, that the problem of reality "in itself" must be, not solved, but eliminated. We cannot know reality "in itself" because it does not exist; and it does not exist because the words "reality in itself" express no concept, are meaningless words. The existence of phenomena consists in their being phenomena, that is to say, in having that relation with every subject in virtue of which they are phenomena, *i.e.* are known or knowable by the subject. Phenomena are all connected with each other in the unity of the subject; but the subject is not a "thing" standing by itself, outside phenomena; it is their unity, a law of their own— a law to which phenomena are as essential as the law is to phenomena. Many subjects exist, and they are all conjoined in the higher unity of Being. Being, of which every subject and every phenomenon is a determination, may perhaps also have other essential determinations (and in such a case the single subjects and their phenomena would not be essential determinations of it). But, in any case, it is Being—a common character of subjects and of phenomena, and, as such, not foreign to phenomenality. Moreover, if its only determinations are subjects and phenomena, Being exists only in so far as it is common to these its determinations, or in so far as it is necessarily implicit in each subject; it is still, as every subject is, a law of phenomena. Let us suppose on the contrary that it also has other determinations. In order to assert this, we must know it; and we could not know it, if it were not necessarily inferred from the fact of phenomenal cognition. Under the hypothesis just considered, it is no longer true that to be in relation with the single subjects (which in that case might even not exist) is essential to Being; but it remains true that to be in relation with Being is an essential constituent of every subject; that, in other words, every subject implies Being; *i.e.* that the subject does not go out of itself, does not know anything absolutely different from itself, not even in so far as it knows Being in other determinations than single subjects and phenomena. God might not have created man. Since He has created him, He has made Himself a constituent of man; and man, even in knowing God, knows, not a reality which transcends him, but himself.[1]

It is absurd to speak of a knowledge of things in themselves, of realities existing independently of our apprehension of them.

Let us admit that a subject S and a reality in itself R exist at first in a state of mutual independence, and that then, in consequence of a process which does not concern us, S arrives at the cognition of R, of R " as it is." The cognition of R, that is to say R as known, has become *ipso facto* a constituent of S. That S, which possesses the cognition of R (and, in so far as it possess this cognition, has changed from what it was previously), possesses in this cognition a constituent of itself; its cognition of R is simply an element of its cognition of itself. The illusory difficulty arises from not understanding that the fact of obtaining a cognition constitutes a change of the subject. It is usual to say: I, who before did not know and now know, am still I, still the same. No doubt, I am still the same in *one* sense, but not in *every* sense. I am still the same in so far as the unity of my consciousness has not been broken up; a form has remained. But the content has been modified, though it is not entirely changed (and though the change is in general, on each occasion, of little importance; so that it is almost lost to sight). Now, the form which lasts exists only as the form of a content. The subject is not pure form, it is both form and content. A cognition which the subject obtains, a reality which the subject comes to know " such as it is," become at once constituents of the subject as content (of its content); and therefore the knowledge which a subject has is always a knowledge of itself. To conclude, the " known thing " can be resolved into a formation (properly, a distinction,) within that unified experience which is the subject.

## 11

### THE DOCTRINE OF SENSATION

The " whole " problem of knowledge breaks up into the system (system, not aggregate,) of many problems. Each of these is

[1] All this, expressed so briefly, is not very clear. It will be made a little clearer here below. But in order to understand completely, it is necessary to study the *Great Problems* and the present book.

"partial," in the sense that it penetrates only into one aspect of knowledge, but not in the sense that it investigates a part of knowledge separable from the rest. It is impossible either to solve at once the whole problem, which must be decomposed into the different partial problems, or to solve a partial problem separately, for the solution of a partial problem has its true meaning only in so far as we recognise in it an element of the solution of the whole problem. The inquiry becomes necessarily involved in itself; whence a real difficulty arises both for him who wishes to expound it with clearness, and for him who wishes to understand the exposition of it.

How does so-called external (extended) reality become known? Through the sensations; though it is true that even the cognition of external reality implies much more than mere sensations.

The doctrine of *Sensation* which is developed with sufficient amplitude in the *Great Problems*, has been completely misunderstood by most readers; it has been considered as a repetition of SCHUPPE's doctrine. Now, Schuppe resolves the particular subject into a simple point of interference of sensible elements. On the contrary, according to me, the subject itself is a centre of spontaneity, essential to the sensible elements, for these are produced by the interference of single spontaneities. The difference is not secondary, it is radical. In what way can such a serious misunderstanding have arisen?

In that chapter it was not possible to anticipate the doctrines which were needed to complete it, and so to define its meaning more precisely. It was not possible, for the further doctrines would have seemed gratuitous hypotheses, they would not have been understood for what they are, unless the ground in which only they could take root and live, had been cultivated before; in short, they required a preparation, of which that chapter is an indispensable part. But critics ought not to forget that, though the chapters of a book must be read one at a time, they are not intelligible separately. It would have been necessary to pay attention to the connection of that doctrine with the others which are developed, or even only mentioned (mentioned however clearly enough) in other places—to consider the whole book as a whole. Then my doctrine would have been understood (one who did not neglect these cautions, has in fact understood it).¹ And GENTILE might have spared, at least in great part, the two full pages spent on the criticism of that doctrine. To defend this doctrine, I must deny, according to Gentile, "that the constitution of the sensible, as sensible, depends on the activity of a sentient being"; I, who assert that sensibles are the results of the interference of single conscious spontaneities, that is to say, of the activities of subjects! And I must "show, against Aristotle, the possibility of thinking matter without form"; I, who assert that each subject (a unity, that is to say a form,) and Being (that is to say, the supreme unity of subjects, also a form,) are essential to the phenomenal universe!

Gentile adds: "It is certainly not sufficient to *say* that the same element which we find in consciousness ... that very identical element, is also outside consciousness."² My answer is

¹ As a rule, when readers disagree with the author as regards the intelligibility of a book, the fault is of the author. This rule is not without exceptions, especially as concerns the fortune of an Italian book, and a book of philosophy, in Italy. However, I too recognise in that chapter of my book some defects which, though of secondary importance, may have been partly the cause of wrong interpretations, and which I shall soon correct in a second edition. For those defects of which I am not aware (and which may perhaps be the most serious), there is of course no remedy. [The chapter has been revised for the English edition.]

² In the review already quoted, p. 225. One who had before him the review by Gentile, and who wished to offer him a proof of his own zealous discipleship, has gone further: "Si on lui demande la preuve de l'identité entre la chose en tant que sensible et en tant que renfermée dans la conscience, il [that is to say, the author of the *Great Problems*] répond en faisant appel à l'expérience. Réponse dont il peut se dispenser, pour la bonne raison que l'expérience n'aperçoit que la chose présente à la conscience." (B. NARDI, *Rev. Néo-scolastique*, Louvain, 1910, n. 68, p. 583.) The witticism is all very well; but to equivocate, more or less in good faith, is not to discuss. A man who hears another speaking has an experience; therefore, since "l'expérience n'aperçoit que la chose présente à la conscience," does he never know, or can he not know, what the other thinks? My excellent critic talks as if experience could be resolved into the fragmentariness of single apprehended facts. But single facts are only the matter of experience, in which we must further consider the form. If we were reduced to matter alone, each of us would think that he is shut up in himself; each one would think himself the only subject. Indeed, no one would distinguish himself from an external world of his own, no one would know anything (for cognition implies a form), that is to say no one would exist as subject. But matter is never completely chaotic; and each of us with the help of others gradually systematises it more and more perfectly. So we arrive at the distinction between the act of *apprehending* which belongs to each single subject without possibility of communication, and what is *apprehended* which is or may be common; we arrive at the conviction that the apprehended external world is one alone, the same (except for the differences mentioned in the text) for all. This conviction implies much more than an aggregate of disconnected sensations. But it implies the sensations too; and therefore can and must be said to be founded on experience, provided that experience be not understood, quite unreasonably, as including only its matter (an abstraction!). My excellent critic may, if he likes, call my appeal to this conviction "appel à l'expérience"; but he ought not to have forgotten that the

this. First, the phrase "outside consciousness" is used without explanation where explanation was impossible; but, on reading further, one sees that "outside" refers to the clear consciousness of a particular subject; I do not admit facts outside all consciousness. Second, I do not merely "say"; I demonstrate. And my demonstration, which is extremely simple, is not therefore any less conclusive. All the manifold subjects (manifold, for each one has his own internal world,) recognise one and the same single, extended external reality. This external reality (in so far as it is apprehended as such) can be resolved for each subject into the complex of sensibles sensed by the subject itself. If the existence of each sensed sensible could be resolved into its being sensed, the external worlds would be as many as the subjects; and each one would belong to a subject as exclusively as the act of sensing. The extended world apprehended by a subject would be internal to the subject, in the same way as, for instance, feeling is internal. In order that the oneness of extended reality (whereas the internal worlds are many) should not be a meaningless word, we must admit that the existence of a sensible sensed by the subject A cannot be resolved merely into its being sensed by the subject A; or again, that one and the same sensible can be sensed by several subjects; or again, that the sensible is fundamentally the same both in the consciousness of A and outside it, that is to say in the consciousness of some other subject. I say, *fundamentally*. Differences, in some cases even remarkable differences, exist, and I have never denied them; but they do not impair the doctrine, for, on the contrary, they can be deduced from it.

conviction exists, in whatever way he may think it to have arisen, and that it must be taken into account; if he had reflected a little, he would have perceived that the meaning of my doctrine is precisely to express that conviction; I cannot tell why he did not reflect. I shall transcribe another phrase from his review: "M. Varisco se représente l'être comme un substrat dans lequel la monade est inserée" (p. 584). I assert most explicitly that Being, the supreme *form* of the phenomenal universe, is a *concept*. My critic does not say, nor is it easy for me to guess, on what he bases his interpretation, which I shall simply call strange. I have already said that he had before him the article by Gentile (indeed he had probably before him only this article). But Gentile does not entirely dissent from me on this point ("Varisco," he writes, "has seen that [concrete being] either is not, or is a determination of the One or indeterminate Being"); and the difficulties he raises against my metaphysics can be reduced to the charge, that my metaphysics are not sufficiently monistic. It is singular that reproaches of the same kind are made against me and exaggerated in the *Revue Néo-scolastique;* though I should have expected that my metaphysics would be disapproved by a neo-scholastic as not sufficiently pluralistic.

## 12

### THE DOCTRINE OF VALUES

The doctrine of values, as it is set forth in the *Great Problems*, is certainly capable of development; but it requires no development to be understood and established as a most essential constituent of the system; this is the reason why it is scarcely mentioned in the present volume.

The doctrine has been criticised by GENTILE, and his criticisms seem to have a certain weight. But in part they are destroyed by what he himself remarks: "Varisco is careful to warn us that he neither separates nor hypostatises the consciousness of the sensed . . ., the consciousness of activity . . . and the consciousness of value or feeling; for, on the contrary, according to him, they presuppose one another and are inseparable from one another."[1] As concerns the rest, they are conclusive only on the presupposition that the doctrine followed by me is inferior to that of Gentile, *i.e.* on the presupposition of the very point now under discussion.

According to Gentile, I stop at the consideration of "values without God! which is as much as to say . . . values without value. For . . . there can be no concrete value which is not a concrete determination of the principle of value itself. His," that is to say my, " value is the value of empirical personality, which is itself not personality, for empirical personality presupposes absolute personality."[2] Let us consider this point.

Concrete (empirical) value is the value of a concrete (empirical particular) subject. A concrete subject is the unity of an empirical

---

[1] Review quoted, p. 229. It is true that he immediately adds: "This is all very well. But feeling *in any case* [italics mine] is not consciousness according to him: feeling is a *prius* with regard to consciousness (compare, for instance, p. 70). It is one thing to suffer, another thing to be aware of suffering, though it is impossible not to be aware of it. And the root of that *ego* without which no consciousness, at least no consciousness possessing value, exists, would consist precisely in this feeling, which is such by consciousness." I do not accept this interpretation. I do not deny that it may seem justified by some expressions of mine taken separately; for this very reason I have not neglected the "cautions" mentioned by Gentile. Among elements which are co-essential (and co-eternal, outside creation) it is impossible to consider one as preceding another. No doubt co-essentiality does not exclude the possibility of distinguishing. *E.g.* a needle pricks *qua* pointed, not *qua* long. Is therefore pointedness, with regard to pricking, a *prius* in respect to length? Obviously no, for pointedness is impossible without length.

[2] Review quoted, p. 230.

multiplicity, of a multiplicity of concretes. That multiplicity which is certainly a constituent of the subject, is always intrinsically ordered, or well ordered, in a certain sense and to a certain degree; otherwise the subject would not exist. But it may not be entirely and on every side well ordered. Indeed, a certain partial, more or less extended (but always partial), disorder must be considered as essential to the subject. The non-completeness of order depends, theoretically, on the fact that the constitutive multiplicity is always in great part subconscious,[1] practically, on the fact that the ordering energy of the subject is limited.

The subject has a positive value, conforms to truth and goodness, in so far as it is ordered;[2] it has a negative value, conforms to falsity and evil, in so far as it is unordered.

The subject does not simply ascertain its own intrinsic constitution; it makes a valuation of this constitution, it says to itself: this is right, that is not right; this is true, that is false; this is good, that is evil. It judges its own constitution according to a criterion which is necessarily higher than its own actual constitution. The standard cannot but be intrinsic to the subject, for it is applied by the subject itself; but, on the other hand, it must be founded on a condition which cannot be reduced to the pure and simple fact of that certain internal constitution, for it serves to judge the constitution itself.

---

[1] The incomplete clearness of consciousness is an obstacle to order; this however does not mean that disorder is essential to subconsciousness, nor that the spheres of subconsciousness and of disorder coincide.

[2] "Varisco does not feel that even theoretical consciousness implies . . . value." From what I have just said, which is, in substance, the repetition of what I had already said several times, it appears that Gentile has misunderstood me; perhaps by my own fault; in any case I was not wrong in remarking the ease with which I might be misunderstood. "According to him theoretical value exists, but it is not original"; in fact, I assert that "theoretical consciousness has a value, because it is the consciousness of a subject which already possesses a value,— which possesses this value, because its consciousness is also practical; it is the consciousness of an activity, of which value constitutes an essential initial character." These are my own words which I do not withdraw; but their meaning is to reassert the inseparability of theoretical from practical consciousness (compare note in the preceding section). The practical aspect is "initial," that is to say, cannot be a product of the mere theoretical aspect; vice versa the theoretical aspect too cannot be a product of the mere practical aspect; and therefore it also is "initial." In short, we distinguish theoretical from practical consciousness; but neither of these two forms of consciousness is possible without the other. We cannot say that *both* a theoretical consciousness and a practical consciousness exist, nor, much less, that either of the two precedes: there is a consciousness, of which the theoretical and the practical aspects (which last must be sub-distinguished into activity and feeling) are co-essential and inseparable characters.

If we combine these two characters of the criterion it is easy to recognise—(1) that the (empirical) subject is subordinate to an OTHER ; for, if this were not the case, it would recognise no other condition but its own constitution such as it is in fact ; (2) that its being subordinate is not a violence endured (as *e.g.* for a stone to be cemented together with others into a building is a violence) : it is a constituent of the subject itself, and an essential constituent.

As subordinate to an " other," the subject is not the only being. An " other " exists. And this " other " is, or implies, the Absolute. For the criterion which is applied by the subject is, at least in part, absolutely irresistible : theoretical thought cannot escape logical necessity. But the criterion is intrinsic to the subject ; the subordination to an " other " is a constituent of the subject. Therefore the subject exists only in so far as it is subordinate to the " other " and therefore to the Absolute ; it is relative, and necessarily implies the Absolute.

The (empirical) subject presupposes the Absolute. It presupposes the Absolute as an " other " in a certain sense, and as a " non-other " in another sense. The Absolute cannot be resolved into the single subject considered in its irregularity ; and in this sense it is " other " than the single subject. But it is necessarily implicit in the single subject ; and, in this other sense, it is an essential constituent of every single subject.

So far I believe that if GENTILE will not let himself be influenced by differences which are differences of language more than anything else, and as such, are indeed inevitable (both he and I are particular subjects, each having its own idiosyncrasies,) but irrelevant to the form of the doctrine, he will recognise that he agrees with me. The " serious " divergency begins when we try to determine the concept of the Absolute.

We have a common fund of doctrine, which we shall represent by A. Two different conclusions are drawn from this fund (with respect to a more precise determination of the concept of an Absolute)—that of Gentile, B, and my own, C. The only criterion for the decision between B and C, is to be sought in A. It is no use to oppose B to C, as Gentile seems to me to have done ; that C cannot be reconciled with B, is indubitable ; but I assert that C, and not B, is the only and true legitimate consequence of A.

## 13

### THE PARTICULAR SUBJECT AND THE "OTHER"

The particular subject is confronted by an "other"—an "other" on which the criterion, intrinsic to the subject, is founded, and which is used by the latter in order to judge itself—consequently, an "other" which, though it is in one sense undeniably "other," is still implicit in the subject as a constituent of it. Each subject recognises immediately as "other" a multitude of concretes. Among these concretes there are more or less developed subjects, and phenomena depending on the activities of the subjects themselves. According to what we have seen at the proper time, the hypothesis that there are concretes of another kind, irreducible to subjects and to the interferences of their activities, is not justified, nor justifiable, nor significant. The phenomenal universe can be resolved into a multitude of subjects which imply each other; whence it follows that the multitude constitutes a system. Each subject is Unity of the phenomenal universe; the "other," for the subject, is the phenomenal universe, deducting from it that particular unity which is the subject itself.

Let us come to the Absolute.

Necessary truths exist (we shall not inquire whether every truth is necessary); this is proved to every subject by its own thought. Truth, whether it is necessary or not, exists only in so far as it is known by some subject. It is therefore necessary that some subject should exist; for, if every subject were to vanish, every truth also would vanish; now, necessary truth cannot vanish. The necessary truths known to a subject are many; but they must constitute a system which is one in itself. That which is necessarily true for one subject is necessarily true for every subject, and holds good unconditionally of every phenomenon. Thus, there are not as many systems of necessary truths as there are subjects, but one single system. So we are led necessarily to a disjunction:

(1) Each subject is a necessary being; and subjects imply each other, so that the existence of one is a condition of the existence of every other, and is conditioned by the existence of all the others; each is a unity of all. Or else—

(2) Necessary being, the Absolute, is one single subject—God.

Let us examine the second hypothesis; and let us try to understand with some definiteness the relations between the Absolute and the phenomenal universe, between God and the subjects.

## 14

### NECESSARY TRUTH AND GOD

Necessary truth exists in so far as God knows it. The existence of necessary truths is the existence of divine Thought, is the existence of God itself. The subject, in knowing a necessary truth, knows God, however imperfectly.[1] God, in Himself, is a rigorous unity; but not the dead and abstract unity of a point: He is a unity which is at the same time infinite riches; and something of these infinite riches is revealed to the subject. A constituent of the divine is at the same time a constituent of myself; it is not, however, the only constituent of myself. I distinguish the necessary truth which is known to me, and my cognition, my subjective thought, which can know necessary truth, but knows it only in part, and may even, but still only in part, deny it.

The existence of that constituent of myself which is necessary truth, is the very existence of God. And what is the existence of that other constituent of myself which is the cognition of necessary truth, my subjective thought?

No doubt, God knows my subjective thought; indeed, it would not exist if God did not know it. My subjective thought, too, is included in the divine consciousness, and exists in so far as it is included in that consciousness. It is also a constituent of divinity.

But are God and I then one? There are reasons against and reasons for this hypothesis; let us touch briefly on both.

(1) Against. God has (or is) consciousness both of the truth which is known to me (that is to say, of Himself) and of my consciousness of that truth (that is to say, of myself). The truth which is known to me is (let us even say, with some restrictions,) God; under this aspect, God and I in some way coincide. On the contrary, my consciousness of truth and God's consciousness (God as consciousness) do not coincide; for, since the first is included in the second, the second is not included in the first. God sees not only the truth which I see, but my seeing it. When I see truth, I see God

---

[1] Further on I shall say something to those who think differently.

with greater or less clearness; but I do not see the vision which God has of my own vision. Further, if the vision of a subject were identical with the constitutive vision of God, the vision of one subject would be identical with that of every other. And individual visions or consciousnesses are irreducibly distinct—separate, certainly not with regard to the content, but as consciousnesses, as containers.

(2) For. The first of the reasons against assumes that in the particular subject known truth and subjective thought are different things. Now, it is easy to convince oneself that known truth is simply a law of subjective thinking: I know truth in so far as I think thus and thus. Our opponents admit that truth and cognition are identical (*unum et idem*) in God; but this result would not follow, unless the two were identical also in the particular subject. The second reason, if valid, would exclude the possibility of recognising sameness of content: if the thinking of Peter and the thinking of Paul were irreducibly two, in so far as each is a thinking, how will Peter and Paul be able to perceive that they both think one and the same truth?

What must we conclude?

## 15

### DIFFICULTIES OF THEO-PANTHEISM

Both doctrines admit the personality of God: the first is in substance traditional Theism; to the second we shall give the name Theo-pantheism. The reasons of Theo-pantheists ("for") have an undeniable force; but they cannot be reconciled with the separateness of personal consciousnesses, which is also undeniable. All would go perfectly well, if only one subject existed; but the subjects are several.—To oppose a bare fact to reasons is no answer—is the reply. But I do not oppose the fact to you; I ask that you should give a satisfactory reason for the fact. That you find yourselves unable to give this reason, constitutes a reason against you. The object at which we aim is to understand known multiplicity, to understand how multiplicity can be known, and can imply that necessity which we recognise as implicit in it. Either you give the reason for multiplicity, and, in particular, for the multiplicity of subjects (which is the fundamental one, that which explains all other multiplicity); or your doctrine, whatever may be its intrinsic coherence, is not the doctrine which we are seeking, and consequently must be rejected. The multiplicity of subjects is apparent! I grant it to be all that you like; I simply require that you should give me the reason for it. The difficulty of discovering this reason constitutes the only real difficulty, against which we are contending; and do you expect me to be satisfied with a word as the only solution?

Variation [*accadere*] is, as we know, phenomenal: its existence consists in its appearance to some subject. Well? I have shown in the *Great Problems*, and again more amply in the present volume, that variation, phenomenal variation of course, implies a multiplicity of absolute beginnings. This is as much as to say that it implies a multiplicity of spontaneous subjects. If we take away the multiplicity of subjects, we take away that multiplicity of phenomena of which the necessary truth known to us is the law; and therefore this truth vanishes also. It is true that variation implies necessity too, and consequently unity, over and above the multiplicity of absolute subjects. A doctrine which were to give no reason for necessity, which were to reject unity, would be unsatisfactory. Hence will a doctrine which considers unity alone, which gives us a concept of it excluding multiplicity, be satisfactory? It is only a question of phenomena, is it not? And *de minimis non curat prætor*. But here the question is about minima which are essential elements of the whole. There is not only this stone, and that, and that other: there is the mountain. I know this. But can we attend to the mountain if we dispense with each of the stones without which the mountain would not exist?

Further, if we admit the uniqueness of the "true" subject, the varieties by which one subject is distinguished from another, and "seems" another, become irrelevant. What are pleasures and pains, physiological or of any other kind, its own and those of other subjects, to a subject? Trifles! I say, its own and those of other subjects; for, if a pleasure or a pain of Peter has no real value for Peter, they cannot have it for Paul either; since he recognises a value in the feeling of Peter only in so far as he recognises the value of the same feeling for Peter. These are insignificant trifles for one who has arrived at the "true" consciousness of himself, at the clear comprehension of his own divinity.

This is all very well. But the life of every man and the story of humanity can be resolved into a struggle,—a struggle of each and all against nature, of each and of many united together against some one else and against others united together, of each against himself,—a struggle, the only reason for which consists in its feeling-value. In heaven's name, do not ascribe to me what I have never said or thought, what I have always opposed with all my powers. Man has something better to do than to seek pleasure or to avoid pain. But what for instance did the three hundred at Thermopylæ wish to obtain, and why did they die? Since life could not be saved without losing honour, they preferred to die. They honoured their country, and they tried (with success; but they did not know whether they would succeed,) to save it—to save it, that is to say to preserve that unity which secured the honour of the single citizens. And what is honour? A man who tortures another, dishonours him, does violence to his person. Would he dishonour, would he do violence, if to be tortured were not an evil for the other?

The one Subject, that which in each of us (according to what we are told) is the true Subject, the only one which has a value, cannot be violated nor outraged by anything. For all that happens, in the first place, happens only in appearance, does not touch the extra-phenomenal, impassible reality of that Subject; in the second place, it has its root in the Subject itself, not in anything else. All that happens is a means (theo-pantheists say, though they ought to say, seems a means) by which the Subject may unfold its own life which is realised in the apparently distinct consciousnesses of single subjects. In consequence, the facts of human life have all the same value; that is to say, they are all without real value. The man who sacrifices himself for the good of others (for instance, to relieve the physiological pains of others,) and the abject calumniator have an equal value, in so far as both are means, as we said, and both necessary means; for the one Subject is free in so far as it depends only on itself, but its being free consists in its apparent self-unfolding, according to an intrinsic necessity. The distinction of good from evil is useful for us who are apparently many, distinct from one another and from the one Subject; but it vanishes with respect to the one Subject, for which everything is good, because everything aims infallibly at the true end—at the manifestation of the Subject itself in the phenomenal world.

It is useless to ask what life and history would become, if we were to convince ourselves that this doctrine is true, and were to act in conformity with that conviction.

Whatever they may be in any case, life and history have no intrinsic value (as life and history); for, since they have had no beginning, they cannot tend towards an end. Does their finality or their value consist in their being the forms in which the extra-temporal consciousness of the absolute Subject appears ? But I ask whether the existence of the absolute Subject is reducible to its appearing in the single consciousnesses of phenomena, yes or no ? To be sure, the system must be ONE ; and we shall have to explain this unity to ourselves. But, under this hypothesis, the unity, whatever it may be, exists only in so far as it breaks up into a multiplicity of consciousnesses ; therefore it is not in itself unity of consciousness. In the second case, it is impossible to avoid a further more serious question : why does the absolute Subject give rise to the appearances of life and of history which it does not require, and which are destined to remain without consequence ?

16

THE PHENOMENAL UNIVERSE AND REALITY

Let us now consider the first of the two hypotheses formulated in § 15 : Each subject is a necessary being ; and subjects imply each other, so that the existence of one is a condition of the existence of every other, and is conditioned by the existence of all the others : each is unity of all.

And, first of all, let us interpret the formula in a restricted sense : each subject is necessary *to the existence of the phenomenal universe.*

Understood in this sense, we must consider it not as an hypothesis but as an intuitive truth. We have shown most evidently that the phenomenal universe is possible only through the existence of spontaneities interfering with one another. Now, the expression " connected spontaneities " means elementary consciousnesses or subjects, each of which is the unity of the rest. Each subject thinks Being, for no developed or enveloped thought, no consciousness exists without the thought of Being. Moreover Being is the indeterminate element common to all subjects and to all phenomena. Whence it follows that each subject, in the act of thinking Being, in the end thinks both itself and the others, but the others in so far as they are essential to itself: we have here the identity of thought and of content, on which theo-pantheism rightly insists.

Now the question arises whether the phenomenal universe exhausts reality or not. But in order to understand correctly what such a question means and by what it is justified, we must point out clearly what is by now out of question. The concept which we have formed of the phenomenal world gives us the full reason both of its multiplicity (that is to say, of its phenomenality, of the possibility of events, of life and of history,) and of its unity (that is to say, of the necessity which we recognise in it); it allows us to assert the fundamental identity of reality and cognition, and yet to recognise that relative distinction between the one and the other which cannot be denied, since cognition belongs to a phenomenal subject.

And thus it seems that the hypothesis of a non-phenomenal reality is gratuitous, and therefore to be excluded.

But if we do not admit a non-phenomenal reality, each subject becomes a necessary being; in other words, subjects have always existed, the phenomenal universe also has always existed, and in consequence it has no finality, no value as a whole.[1]

[1] Being (our common concept of Being)—(1) according to the hypothesis that no non-phenomenal reality exists, necessarily determines in itself centres of spontaneity, *i.e.* subjects; (2) according to the hypothesis that a non-phenomenal reality exists, cannot but have (over and above those determinations which are subjects and phenomena, and which in this case are not essential to it,) essential determinations which make a person of it: it is God. So I wrote in the *Great Problems*. This doctrine has been criticised as an extravagance. No concept, it is objected, no mere logical form, can create centres of activity; and no personal consciousness can be ascribed to it: "if being is God, it will be transcendent," that is to say, it will be no concept of ours. My doctrine is this: either each single subject is a necessary being necessarily implying the others, or one only necessary subject exists, God. In both cases, each subject has in common with all the others a character which in the second case is common also to God—the character of Being; a character, the common possession, or existence, of which consists in being thought by each subject (let us say more exactly, consists in the essential constitutive thought of each subject), and which is in short the concept of Being. A concept does not exist independently of a subject which thinks it; but hence it does not follow that the concept is "mere logical form"; that it exists only in thought, and not also in reality; a doctrine which ends in agnosticism, and is in substance meaningless. "God," supposing Him to be personal, "will be transcendent"; I admit it, and indeed I have maintained and do maintain it; but I mean transcendent in the sense that the consciousness of the single subject, included in the consciousness of God, does not include the latter, and therefore is not identifiable with it; and not in the

## 17

### DETERMINATIONS OF THE PRINCIPLE OF BEING

From the doctrine which we have just summed up for the hundredth time, we infer that there is a principle of value (of all value), in so far as there is a principle of existence, and in so far as there is a principle of activity or of variation; for these principles can be resolved into one single Principle—into Being.

A "concrete being" which is not a "determination of ... indeterminate Being" is impossible; in the same way, a "concrete value" which is not a "determination of the principle of value itself," that is to say, again of Being, is impossible; and we may add that a spontaneity which is not a determination of the principle of variation, that is to say, again of Being, is impossible. GENTILE is right; but he says just what I say.

The difference between him and myself concerns, not the "Principle" ("Being"), but the existence of "determinations of the

sense that in the subject there is *nothing* of God. The Being which is thought by the subject is, as Being, *i.e.* in so far as it is indeterminate, numerically the same in the consciousness of the subject and in God; although it is true that those determinations of Being which make it a person, God, are not, at least not essentially, thought by the subject. We had said that Being necessarily determines in itself, either a multiplicity of subjects, or those characters which make of it a person. The expression "to determine necessarily" has been understood as if it meant to produce. But that which is determined necessarily, or which in other terms exists necessarily in a (more or less) determinate form, exists *ab æterno*; it is not produced and cannot be produced (therefore even the Son of God, co-eternal with the Father, is said to be "*genitum, non factum*"). When one says that a thing exists necessarily, we can ask him why he says it. And if the why should not be adduced, the existence of the thing would not be necessary. Why do we say that either a system of subjects exists necessarily, or God exists necessarily? Because to assert the possibility that neither a system of subjects nor God exists, is the same as to assert the possibility that nothing exists. Now, it is impossible that nothing should exist, for Being is necessary. As to the necessity of Being, we cannot demonstrate it; this truth is not founded on reasons, for it is reason. I hope I have made myself clear. And so it seems to me that I have answered also an observation by DE SARLO, who (compare *Cultura Filosofica*, Florence, 1910, n. 1, p. 59) does not think that the spontaneities of subjects can be derived from necessity. The true terms of the question are these: either God exists, and is free necessarily, not certainly through an external force, but through the necessity of His own nature; or spontaneous monads exist *ab æterno*, which monads, supposing them not to have been created by God, are spontaneous through the necessity of their own nature. Either divine freedom, or the spontaneities of monads, exist in virtue of a necessity; that is to say, it is impossible to suppress both without reducing everything to nothing. Indeed I should say that I easily understand a spontaneity, the existence of which is necessary, but I do not understand so easily a created spontaneity.

Principle " (of " Being "), other than those by which the phenomenal universe is constituted.

I say (more exactly, the doctrine expounded says) that Being, as the principle of existence, exists in so far as those determinations of it which are the subjects exist, and not otherwise ; as the principle of variation, it exists in so far as the spontaneities of subjects exist, or in so far as phenomena happen, and not otherwise ; as the principle of value, it exists in so far as the values of subjects exist, and not otherwise. It seems to me that each of the three aspects of Being has been equally taken into consideration, and that therefore the accusation of inconsistency is out of place.

It is true that single values are transitory, in the same way as the single manifestations of spontaneities, that is to say phenomena, are transitory ; while, on the contrary, those secondary forms of unities of phenomena which are subjects, are, as unities or as forms, permanent. But this is a necessary consequence of the hypothesis that the only determinations of Being are those by which the phenomenal universe is constituted ; or more exactly, of not having ascribed other determinations to Being. That phenomena are transitory, is an essential characteristic of them. Values, supposing them to be realised only through phenomena (I am speaking of the realisation, not of the principle), will be equally transitory. On the contrary secondary unities, or subjects as unities, cannot be transitory ; a secondary unity cannot be a result, since it is a prerequisite of the course of events. The characteristics of the phenomenal universe are all consequences of the same necessity—the transitory as well as the non-transitory characteristics, which all imply each other. It is superfluous to notice that, while single values and single phenomena are transitory, the existence of single values and of single phenomena is an essential non-transitory characteristic of the phenomenal universe.

The permanent value of Being can be resolved into the continual presence in the phenomenal universe of inter-connected single values, each one of which is transitory by its own nature—into the continual presence in it of all possible forms or varieties of them, which are unceasingly transferred from one subject to another.

A doctrine from which we necessarily infer that Being has no value and no activity or existence except in the sense explained, seems as inadmissible to me as to others. I believe (as I have said) in the permanence of values. And in order to assure this permanence (as I have said) it is necessary (" or would it be necessary ? " as Gentile comments in a parenthesis. No; I have said and I repeat, it is necessary ; such is my conviction) to admit that Being possesses other determinations than concretes ; or in short, to admit the personal existence of God. "But," Gentile comments here, " it is not manifest how this can be admitted. . . . Varisco does not think that it is yet possible to place oneself at this point of view."[1] Others have accused me of inconsequence on this point, for I admit the permanence of values, I admit that the permanence of values is not possible without God, and nevertheless I consider the existence of God as a problem which is not yet fully ripe for a rational solution.

I thought I had made myself clear (in the *Great Problems*); however I will explain my position again.

### 18

#### CONCEPT OF GOD

To express one's own conviction about values and about God, no doubt is soon done ; and I have done it. But—in view of the great variety of opinions on the subject (perhaps there is none of them which does not contain some part of truth) which have steadily increased in number and complexity—it is no short or easy undertaking to develop one's own conviction into a doctrine which is intelligible in its real meaning and can be discussed on its intrinsic merits, or, in a word, which does not leave room for misunderstandings. And it is only too likely that I shall not be able to accomplish such an undertaking.

That the undertaking is not easy, appears even from the misinterpretation just pointed out, into which GENTILE has fallen. Since I do not think myself capable of explaining my doctrine about God at once with the necessary clearness and with scientific precision, he thinks that I do not yet understand the indispensability of God ; while, I, on the contrary, believe that the God of Gentile has nothing of God about Him but the name.

According to Gentile himself, what he calls the spirituality of

---

[1] Review quoted, p. 230.

Being, or in a word the permanence of values, cannot be assured without God; and in this we agree (though the agreement is not recognised by him). But he thinks that in order to assure that permanence God can and must be conceived in accordance with his own conception; that is to say he thinks, if I interpret his thought rightly, that "true" philosophy coincides with the Theo-pantheism of which I have given above a summary exposition and a criticism. On the contrary, I believe that Theo-pantheism, though it declares itself to be a doctrine of spirit, is not such; that its consequences coincide with those of the doctrine above recapitulated (§ 18, and expounded both in the *Great Problems* and in the present volume,) which recognises as the only determinations of Being those by which the phenomenal universe is constituted.

There is a traditional Theism, to which, in fact, I adhere. But we must take into account the already mentioned difficulties which Theo-pantheism opposes to Theism, other difficulties which I have mentioned in other works, and yet others. I do not believe that these difficulties are absolutely insuperable. Indeed, for my own part, I believe that I have overcome them. But to express one's own opinion, asserting that it has the value of a demonstrated theory, is one thing; to express it in such a way as to make it really a demonstrated theory, is another.

Such being the case, it seemed to me that the first inquiry to make was precisely that which I have undertaken—to study the phenomenal universe in its entirety, that is to say, human cognition, experience, with regard to the necessity which is manifested in it; and to explain clearly to ourselves what is implicit in it, *i.e.* that which, though it is no fact of experience, nor a complex of facts, is the condition which makes experience or human cognition possible.

In order that experience may be possible, or in order that the phenomenal universe may exist, we must admit, according to the results of our inquiry, that all phenomena are determinations of one and the same Being; that they are produced by a multitude of conscious activities interfering with one another, that is to say by a multitude of subjects which imply each other, and each of which is a unity of all the rest and of the phenomenal universe; and that the mutual implication of subjects depends on the fact that subjects are essentially consciousnesses—distinct as such—with one and the same content, Being, which in its turn is the common character of subjects and of phenomena.

We have still to discover whether Being has, or has not, only those determinations by which the phenomenal universe is constituted. Under the second hypothesis, the determinations just mentioned are not essential to Being; Being, in the fullness of its essential determinations, is God : this is Theism. If we admit Theism the course of events which takes place in the phenomenal universe is, in its totality, directed towards an end. Such an end is, on the contrary, irremediably wanting under the other hypothesis—the pantheistic hypothesis.

### 19
#### THE CHOICE BETWEEN THEISM AND PANTHEISM CONSTITUTES THE SUPREME PROBLEM OF METAPHYSICS

The problem of metaphysics (the really " great " problem, on which the solution of the others which have a more obvious practical importance, and which we have called " great," depends,) must therefore be formulated as follows :—to decide between Theism and Pantheism, both understood in the respective senses which we have just determined.

We have not solved this problem ; that is to say, we have not constructed metaphysics. And anyone who cares to say that consequently we have done nothing, may say so. He will be greatly mistaken. We have reduced the problems of metaphysics to one and only one, to the problem just now formulated with a clearness and a precision which we dare to say have never been attained so far.

Two results which seem to us of some importance, can be drawn from our, no doubt, very modest, work. One result is the elimination of Theo-pantheism, that is to say, of an intermediate form which is necessarily resolved, either into an irrational Theism (a Theism in opposition to the only postulates, on which Theism can be based,) or into precisely that pantheism of which we have given the concept.

Theo-pantheism can be considered as the doctrine of HEGEL. Here I needs must pause a moment to touch on " what is living and what is dead " in Hegel's doctrine.[1] The real merit of Hegel, in my eyes,[2] consists in having forcibly insisted on the moment of unity in the conception of reality, in having understood and clearly pointed out the fundamental identity of reality and cognition, consequently, and chiefly, in having established it that the unity of reality can only be the unity of the subject. The method by which he reaches these conclusions, and the form under which he presents them, do not seem to me satisfactory;[3] but they do not constitute the nerve of the doctrine. And the doctrine which I have developed concerning the phenomenal universe is (at least in my own intention, but I think also in its result,) a more precise and more exact form of that which is still living and will always live in the doctrine of Hegel—a form which is free from all ambiguity and contradiction. It refutes Hegel's doctrine, but only in so far as it determines better and completes that doctrine.

[1] I do not discuss here, but shall perhaps discuss another time, CROCE'S work with that title.

[2] Not only in my eyes; BRADLEY and CAIRD, for instance, are of the same opinion.

[3] I have explained on other occasions the reasons why I do not approve the method. As reasons against the method, they seem to me still valid; my mistake was a failure to distinguish adequately between that which is, no doubt, open to criticism and should be abandoned in Hegel and the living and permanent kernel. My criticism of the form in which Hegel presents his conclusions will be apparent on the whole from many parts of the present volume, as well as of the *Great Problems*. Since I have my pen in hand, and in order to define my position with regard to Hegel better, I must notice an observation by P. RAGNISCO (*Note nel cinquantesimo anno del suo insegnamento*, in *Atti del Regio Istituto Veneto*, 1911–12, T. LXXI, f. II, p. 180): ". . . I approached H. SPENCER. . . . Indeed . . . I saw that HEGEL'S doctrine was too insecure. My good sense could not swallow too violent paradoxes." It happened that my own thought was transformed in the opposite sense (though I had never been an admirer of SPENCER). Let us dismiss the method and form of HEGEL, on which I have already expressed my opinion. To whom does the substance of Hegelianism seem paradoxical, and why? To the man who has not asked himself how cognition is possible; because to the man who has not put this question to himself, and is satisfied with actual cognition, the disconnected multiplicity which cognition presents to him does not seem to imply any difficulty. "Good sense" knows, but it gives no account of its own knowledge; and since it gives no account of it, that which must be admitted in order to give such an account, and which, though implicit in cognition, is not an immediate object of cognition, seems gratuitous, capricious and unintelligible. To understand that the manifold "known" realities must constitute unity in order to be known, to understand how they constitute it, are problems which good sense does not propose to itself; but which are not against good sense. In fact, since good sense exists, since it has (who doubts it?) its good reasons to allege, its existence must be possible. HEGEL'S paradoxes have no other object than to make us understand the possibility of good sense. Nevertheless they may be "violent"; the solution of the problem which HEGEL gives us may not be the true solution. But I believe that in its substantial part it is true. In any case the difficulties opposed or opposable by good sense which has nothing to do here, do not count.

The other result of which I was speaking, connected with the first and in substance identical with it, is to have made the reasons of Pantheism, the essentials of its form, its true meaning, and its consequences clear. Since we are reduced to the necessity of choosing—of course, after adequate reflection—between Theism and Pantheism, we must form a perfectly clear and (at least so far as essentials are concerned) complete concept of both. With regard to Pantheism, the exposition which I have made of it, and the demonstration which I have given of the impossibility of any other form of Pantheism, leave little to be desired; in any case, they are something. Ought I to have undertaken an analogous inquiry with regard to Theism? I do not deny it. But the discussion of Pantheism has led, in part, to a discussion of Theism also. And I think I have pointed out the only possible form of Theism.

You had then the elements necessary for the choice; why have you not chosen?—Why? I doubted (not without reason, as we have seen,) whether the doctrines which I was expounding, *i.e.* the premisses, would be thoroughly understood in their true meaning; and under these conditions there was no reason for drawing from them the ultimate consequence which would have seemed unjustified, and perhaps would not have been understood. No doubt, we must draw a conclusion, but we should do so with full consciousness of what we are saying and of the reason why we are saying it. The end which I had set before myself both in the *Great Problems* and in the present book, was to clear the ground of a crowd of idle questions, misunderstandings, and presuppositions which obstruct it and make it difficult to take our bearings, to find a straight way in it. If I have attained this end, I shall have done something, though not everything. I should be satisfied with the result; and even the reader, if he is conscious of the difficulties which we have to overcome, might be satisfied with it.

## 20

#### THE IMMANENCE OF GOD RECONCILABLE WITH RELIGIOUS BELIEF

With regard to Pantheism, what I am going to add may perhaps help to eliminate a misinterpretation. "My doctrine," as I have said on another occasion, " ought to be interpreted in a pantheistic sense only on the hypothesis (which I do not accept, though I have not refuted it,) that values are not permanent."[1] This explanation did not seem satisfactory to a critic of mine who objected that " Prof. Varisco does not admit that absolute distinction between God and the world, . . . which alone excludes pantheism." And referring to certain biblical quotations of mine, he added that in the Bible " there is not one single passage where it is insinuated that God is immanent in any other way than through a relation of presence and of operation."[2]

My critic supposes that I understand the " existence " of God in the world in another sense than that of " operation." But it is not so. God is in the world in so far as He operates in the world ; he who admits that God operates in the world (and what theist could maintain the contrary ?) agrees with me in admitting that God is in the world in the sense in which I say that He is in the world. I do not quite understand a real " existence " which does not consist in " being active," in operating or in doing ; however, such an " existence " is an hypothesis to which I have never been obliged to have recourse in the *Great Problems* or in the present work ; and which consequently seems to me useless and gratuitous. The critic himself admits that we know things in so far as things produce certain representations in us ;[3] since the existence of things is known to us only in consequence of their operations on ourselves, it can consist only, in so far as it is known to us (that is to say, in so far as we have any reason for speaking of such an existence), in their being active.

---

[1] From a letter to the Editor of the *Rivista Néo-scolastica*, published in that review, Firenze, 1911, n. 2, p. 256.

[2] G. TREDICI, *Cristianesimo e morale*, *ibid.*, n. 3, p. 442. I take with pleasure the opportunity to express my thankfulness to Prof. TREDICI, who wrote a careful review of the *Massimi Problemi* (*ibid.*, 1910, n. 2, pp. 170–6) and also had discussions with me at other times (*ibid.*, n. 1, pp. 92–6), and to Father P. GEMELLI, editor of the *Rivista n.-scol.*, who has always accepted my answers, Besides the real disagreement mentioned in the text, a verbal disagreement exists between Prof. Tredici and myself. A doctrine which ascribes to God a consciousness distinct from the human (I have explained above in what sense I mean distinct), is not called by me pantheistic, but theistic ; Prof. Tredici calls every doctrine pantheistic, in which the " absolute " distinction between God and created beings is not admitted. A question of words ! But the terminology which I use, is not mine only ; it is followed, for instance, also by HÖFFDING (compare *Phil. d. l. relig.*, French trans., Paris, 1908, p. 81).

[3] G. TREDICI, *I Massimi Problemi;* in *Rivista Néo-scolastica*, 1910, n. 2, p. 174.

But we must go deeper.

God, whom we suppose to be personal, is not simply the world He is Being, but Being endowed with other determinations than concretes; and in this sense He is certainly distinct from the world. So, for instance, I see blue. Blue, in so far as it is seen, is a determination of myself; it is not however my only determination; whence it follows that I am not only the blue; I am distinct from the blue, because I am both the blue and more (much more). That my doctrine is irreconcilable with a distinction between God and the world, even more radical than that which exists between each subject and the world, is not to be thought.

But God is the creator of the world. And therefore the operation of God on the world is not to be confused with the operation of a concrete A on another concrete B. The action of A on B presupposes that B exists independently, up to a certain point, of the action itself; for though concretes exist only in so far as they operate reciprocally on each other, it is still true that the existence of B is not exhausted in that determinate action of A on B—an action which might vary in a hundred ways both through the spontaneities which it implies, and through the varying of circumstances. On the contrary, the operation of God on the world does not presuppose the existence of the world; it creates the existence of the world. Consequently, he who says that God is in the world only in so far as He operates in it, either means that God is in the world only in so far as the world exists (which we naturally admit), or I absolutely do not understand what he means.

I do not flatter myself that I have convinced my opponent, nor even indeed that I have made myself understood by him. The disagreement between the two conceptions is, I believe, only verbal; but time, and not a short time, is required in order that all may perceive its intrinsic emptiness. Theologians now understand that the heliocentric structure of the solar system is not irreconcilable with the faith; they will understand some day that divine immanence also—that immanence which cannot absolutely be denied, and is not irreconcilable with divine personality—is not irreconcilable with the faith. But that day must be prepared for; it is impossible meanwhile to solve completely and in a comprehensible way, the dilemma which I have left unsolved (but which is not unsolved for me : I am a theist). My wishes hasten to meet that day ; and I work as best I can to prepare it.[1]

[1] I must submit to the attention of my readers a short essay in criticism (of the *Great Problems*) which shows exceptional penetration. "L'auteur . . . ne semble avoir conscience . . . que son panthéisme l'obligerait . . . à nier la valeur objective du principe d'identité. . . . En vertu de ce principe, Dieu est Dieu, la créature est créature, on ne peut identifier le fini et l'infini. . . . Bien plus " (take note !) " si le principe d'identité est loi fondamentale du réel, la réalité fondamentale doit être en tout et pour tout identique à elle-même, elle doit être l' *Être même* qui n'est susceptible d'aucune multiplicité, d'aucun changement ; . . . et donc la Premier être est essentiellement distinct du monde. . . ." (R. P. GARRIGOU-LAGRANGE, in *Revue Thomiste*, Toulouse, 1910, n. 6, p. 810.) The complex and difficult problem of understanding how unity and multiplicity, necessity and accidentality, permanence and variation are compossible, is solved in these two lines with an assurance which may be compared with that which is shown in judging a book without even looking through it. The critic in fact believes that my aim was to " identifier le fini et l'infini " ! But the last sentence is specially precious. In order to infer from the principle of identity that " là réalité fondamentale " (it alone, mark, or else we fall into pantheism,) must be " l'Être même," incapable of multiplicity and variation, that principle ought to be, not " la loi fondamentale du réel," that is to say of all reality (for then the world too would not admit of multiplicity or variation), but only the law of fundamental reality. The syllogisms of my critic have four terms, or four feet ; which makes them firmer. If vice versa the critic admits that the principle of identity is only the law of fundamental reality, but not " la loi fondamentale du réel," I shall conclude that God is indeed God (for the principle of identity holds good of Him, who is the fundamental reality) ; but further that a created being is no created being (for the principle of identity does not hold good of a created being, which is not the fundamental reality). If the critic happens to see the present note, he should not jump, as he is apt to do, to the conclusion that the *Great Problems* is written in the same way ; no, the merit of such delicate subtleties is entirely his own ; I, for my part, should not have been able to raise myself so high. And, if he means to become acquainted with the *Great Problems*, he must have patience and read it ; it is not a " réalité fondamentale " about which it is possible to argue *a priori*.

THE END

# INDEX

Absolute, The, and Being, 207.
Accidentality and necessity, 154, 182.
Activity and cognition, 54.
Activity and resistance, 56.
Agnosticism, philosophically absurd, xxi, 195, 293.
Appearance and appearing, 201.
Aquinas, S. Thomas of, v *n.*, xv *n.*, 122 *n.*
Aristotle, xv *n.*, 262 *n.*

Bodies, existence of, x, 67.
Bonatelli, 5 *n.*, 244 *n.*
Bradley, *Appearance and Reality*, 204 *n.*, 205 *n.*, 207 *n.*, 219 *n.*, 224 *n.*, 229 *n.*, 320 *n.* 2.

Caird, E., *Hegel*, 204 *n.*, 233 *n.*, 320 *n.* 2.
Causality and rationality, 143.
Christianity, 270 *n.*
Cohen, H., *Logik der reinen Erkenntniss*, 95 *n.*
Comte, 197 *n.*
Consciousness and subconsciousness, xiii, 11, 40, 97.
Cournot, A., *Ench. d. idées fondamentales*, 150 *n.*
Croce, B., *Filosofia della Pratica*, xxii *n.*, 275 *n.*

Dalai Lama, 28.
Dante, *Inferno*, 50 *n.*
De Backer, S. J., *Instit. Metaph. spec.*, 175 *n.*

Determinism and indeterminism, 158.
Duhem, 269 *n.*

Epistemology and metaphysics, 297 ff.
Epistemology, a theory of the subject, 4.
Error, meaning of, 183.
Ethics, not independent of metaphysics, 272 *n.*
Experience and thought, 13.
Experience, unity of, 66.
Explicit cognition and reality, difference between, 98.

Facts, 86.
Fichte, 275 *n.* 2.
Fictitious problems, 288 ff.
Finality, 250.
First principle, 1 ff.

Galilei, 288 *n.*
Gentile, 303 *n.*, 305, 307, 317.
God, concept of, 322–4.
God, meaning of the word, 257 *n.*

Haeckel, 168 *n.*
Hegel, 168 *n.*, *Encyclopædia of Philosophic Sciences*, 242, 243 *n.*, 250 *n.*, 319, 320.
History, an immense tautology, 251.
Hobbes, 56 *n.*
Höffding, *Philosophy of Religion*, 322 *n.* 2.
Hume, 290 *n.* 1.
Huxley, 281.

I, a centre of the universe, 9, 208.
I and the world, co-essential to each other, 38.
Idealism, criticism of, xxi.
Immanence of God reconcilable with religious belief, 321 ff.
Immortality of the soul, 288 ff.
Implicit and explicit elements of knowledge, 97.

Judgment and cognition of the judgment, 86.
Judgments, the system of, the ultimate test of truth, 90.

Kant, *Critique of Pure Reason*, 22 n., 23 n., 78 n, 115 n., 194 n., 195 n., 197 n., 269 n., 275 n. 2, 279.
Knowableness, the essence of reality, 98, 105.

Leibniz, 39.
Leopardi, 130 n., 252 n.
Logic and practice, 249 ff.
Lotze, 277 n. 2.

Mach, 269 n.
Man, what is he? 36.
Metaphysics, concept of, 193.
Metastasis, 184 n.
Monads, spontaniety of, 315 n.
Monist, in what sense the author is a, 167 n.
Morality and religion, 272 n.
Multiplicity of primitive unities, 42, 179.

Necessary truth and God, 309 ff.
Necessity as founded on the unity of the real, 115.
Necessity of relations, the, as reconciling unity and multiplicity, 154.

One, The, and phenomenal reality, 239–40.

"Other," the, and the particular subject, 308–9.

Pantheism and theism, 258 ff.
Parmenides, 168 n.
Permanence of values, 305–6.
Pessimism, the fundamental reason of, 252 n.
Phenomena, possibility of, 209.
Phenomenon, what is a, v.
Philosophy, definition of, 2–5.
Physical sciences, character of, 68, 156.
Plato, xv n., 11, 28.
Pluralistic metaphysics, 167.
Poincaré, 269 n.
Polycentric system, the universe a, 50.
Positivism, the element of truth in the method of, 295 ff.
Possibility of cognition, problem of the, 293.
Problems, particular and universal, 286.

Ragnisco, 320 n. 3.
Realistic and subjectivistic aspects of the author's doctrine, 115–16.
Reality and appearance, 73.
Reality and cognition, coincidence of, 91, 128.
Reality and the phenomenal universe, 313–14.
Reality "in itself," an absurd concept, 300–1.
Relativity of knowledge, meaning of the, 198.
Religion and philosophy, 267 ff.
Righi, Augusto, *The Modern Theory of Physical Phenomena*, 196 n., 269 n.
Rosmini, *Nuovo Saggio*, 86 n., 178 n.; *Sistema filosofico, Antropologia, Psicologia*, 178 n., 208 n.
Royce, *The Spirit of Modern Philosophy*, 29 n., 35 n.

## Index

Schuppe, 302.
Science and epistemology, 295 ff.
Self-consciousness, 9.
Sensation, the doctrine of, 301 ff.
Sertillanges, *S. Thomas d'Aquin*, 121 *n.*, 122 *n.*
" Small perceptions " of Leibniz, 39.
Socrates, 5.
Space and time, 78.
Spencer, Herbert, 197 *n.*, 272 *n.*, 320 *n.* 3.
Spinoza, 168 *n.*, 221 *n.*
Subject, the, and the ego, 24.
Subject, the, and the world, 37.
Subject, the, as the unity of the universe, 177.
Subject " in itself," the, and the phenomenal subject, 217.
Subjectivism, interpretations of, 22.
Subject-object and Peter-Paul, the dualities, 46.
Supreme problem of metaphysics : the choice between theism and pantheism, 319–20.

Tari, A., *Saggi di Estetica e Metafisica*, 275 *n.*
Taylor, A. E., ii.
Theism and pantheism, 258 ff.
Theo-pantheism, criticised, 310 ff., 319.
Thought and reality, 14.
Truth and error, xix, 108–9.
Truth, intrinsic and historical, 129.
Truth, ultimate test of, 90.

Unity and multiplicity, xiv, 134 ff.
Universal subject, concept of the, 224.
Universe, the, as the unity of a multiplicity, 176.

Value of the subject and of the universe, 253.
Values, the doctrine of, 305 ff.
Variation, interpretation of, 212–14.
Varisco, *Scienza e Opinioni*, 5 *n.*, 269 *n.*

PLYMOUTH
WILLIAM BRENDON AND SON, LTD.
PRINTERS